SAMPURAN VASTUSHASTRA

SAMPURAN VASTUSHASTRA

Dr. Bhojraj Dwivedi
M.A. (Sans.), Ph.D (Astrology)

DIAMOND BOOKS

ISBN: 81-7182-195-2

© Publisher

Published by : **Diamond Pocket Books (P) Ltd.**
　　　　　　　　 X-30, Okhla Industrial Area, Phase-II
　　　　　　　　 New Delhi-110020
Phone　　　　　 : 011-40712100
Fax　　　　　　 : 011-41611866
E-mail　　　　　 : sales@dpb.in
Website　　　　 : www.dpb.in
Edition　　　　　: 2016
Printed by　　　 : Adarsh Printers, Shahdara, Delhi-110032

SAMPURAN VASTUSHASTRA - DR. BHOJRAJ DWIVEDI

FOREWORD

Sampuran Vastushastra (The complete science of house construction) is the first book based on the study of ancient architecture in which the Art of building a house (Bhawan Sthapatya Kala) has been thought over elaborately. This book gives an insight into the various aspects of this science i.e. direction of the entrance of the new construction (Griha Pravesh), evaluation of site, direction of kitchen, water tank, place of fire in the kitchen, direction in which to sleep, merit of land (Shastriya Vidhan) timing-auspicious time for constructing a house.

Internationally renowned and learned Dr. Bhojraj Dwivedi has written and compiled this book, enshrining all these aspects with pictures, in a very lucid way. Two things, Fate and 'Vastu' (the house or land), affect the life of person, each responsible for 50% happiness in life. If 'Vastu' is poor the result as compared to efforts will be half, even if the stars of fate are exalted and bright. As against this if Vastu is right, and the planet position is unfavourable, the ill effects will not be so bad as to that when both are poor. This means that if a house is constructed according to the theory of Vastu, man's fate can be definitely brightened. A person should take care of front face of the house, adjacent roads, doors of houses, at the time of buying a plot. An authoritative presentation regarding importance of hindrance of door (Dwar vedha) angle (Kona vedha), shade (Chhaya-vedha), trees (Vriksha vedha), pillars (Stambh-vedha) is given in this book.

—Publisher

— GRATITUDE

While Goddess Saraswati continued to kindle the light of inspiration, my wife Srimati Janaki Devi's untiring soft and humble help did a lot in writing this book. My son, Pandit Ramesh Dwivedi, has toiled a lot in typing, photocopying, proof reading, and composition at the cost of his study and own work. The indirect help provided by my daughter-in-law, Smt. Raksha Dwivedi is also commendable. I am grateful to my dear friends, admirers, and the wise readers who have always directly encouraged my writings through their numerous praiseworthy letters.

A set of 12 books, covering different aspects of 'Vastushastra', are being published. I certainly desire to mention those reference-books and extend my complements and gratefulness to the ancestors of old classic creations, from which I have taken help in writing this book. These are :

(1) Brihat Samhita
(2) Bhartiya Vastushastra
(3) Maansaar
(4) Rajvallabh
(5) Vastusar
(6) Vishvakarma Vastushastra
(7) Aparajit Prichha
(8) Prasad Nandan
(9) Samrangan Sutradhara
(10) Agni Purana
(11) Maymat
(12) Vastusandesh
(13) Feng-Shui
(14) Bhartiya Sthapatya
(15) Shilpratna
(16) Bhuwan Pradip
(17) Vishvakarma Prakash
(18) Kashyap Shilpa
(19) Muhurta Martanda
(20) Vastuvidya
(21) Tantra Sammuchnaya
(22) Narad Samhita
(23) Vanijyavastu Shastram.

I record my ineffable gratitude to Sri Sanjay Kumar Singhal, in rendering my Hindi work into English with simplicity of style. I acknowledge the work done by Shri Ajit Singh for suggesting improvements in the English translation for the Second Edition. Finally, not the least important, I am grateful to Shri Narendarji, Managing Director of Diamond Pocket Books whose special inspiration has facilitated the presentation of this beautiful book to reach the awakened readers in such a short time.

—**Dr. Bhojraj Dwivedi**

130, First 'A' Road, Marudeep Apt.
Sardarpura, Jodhpur-342003
(Rajasthan)-INDIA
Tel.: 0291-637359
Fax: 0291- 431885
Email : agyat@wilnetonline.net

PREFACE

Vastushastra has become very popular these days. Conferences and seminars are being organized frequently at various places. It creates astonishment and happy moment on seeing the title of Vastu-Specialist, Vastu-Vidya Visharad, Vastushastra Marmagya etc. on their visiting cards or letter pads of those growing and up-coming untraditional astrologers, through various Pocket Books now-a-days. It seems that we have come back again to Vastu Yuga (Architecture-period). 'Which are the five most beautiful things, pleasant to the eyes in this world' was the question in a conference participated by learned men. After much discussion the conclusion reached was (1) Beautiful face (2) Beautiful children (3) Beautiful flowers (4) Beautiful sunrise and (5) Beautiful houses, are the five most beautiful things of this world, of which the first four are natural and god-gifted, while, the fifth and the last one is man-made. With this illustration, it becomes very clear and obvious that, how important and high ranked Vastushastra is, from the aesthetic point of view, among creation of human beings. In fact, Vastushastra is most charming, amorous and pleasant and it is possessed by its permanent value and most attractive elements of human civilization.

Once an inquisitive hermit asked Vishvakarma, the architect-God, "If Vastu is a divine study, why this should be taught to men? And what is its utility for human beings? God-Vishwakarma replied, to this, in the following way:

चतुर्वर्ग फल प्राप्तिः सलोकश्च भवेद् ध्रुवम्।
शिल्पशास्त्र परिज्ञाना न्यर्त्येडपि सुरतां व्रजेत॥
**Chaturvarg Phal Prapti Salakosch Bhawed Dhruwam
Shilp Shastra Parigyana Nytaryeapi Surtam Vrajet.**
—*Vishwakarma Vastushastra, A 2/slok 30*

Human being gets Purushartha Chatushtaya (the four elements to complete the human life)—Dharma (religion), Artha (property), Kama (desire) and Moksha (salvation), from the knowledge of Shilp Shastra (science of crafting) and Vastushastra. It helps them, in carrying a meaningful life along with the enshrining and imbibing of divine-forces (Devatwa), in this Mrityu lok (this planet where death is sure). With this amazing work, he is able to help and do welfare of others. More is said also:

इदं पवित्रं परमं रहस्यं यः पठेन्नरः।
स्यात्तस्याविततथा वाणी सत्यं सत्यं वदाम्यहम्॥

**Idam Pavitram Param Rahsyam Yah Pathennarah
Syattasyavitatha Vani Satyam Statyam Vadabhyaham**

—*Vishwakarma Prakash, A 39/slok 111*

Human being understands, this wonderful and pure science, by reading and going through it properly. His words become the truth, leading to success and never go in vain.

CONTENTS

Relation Between Vastushastra and Religion	13
Character and Nature of Vastu	26
Evaluation of Site : Various Aspects	31
Laying Foundation for houses	58
Entering the House: Griha Pravesh	62
Hindrance in Free Movement :	
Air Sun-rays, Dwar-Vedha	64
Entrance Gate : Pravesh-Dwar	75
Commercial Complex	81
Effect of Direction on Houses Falling on Roadside	94
Vastu and Business Setup	99
Scientific Secret of Swastik	107
Eradicate Vastu-faults	114
The Importance of Directions in Constructing a House	119
Pictorial Depiction of Vastu (Shape of Plot)	173
Selection of Plot (Site)	180
Bed Room	206
Miracle of Feng-Shui	208
About the Author	213

Chapter 1

Relation Between Vastushastra and Religion

Vastu—is not only house-craft but also a religious ritual. Architecture and Vastu-science are two different things. An architect can build a posh house but can't give guarantee of happy life to the people, living in that house whereas Vastu-science confirms and gives a guarantee to this. Architecture (house building) has been supposed to be wordly act, among all the human civilizations of this world, while architecture in India is a religious-activity. In India, architecture's value holds the attainment of Purusharth Chatushtaya. We will not understand the secret of 'Vastu', until and unless we understand this religious secret. If Vastu science is carved out of the House-construction-Art, its value becomes zero. Without it, construction is nothing but a stockpile of bricks, stones, iron and cement. In this context, the example of Sacred Thread Ceremony (Yagyopaveet' Samskara) is appropriate as an illustration. This ceremony is, in vogue, among Brahman or twice-born (Dwij). Considerable sum of money is spent on this very big ceremony. Marriage can be performed many a times but 'Yagyopaveet' (the sacred thread ceremony) is held only once in life. It is said:

जन्मना जायते शूद्र, संस्कारात् द्विज उज्यते।
वेदपाठी भवेद् विप्र: ब्रह्म जानाति ब्राह्मण:॥

Janmana Jayate Shudra, Samskarat Dwij Ujhyate
Vedpathi Bhawed Viprah, Brahm Janati Brahmna.

A man takes second birth with the Yagyopaveet Samskara. He acquires divinity. If religiosity were disentangled from Yogyopaveet Samskara then it would be a sheer thread of cotton with a value not more than twenty-five paise. Hence one should imbibe this formula

    (1) Yagyopavit   —religiosity   =zero
    (2) Architecture   —Vastu   =zero

It is obvious that, if the religious part is taken out from Vastu-kala then it is no more than a heap of iron-cement-sand. It's value becomes zero. Undoubtedly, (Yagyopaveet Samskara gives second birth to man and he becomes twice born (Dwijatwa) and obtains Divinity (Devattva). Due to lack of faith, regard, respect and religiosity, the big ceremony, of Yagyopaveet and Rakshabandhan have become mere rituals of thread binding which reflects to no value. There are three types of Proof (Praman), for the evidence of truth, in this world-Pratyaksha (visible), Guess (Anuman) and trust-worthy expression of words (Apta Vakya). Vastushastra is a visible science (Pratyaksha), based on trust-worthy speech. Seers seeking truth kept alive, this Vastu-science, by constant efforts with a feeling of gratefulness to those hermits. We have to maintain and extend forward the pure current, of this knowledge and science. Then only, the purity of the Vastushastra will remain undiminished.

Hidden Religious meaning associated with House Construction Art should be understood:

House construction is a religious work in India, in which the secret of attainment (Siddhi) of four 'Purusharth' Chatushtaya Dharma, Arth, Kama, and Moksha, will have to be understood elaborately.

(I) **Religion (Dharma):**—A man should have religious belief. Spiritual and inner (soul) happiness should be felt by the people, living in the house. The people, living in that house, should be rid of the distresses related to physical, divine and spiritual forces. Common people should bow down, with a sense of respect and belief, on seeing the person living in such a house. There should not exist any dispute, quarrel and natural enmity against each other. You must have heard that, even violent animals, used to forget their natural enmity and the sense of harming each other in the hermitage (Ashrams of Rishis). The lion and the goat, the snake and the mongoose used to sit together in the same Ashram. This is an apparent and clear example of religious benefit of Vastu.

(2) Wealth (Arth):—A person should rise and prosper with increase in wealth, the moment he enters the house i.e.Grihpravesh. It should not lead a man to continuous debts after construction of the house. A house is considered as worthless and bad if a person becomes bankrupt economically. Opposite to this lies the worthiness and meaningfulness of a house which increases the source of income, market value, glory and fame of the person occupying the premises.

(3) Desire (Kama):—Much happiness and pleasure of wife should be associated with a person. There should be increase of son and grandsons, along with increase in his pleasure, prosperity and material-happiness. It should not bring forth quarrel among family members and relatives, court-cases, and engulfing a person in mental tension. This shows that the geomancy (Vastu) of that house is poor. The fruitfulness and meaning of a house lies when a person's wife, and kids abide by him and give him respect.

(4) Salvation (Moksha):—An auspicious Vastu leads a person to Moksha. Right behaviour of good family, leads to regal attainment. Vastushastra helps a man to acquire these four objects. Hence its utility is indescribable. According to religious opinions (the sloka in Sanskrit वास्तु पूजां प्रकुर्वीत गृहारम्भे प्रवेशने च) **'Vastu pujam Prakurvit Griharmbhe Praveshne cha'** says that the land must be examined and worshiped before buying. Land-worship and foundation-worship should be performed at an auspicious-moment before house construction. Installation with proper rituals, Vastu worship, Gayatri-Japa (Muttering of Goddess Gayatri Mantra), worship of Lord Ganesha, Rudra Japa, worship of Vishnu, Nav-Graha worship and complete invocation to calm down the planets should be performed after house construction. One tenth invocation of 'Japa' (Yagya or sacrifice) is desirable. It's one tenth should be spent, on feeding Brahmans with gifts to them. A tenth part of total expenses of house construction, as directed in Shastra should be spent on installation work. In 'Vishvakarma Prakash' it is written clearly that

अश्रियं मृत्युमाप्नोति विहनतस्य पदे पदे।
वास्तु पूजां अकुर्वाणः तवाहारो भविष्यति॥

**Ashriyam Miritiupnoti vihantasya pade pade
Vastu Puja Akuran Tavaharo Bhavishyate**
—*Vishwakarma Prakash 1/ shlok 17*

The person who does not worship Vastu, out of greed, atheistic attitude and negligence, finds his prosperity and power destroyed. He meets many troubles and stumbles in every work. With the anger of Vastu-Purush (God of Vastu), they get into miseries and meet untimely death.

The basic difference between Western culture and Indian culture, relating to Vastu-art is that the former is self-centred, narrow, non-religious and having no benevolence. To feed grains and water to birds, to give bread to dog and cow, to pour water on trees like pipal, to worship 'Tulsi', a sacred plant or basil and to get blessed by satisfying Brahmans are not part of western culture.

Nature of Vastushastra in Modern Age

In ancient period, Vastu science, architecture as described in Vedas Puranas and classical books was considered to build huge and palatial buildings, forts, schools, ponds, wells and gardens including ordinary residential places. The art of architecture and house-construction got deformed gradually under the influence of foreign irregular fashion. Due to a rapid increase in population, the land has become scarce in towns, so multistorey-buildings and flat-system has been developed. The haphazard glare of the Western World and mansions built of cement and iron have led to a break in the classical rules and regulations, leading to unhappiness and trouble ridden people, living in those big flats erected unclassically. The meaning of human-life is gradually being destroyed and people got bored sooner than later.

Many researches and thoughtful works have been undertaken abroad on Indian-Vastushastra. Germany was the first country to take a lead, resulting in the spread of Indian Vastu-science, through oriental-language and other foreign languages. To ensure a peaceful life, good and sound-sleep, houses even in foreign countries are being now built keeping in mind the direction of main entrance, place of water reservoir, kitchen, a suitably placed fire-spot, and bed room based on magnetic field (North-west) and all these aspects are based on Indian Vastu Shastra.

House construction on Vedic rules in America

Progressive ultramodern scientific countries of the world have started to build their houses with a fervour from our Vedas. Recently on January 20, 1995, the architects of America have claimed their houses made in Los Angles are the first of their kind and are based on the Sthapatya Shastra (science of architecture) as enunciated in Atharvaveda: Sri Kirit Kumar Patel wanted to worship the God 'Surya' in his suburban house but he was unable to fulfil the desire in his house facing west. Hence he emphasised on building a house facing east to architect Moriss Shilder of Philedelphia. He took help of three thousand years old Vedic rules of Vastushastra. The principles of Sthapna Shastra 1000 B.C. reported in Atharveda helped him, which turned out to be a spiritual experience for Shilder. He says, "Sthapatya-Shastra enshrines the description and process, affecting favourably the feelings of people. i.e. feeling of hunger in dining hall, feeling of collectivity in sitting room, feeling of alertness in study room and feeling of relaxation in bed-room, are remarkable. The centre place of house is called place of Supreme being or essence (Brahmsthan). His firm has utilised the various rules and doctrines mentioned in Sthapatya-shastra of Atharvaveda so that Mr. Patel could shape his imagination and reminiscences.

Water place should not exist in Agnikona (Fire Square)

Recently one Jain, a big merchant, was building a marvellous palatial house at his birth place (village) but it could not be completed even after efforts over three years. Although he possessed sufficient required money, there was always non-availability of materials and engineers at the nick of time. Even if everything was in order, then some mishap like death of a worker or machinery-breakdown created a problem. On the whole, the house couldn't be completed in during three years but it certainly piled up a lot of problems for him.

The Jain couple came to me and narrated their problem. I expressed a strong desire to see the site. After a nine hours long journey to their village, I found that boring for water had been done in the fire square of the house. His problems mitigated after boring was done. A son of sethji was injured after falling from a roof. I shifted that boring to Ishanya (N.E.) direction (Kona) and removed the water tank lying under the center of the roof and the problems of sethji vanished. Many a times, small faults lead to disaster. According to Shastras, place of water is in Ishanya (North-East), North, East and West but water-resource placed in **Agneya kona** (South-east) causes, loss of son, fear from enemies and other problems. In Naishtritya (South-west) it causes loss of son, in south it causes loss of wife, in Vayavya (North-west) it leads to trouble from enemies and in the middle of house, it destroys the accumulated wealth.

Utility of Vastushastra in modens age

Man can make doors, windows and build a house on the land bought by him voluntarily in villages, block, kasba and small towns, based on the rules of Vastushastra. But there is limited choice for the buyer to modify the house and the flat entirely built by Housing Board in big cities. Many letters generally come to me from Bombay, Madras and Calcutta saying that after purchase of a flat their business has gone down, wife is engulfed with diseases, abortion has led to no child, mental tension is mounting, marriage not successful, diseases and enemies have emerged. In such a condition misfortune can be overcome, by rectifying the angle and direction, changing the number of stairs, windows, changing the direction of bed in the bedroom and changing the water-place, fire-place, place of worship and consider other factors.

Office-below-beam should be avoided

You must have read the story of Hiranyakshap and Prahalad in Puranas. Hiranyakshyap had the blessing that his death would occur neither in day nor in the night, neither from a male nor from female, neither in sky nor in nether world, neither on land nor in water, neither inside house nor outside it. Lord Sri Vishnu had to take 'Awatara' (incarnation) of Narshingha (half man-half lion) to kill him, during the dusk period, on the corridor (entrance of room) putting him in His lap as a door does not fall either inside the room or outside it. Hence from the puranic period BC 2000, to sit under rending point (Pat), on the door sill or under beam is avoided and the construction of house started in the dusk is not encouraged and is prohibited. To sit under beam is to invite death, shortening the age and inviting bad omen. My experience says that in offices revolving chair, and the seat placed under beam is dangerous. It creates unfavourable situations and hampers the smoothness of the work. Sometime ago an industrialist came to me and told me about his factory not running well inspite of best efforts. Due to constant labour-problem, factory was at stake, even after all means were employed to satisfy the labour. I myself saw the factory and after observation found that there was a wide beam, in the central hall, under which the employees used to work. A beam itself remains tense and thus keeps the persons underneath in tension thereby reducing their output drastically. I changed the workers hall by shifting it to another place. There was an amazing change, the workers and labourers started reaching the factory in time and the prevailing problems never repeated thereafter.

Vastu of Town should be proper

If you observe the map of the world you will find that Sri Lanka is triangular in shape, hence skirmishes and cold war will continue forever due to terrorism. Similarly, quarrels, disturbances, uneasiness and skirmishes have been observed in Chandigarh due to its triangular shape. Sawai Jai Singh established Jaipur, according to Vastushastra, which became the capital of Rajasthan after independence. Its fort and palace are without any scratch. Neither any area had been looted, nor there lies any temple, mosque or fort destroyed. People, living there, are happy and prosperous.

The town, which possesses river, pond or sea in Ishanya (N.E.), and if the southern part is elevated, remains very prosperous and is the main centre of business activity. Bombay in India, and America, on the world map, are excellent examples of Vastu-science. World-famous Tirupati-Temple in India is a unique example of Vastushastra, in whose Ishanya (N.E.) flows the river Pushkarni and is surrounded by hills.

Special Care Should Be Taken of Dwarvedha

Both the builder and owner of a house should take special care of the factors which blocks light and air reaching the door (Dwarvedha), otherwise the results may be disastrous for both. A person known to me built a marvellous house spending several lakhs rupees having a boundary-wall before the main door with a tap beside. A road 25 feet wide was in front with a pipal-tree on the side. A handpump was also bored under that tree. The tree provided shade on the main gate of house after 10 A,M daily. Neither the house owner nor the builder (contractor) took care of this. On auspicious moment the new house was inaugurated. The rituals for entering the house Griha-Pravesh were to be performed with my hands. This door situation struck me and I cautioned them against the bad results on the coming generation of both, house builder and house owner. But there is no time to think about these minor things by the people involved into western music, dinner and disco dance. In the cold atmosphere of winter icecream was being served after dinner. The only son aged 14 years of the house owner ate a lot of icecream which resulted in his getting fever which continued for 3 days. This was initially taken very lightly and the child was given domestic treatment. He was given tablets to bring down the temperature but it used to recur after 2-3 days. Sometimes temperature used to go up in the night even after normalcy during day-time. After one and half months they learned from the family physician after X-ray and other tests that the lungs were filled up with water. With proper treatment, water was removed and the boy survived but the treatment continued for 1 1/2 years. On the other hand the two children of the contractor met with an accident and were admitted to hospital. These incidents should not be termed as merely a chance happening. When I made the perforated-door proper, the house-owner and the contractor got peace. Sometimes trivial things become cause for distress in peculiar ways which affects the coming generation. A rational man should always think that there should not be any tree or plant, corner of wall, pole, ditch, well, garbage, mud, lane, shadow of temple, any type of blockade or impediment just in front of main door. The door should not produce unpleasant sound while opening or closing. There will be good and auspicious result and will protect the family members if the main door is well placed and built properly.

Vastushastra should be Practical

Vastuvigya or those who know about Vastu (Vastu-Scientists) became unpractical, as the importance of Vastushastra increased. Recently, a seminar on Vastu was organised in Jaipur where Vastu-Scientists of Bombay were called. The entry fee for the participants was Rs 1100/- and all were compelled to buy a book of 35-40 pages costing Rs 150/- This book comprised many selected photographs taken from famous books and granthas. This costly book could be xeroxed for Rs 12/- only. Hence the organiser just befooled the serious and inquisitive audience and went back with five lakh rupees in one day. Only recently another serious incident occured with my friend which really stunned me. This friend has got a big factory in the industrial belt of Muzzaffarnagar. He was running in an unfavourable period for last 2-3 years. Some one told that Vastu of factory was wrong. This man, contacted the Vastushastra Experts in Madras, Bangalore, Bombay and abroad too. They quoted in thousands with air travel to visit the place only. At last, a person from Madras acceded to his request. My friend spent more than 50 thousand rupees on the travel, lodging, boarding and consultation of this Vastu-Scientist. This led my friend to loss of seven lakhs of rupees in breaking and demolishing the labour-quarters, latrine, bathroom office, godown wall by hammer and bulldozer as instructed by that Vastu-scientist. Finally he contacted me after eight exhaustive months when no relief was seen. After a brief telephonic conversation, I went over to Muzzaffarnagar. There is an old adage in Marwari language:

'नेडो तीर्थ गांव गुरू, गलियों हंदा देवा
इतरा री महिमा नहीं, संत भाखै सहदेवा।'
**Nedo Tirth Gaon Guru, Galio Handa Dev
Itra Ri Mahima Nahin, Sant Bhakhay Sahdeo.**

(i.e. The pilgrimage near to a village does not have any meaning or importance for the native place. The wise and learned men of the particular caste or village are not given any importance in their own caste and village). There is little importance of the saints in yellow robes or clothes on their person moving about in Kashi. But even a foolish person from Kashi with yellow robes moving in Jodhpur is given much importance and respect and is appreciated. The same case happened to my friend. The person who came from Madras was having little knowledge but big fame. Actually the North-East (aspect) of that factory was out of alignment. Ishan (N.E.) is very important amongst the eight directions. The corner of Ishan (N.E.) is saved with proper care while building hotels, shops, multistorey buildings, factories, industries and commercial complex. If the fault remains in the Ishan (N.E.) related to Vastu even after possessing many a especiality of Vastu in remaining directions, that industry or factory can't progress and will not be profitable and fruitful. All the income will be spent on futile things. Even after the income in lakh and crores the balance-sheet will show zero due to imbalance amount of expenditure. Hence read the book written by me named 'Commercial Vastu' also for details from which some important points are mentioned here:

1. Corner of Ishan (N.E.) should not be higher than other walls of factory-industry, stall, hotel and commercial complexes.
2. Water-reservoir or well in any direction of factory leaving Ishan (N.E.) corner gives bad results.
3. Any fault, ditch or broken part in the direction of Ishan (N.E.) will get handicapped child to industrialist.
4. Lavatory (latrine) in Ishan (N.E.) creates quarrel in family, amongst the workers, in the factory, and the owner of factory will be afflicted by character assasination and diseases.
5. Kitchen in Ishan (N.E.) creates quarrel in house and excessive expenditure.
6. Garbage, storage of stones & thrown away goods should not be kept in Ishan (N.E.) at any cost because it brings defame to the owner and shortens his age.
7. According to Vastushastra rules even sticks of mosquito net, or any type of garbage or dirty things or sweeping brush should not be kept in the corner of Ishan (N.E.).

I rectified the Ishan (N.E.) of that factory which is in order now. The owner is satisfied. What I want to say here is that only going through the book is not enough. A Vastu-Scientist should be sensitive and practical. Demolishing and breaking of walls and houses without reason has no meaning. The house and industry should be observed patiently and minutely. In this materialistic world, a Vastu-Scientist should charge for his labour but it should not be exorbitant and it reason has no meaning. The house and industry should be observed patiently and minutely. In this materialistic world, a Vastu-Scientist should charge for his labour but it should not be exorbitant and it should be quite practical. He should keep in mind that the person has called him is in his distress and engulfed in problems; hence he should work with a helping attitude. Then only this science will be truthful helpful and meaningful.

Some important rules of Vastu-Science

1. Before buying the land, its shape and angles must be examined by the learned Vastu-Scientist according to the rules of Vastu.
2. Adoration of land and the foundation should be performed in auspicious moment before constructing the house. After completion of the house idol should be installed in a ritual way. Worship of Vastu, muttering of Gayatri and Rudra, worship of Lord Ganesha, Vishnu, Navagraha and invocation for cooling down planets, including food and gift to Brahmans should be performed. In Sastra, tenth part of total cost of house should be invested on rituals for house awakening.
3. House should always be built in such a way that it can get maximum natural light, fresh air and rays of the morning-sun.
4. The main door of factory, workshop, mill or school should never be in the corner.
5. There should not be any restriction or blockade in front of door (Dwaravedha).
6. Useless and refusal trees should not be sown on front door-front. For the knowledge about this read my book 'Jyotish Me Bhawan, Vahan and Kirtiyoga' (House, Vehicle and Fame in astrology).
7. The kitchen, furnace, generator, transformer or oil-engine or any item relating to fire should be kept in Agnikona (South-East) of the land.
8. Only North-West corner should be used for animal, chariot, bullock cart, taxi or car-parking etc.

9. The stream or flow of water-whether of rain or collected water should be in the direction of North-East.
10. Administrative room, sitting room, consulting room or the room for talking major and important decisions should be in the north or east direction of the house.
11. The face of worshipper or penancer should be in the direction of East, Ishanya (north-east) or North.
12. Latrine, urinals, drain, manhole or dirty sewage should be in the north-west or south-east corner.

Chapter 2

Character and Nature of Vastu

According to Halaayudh (dictionary)—वास्तु संक्षेपतो वक्ष्ये गृहादो विघ्ननाशनम्। ईशानकोणादारभ्य ह्योकाशीतिपदे त्यजेत् (Vastu Sankshiptat Vakshaye Grihado Vighanasham: Ishan Konadavabhya Hyokashitipade—Tyajet) i.e. In nut-shell vastu is the art of starting constructing a house from N.E. corner so as to save the house from mishaps and troubles caused by the adversities of nature! which saves the house from mishappenings and troubles of nature's sudden adversities.[1] Amarkosha states as—गृहरचनावच्छिन्न भूमे (Griharachna-Vaechinna Bhume) i.e. the uninterrupted plot suitable for house construction is called vastu.[2]

Vastu is that plot, on which the house is setup or the plot considered good for building a house is Vastu.[3] The word vastu is familiar to house hold from the Rigveda period.[4]

Vastushastra is supposed to be the propounder of architecture and the art of house-building. In other civilizations of the world where house construction or town-formation was taken as a type of worldly act whereas the importance of this in Indian culture is taken as a religious act. The Indian seers clarified the cause of houses construction and state that the true meaning of a house lies in getting enjoyment through family and happiness due to dharma, artha, kama,

---
1. हलायुध कोष, पृष्ठ 606
2. अमरकोष, द्वितीय कांड, पृष्ठ 140
3. संस्कृत-शब्दार्थ कौस्तुभ, पृष्ठ 1008
4. वास्तोष्पते प्रति जानीहास्मान्-ऋग्वेद 7/सू 54/1

animals (cows, horses, dogs etc), including the removal of pain and troubles related to place, cold, wind, smoke and fire. [5]

The Indian saints provided a philosophic shape to grammer by imagining the shabda- Brahma (sound of the divinity), they also by imagining this Brahma transformed the Kavya (prose) Nada-Brahma (Sound-Brahma) and music, lifting it to the extremely mystic world or heaven (Parlokik Param Rahasya) from this mundane world. In the same fashion, to increase the stability of the imagination of a person in a house of stone, Vastu-Brahmvaad has been propounded into account. Vastushastra is a process in which limited and moderate land is enlarged into unlimited and huge world-power. That bare-name existing without shape which is controlled in this Vastu-Mandal (vastu-aura) is called vastu-purush (vastu- person). [6]

Dr.Acharya writes in vastu vishvakosha that the word Vastu denotes the villages, towns, forts, ports, fortified city, residential houses as the abode for living. It also moves together with sculpture and stone age art as well. [7]

Subjects of Vastu Shastra

The construction, veneration, rectification and repairing of house, mansion, high palace, fortress, town, temple, well, pond, oblong pond, sculpture and architecture, different types of mandapas, sacrificial shed, seminar house, royal camp, chariot, different types of vehicles, parks, stages etc. are the subject of study in Vastu shastra.

Vastushastra is also a part of Astrology as it is necessary to know and observe the auspicious moments and 'Muhurta' by astrological-calculations for every vastu-construction. Any type of work relating to this should be started only after seeing the proper date and day. What and how should be the face of quarter (Diksanmukhya), are the pertinent questions answered in

5. स्त्री पुत्रादिकंभो आरण्यजन्वनं धर्मार्थकामपुरम्।
जन्तुनामयनं सुखास्यदमिदं शीताम्बुधर्महिम्।। —बृहद्वास्तुमाला, पृष्ठ १
6. भारतीय स्थापत्य—डा. द्विजेंद्रनाथ शुक्ल (प्रका. 1968) हिंदी समिति लखनऊ, पृष्ठ ११
7. वही दृष्ट्य, पृष्ठ 17

Vastu-mandala.

The Science of Vastu is also closely related to geography, geology, and mathematics. The place for building a mansion is fixed after the exanination based on smell, colour, taste and touch of the soil of the land.

The knowledge of Digdashagyan (knowledge of direction), Digsaadhan (means and execution for direction), nature of soil, land, rectification and examination of land, income, Grihpindsaadhan, muhurta for house construction, Karma-Chakra, door of house, Dwara-Vedha, Dwar-dona, determination, of Griha-pravesh, Goshala (cow-shed), Cavalry-construction, places for elephants, laying out of garden, koopchakra (well-construction), Vrikshayurbheda (secret of trees), oodkargalam (place of water), nature of palace, muhurta for establishment, construction of imperial building, bed-geomancy, arch-door-way, box, nest, Mandapbheda, science of images and idols, traditions of worshipping, signs of different gods and godesses gender, jewellery are the subjects of study in vastushastra.

The residential place and the house should be auspicious to the people living in it from the wealth, prosperity, luxury, progeny and happiness point of view. Where and in what direction, the fire, water, place of worship, and bed-room should be situated? Where should be the direction of sunlight and air? How the owner of house will enjoy sound sleep? What should be the shape of the plot and where should be its entrance? In which direction should lie the main-path inside the house? There are many such fields on which vastushastra deals elaborately:[8]

(a) Goal of Vastu:

The house should be congenial to the natural resources with symmetrical architecture and vastu-formula so that the people living in it be healthy, happy and prosperous. This is the aim of Vastu. The aim of vastu is the gain of Ihlok (mundane world) and Parlok[9] (beyond this

---
8. नारद संहिता, अध्याय 31/पृष्ठ 220
9. देवनामालयः कार्यो द्वायमप्यत्र दृश्येता। —बृहत्संहिता अध्याय 56/श्लोक 2/पृष्ठ 380

world, heaven). According to Varaahmihir, Maharashi Narada says

अनेन विधिना सम्यग्वास्तुपूजां करोति यः।
आरोग्यं पुत्रलाभं च धनं धान्यं लभेन्नरः॥[10]

**Anena Vidhina SamayagVastupuja Karoti Yah
Arogyam Putralabh Cha Dhanam Dhanayam Labben-narah**

One who respects vastu rightway gets health, progeny, property, and other useful gains. The people lacking proper Vastu of house, invite death of wife, progeny, destruction of property, tension, disease, unrest and different types of adversities.

(b) Name Of Respected Vastushastra-Scientist

Eighteen learned person of vastushastra have been mentioned in 'Matsyapurana' among which Bhrigu, Atri, Vasishtha, Vishvakarma, Maya, Narada, Nagnajit, Vishalakhsh, Vishaloxh, Purandar, Brahma, Kumar, Nandish, Shaunak, Garga, Vasudev, Anirudh, Shukra, and Brihaspati are reported to be propounders of eighteen vastushastra. As it is mentioned:—

भृगुरत्रिवसिष्ठश्च विश्वकर्मा मयस्तथा।
नारदो नग्नजिच्चैव विशालाक्षः पुरन्दरः॥
ब्रह्मा कुमारो नन्दीशः, शौनको 'गर्ग एव च।
वासुदेवोऽनिरूद्धश्च तथा शुक्रबृहस्पति॥[11]

**Bhragyaistachya vishwakarma mayastha
narado naganjichev vishalaksh purandar
brahma kumari nandish shonako garg evam cha
vasudevomnirudhsch tatha shukrabrihspate.**

Narayhan Bhatt, Ramdaivagya, Keshavdevagya, Mandavya, Lall, Shripati, Brahmshambhu, Kalisdasa, Varahmihir, Todaranand, Bhaskara, Shangardhar etc. are the learned men of vastushastra, having a deep insight of the subject.[12]

---
10. नारदसंहिता, अध्याय ३२/ श्लोक 19/ पृष्ठ 228
11. रूपमंडन—डा. बलराम श्रीवास्तव (प्रका. १९८९) मोतीलाल बनारसीदास वाराणसी, पृष्ठ 1
12. बृहद्वास्तुमालाऌपं—रामनिहोर द्विवेदी (प्रका. 1932) काशी, पृष्ठ 4

(c) Excellent books on Vastushastra

Vishvakarma padhati, Vishvakarmapurana, Vishvakarmaprakash, Vishvakarmmat, Vishvakarmasamhita, Vrihad Vastumala, Vastupradip, Vasturatna, Vasturajvallabh, Rupmandan, Mahajyotinirbandh, Grihratna-Bhushan, Ratnamala, Shilp Ratna, mansaar, Vastumuktavali, Pratishtha-Mahodadhi, Pratishtha kalplata, Pratishthatatvadarsh, Prayogparijat, Shilpasaar, Bhartiya-Sthapatya etc. are the important ancient books on architecture, craft and Vastushastra.

Many important things have been propounded by taking help from Agnipurana, Matsyapurana, Bhavishya purana, and Brihtsamhita. 'Samrangana Sutradhara' is a Vastushastra's old book (Purana) in which Vastushastra is dealt in lucid style, through a discussion between Vishvakarma and his sons.[13] Maymatam and Vastuvigyan are the famous books of this science.

□

---
13. भारतीय स्थापत्य—डा. द्विजेंद्रनाथ शुक्ल (प्रका. 1968) हिंदी समिति लखनऊ, पृष्ठ 12

Chapter 3

Evaluation of Site : Various Aspects

1. Land

Examination of land can be undertaken in four ways. Whether the land is auspicious or inauspicious, is checked by digging a trench or pit with depth of one hand and a hand of length and breadth amidst the plot by the owner, followed by filling this pit with same soil. If the pit needs extra soil, then the land is inauspicious, if the soil is sufficient to fill it upto the level, it is of general type and if the soil goes up the level then the plot is supposed to be very auspicious.

So many things and information are given about land, in Vastushastra and it is said that—'ततो भूमि परीक्षेत वास्तुज्ञानविशारदः' 'Tato bhumi parikshete vastugyanvishharad' which means that the master of Vastushastra should test the land from different aspects.

Sacrificial pit and mandapa's construction should be done on Monday, Wednesday, Thursday and Friday and other auspicious dates barring inauspicious and rejected Rikta (vacant) days, inauspicious yogas like Vyatipat. Examination should be done with five priests or Brahmans. To know the suitability of a land for sacrifice, burn any grass or straw followed by digging of pit upto knees. Fill it completely with water and do Punyah Vaachan (reciting swastivachana). On the very next day if the land is torn or found with any inauspicious thing for example bone, then the land is not good for sacrifice and will lead to destruction of property and age.[1] Land having pits and trenches,

---
1. गृहमध्ये हस्तमितं खात्वा, परिपूरितं पुनः श्वभ्रम्।

thorns etc. should be rejected straightaway. Naryan Bhatt says,'Dig a pit of a hand's length breadth and depth; fill it with water at sunset. If water still remains there till next morning then it is a sign of good luck and if not, it should be taken as inauspicious.!2☐

(a) Things Obtained during digging

While digging the base of house, if termite, python etc. are found, one should not build a residence on that plot. If chaff or husk, snake, eggs etc. are found, it gives excruciating pain. Varatica (cowrie) gives

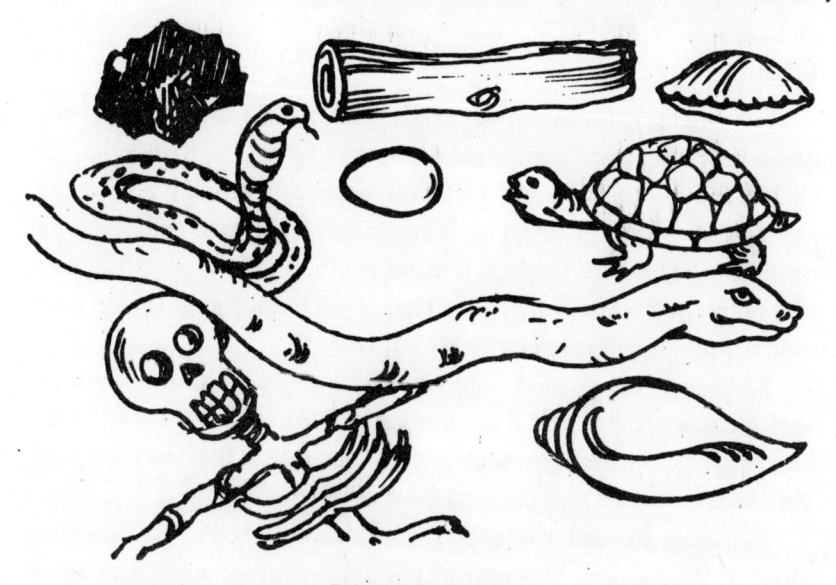

Excavated material

trouble and quarrel. Karpas (torn cloth) causes extreme worry. Burnt wood (coal) gives diseases. Khappar (tiles) creates quarrel and iron found indicates death of owner of house. Bones, skeleton hair etc. found weaken the age of plot-owner. But cow-horn, shankha (conch-shell), Oyster-shell, tortoise are sign of good omen. If stone were found while digging then gain of gold and if bricks were found then prosperity is expected there. Coins provide happiness and

यद्यूनमधिष्ठं तत्समे समं धन्यमधिकं यतृ॥ —बृहत्संहिता 55/श्लोक 92
2. यज्ञकुंडमंडप—सिद्धि, भूमिपरीक्षा/पृष्ठ 26

SAMPURN VASTUSHASTRA   32

copper found increases fame and prosperity.[3]

(b). Land-Examination According to Varna (colour)

1. **Colour:** The land of white soil, red soil, yellowish-green soil and black soil are called Brahman, Kshatriya, Vaishya and Shudra respectively.
2. **Smell:** The smell of soil like ghee, blood, honey or grain and liquor are appropriate for Brahman, Kshatriya, Vaishya and Shudra respectively according to the shastras.
3. **Taste:** Keep a bit of soil on the tip of tongue. The tastes like honey, sour, (acidic) astringent (foul) are put among Brahman, Kshastriya, Vaishya and Shudra respectively.
4. **Straw-Test:** The land comprising kush, Darbh (holy grass) and sacrificial plant, denotes Brahmani; red-grass (Shar or Munj), the plant of red-flowers and snakes are associated with Kshastriya, property, grain and plant with fruits are associated with Vaishya; the evil-plants and trees with all round straws denotes Shudras.
5. **Effect of Land:** Brahmani land provides all types of spiritual and divine happiness. Kshastriya gives kingdom and increases volour and its effect. Vaishya is associated with property and prosperity. Shudra is neglected because it increases quarrel and creates skirmishes. Hard and smooth soil irrespective of colour is always good and appreciated.[4]

(c). Second Method for land-examination

Make a pit as mentioned previously and fill it with water. Then move hundred steps away from that and return again. If the water maintains the same level, in the pit then it is auspicious.[5]

---

3. बृहद् वास्तुमाला, पृष्ठ 21
4. बृहद्वास्तुमाला, पृष्ठ 22
5. बृहद् वास्तुमाला, श्लोक 34/पृष्ठ 7

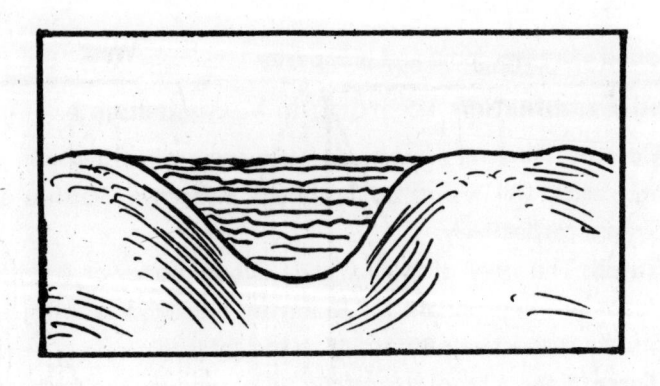

Pit filled with water

Examination according to slope

The slope towards north, east, south and west are auspicious for Brahmana, Kshastriya, Vaishya and Shudra. Brahmana can build house in the land of all the four types of slope. It is good for the rest of Varnas, to build house in the respective slope.[6]

(A). Vastu-Knowledge of Varahmihir

Varahmihir has thought about the four directions in context of four varna but 26 types of land has been mentioned in Vastushastra, by enlarging the shape of this classification which are discussed below—

What the diagram says

1. Black & short denotes high land.
2. Long and fine arrow denotes depression.
3. Elevated land has got cross-sketch.
4. Depressed land is white.

1. Govithi —The land having elevation in the west and slope in the east is called Govithi. Such land increases progeny.

2. Jalvithi—The land higher in east and depressed in west is called Jalvithi and this destroys the progeny.

---
6. बृहत्संहिता, अध्याय 53/श्लोक 93/पृष्ठ 346

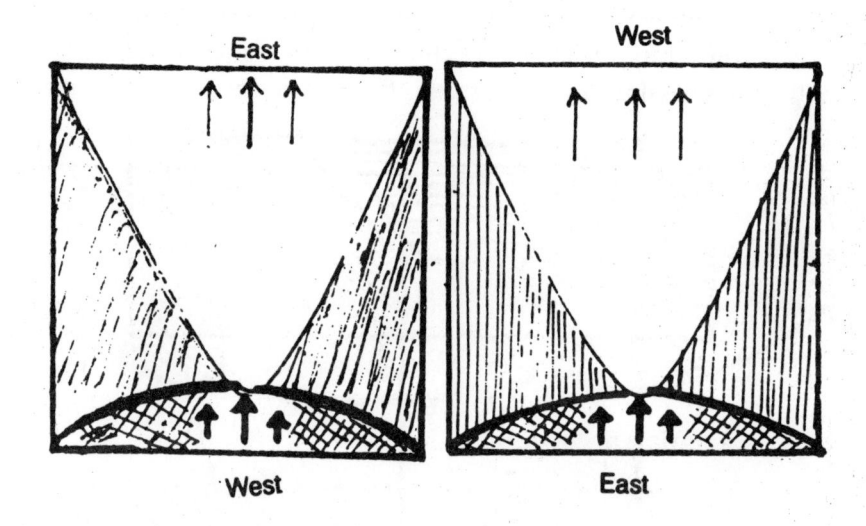

Govithi Land

Jalvithi Land

3. Yamvithi—The land with elevation in north and depression in south, is called Yamvithi and deteriorates health.

4. Ganavithi—The land with elevation in south and depression in north assures good health.

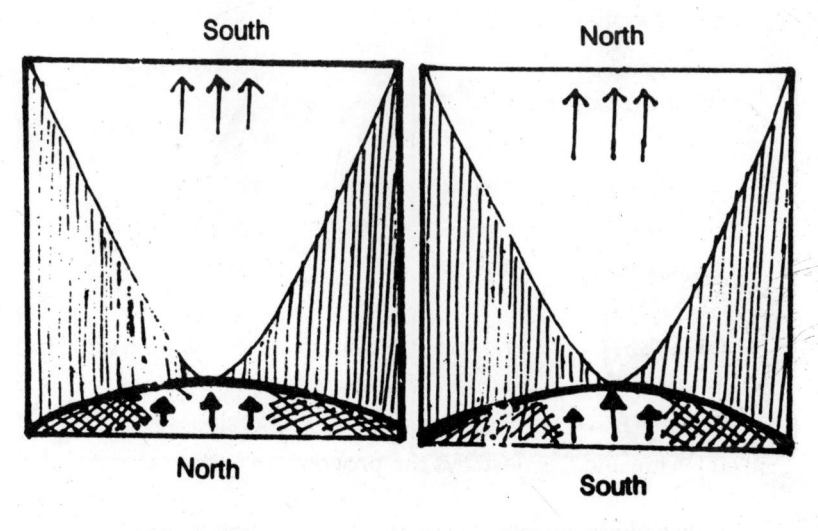

Yamvithi Land

Ganavithi Land

5. Bhutvithi—The land which is higher in Ishanya (NE)-corner and low in Naishritya (SW) is called Bhutvithi and gives sorrow and pain.

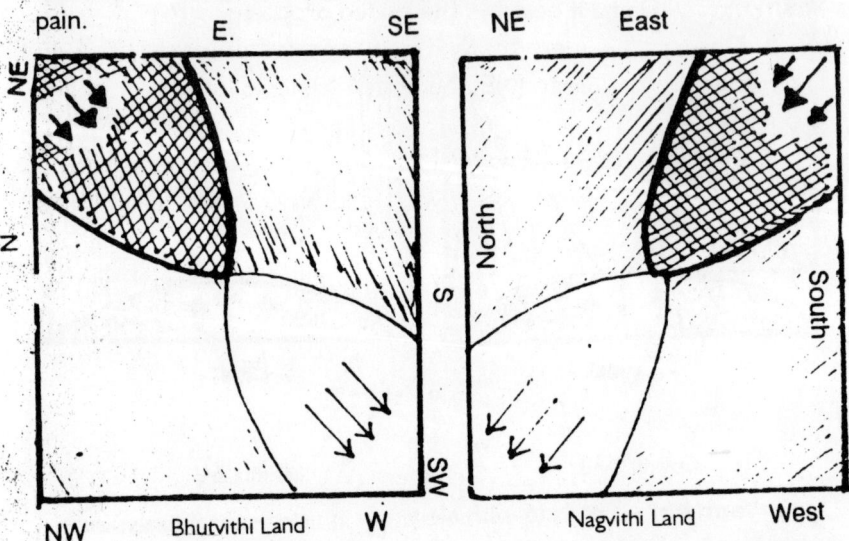

Bhutvithi Land   Nagvithi Land

6. Nagvithi—The land which is elevated in the Agneya (SE) and low towards Vayavya (NW) is called Ng-Vithi and bestows landed property.

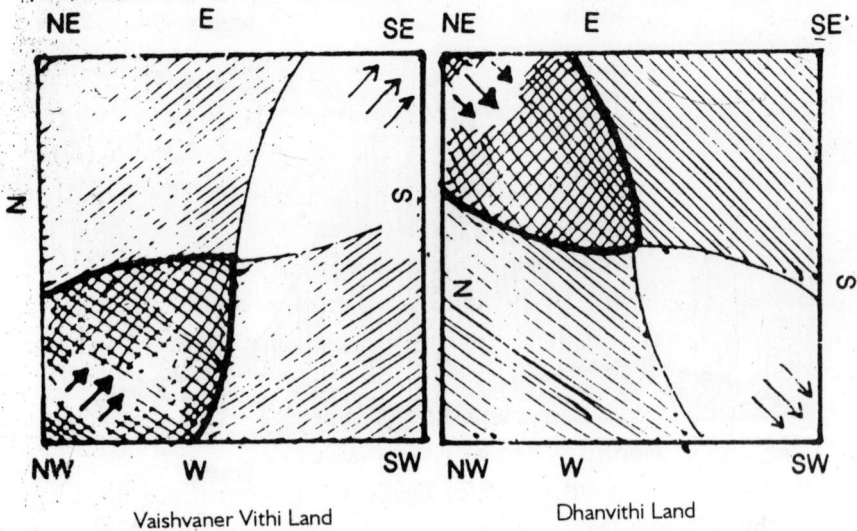

Vaishvaner Vithi Land   Dhanvithi Land

7. Yaishvaner Yithi—The land which is elevated towards Vayavya (NW) and depressed towards Agneya (SE) is called Vaishvaneri Vithi and it destroys the landed property

8. Dhanvithi— Here the land is lower towards Naishritya (SW) and higher towards Ishan (NE). Such land bestows lot of money and property.

9. Pitamah Yastu—The land which is higher between east and Agneya (SE) but low between west and Vayavya (NW) is called

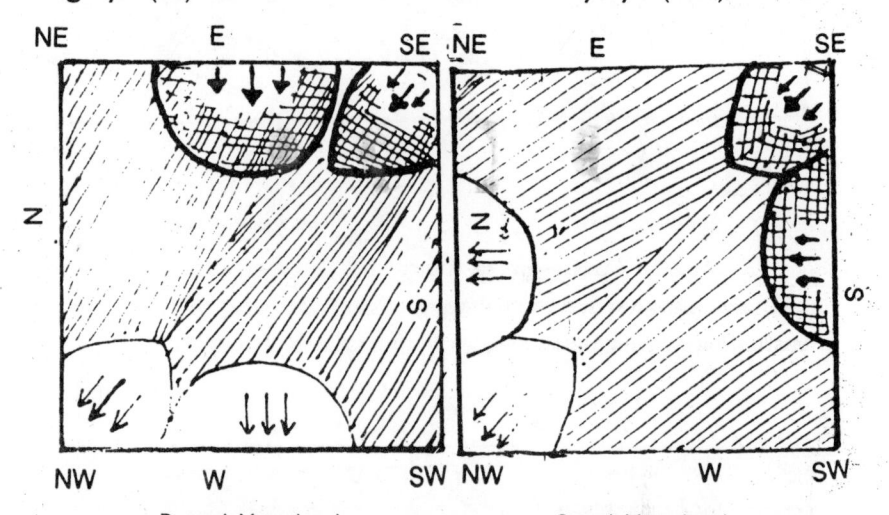

Pitamah Vastu Land   Supath Vastu Land

Pitamah Vastu (land). This land provides happiness to human-beings.

10. Supath Yastu— It is that land which is elevated between Agneya (SE) and south but low between Vayavya (NW) and north is supath. This is suitable for all good activities.

11. Dirghayu Vastu—Dirghaya vastu is the land depressed between north and Ishanya (NE) and elevated between Naishritya (SW) and south. This is extremely good situation and helpful in increasing progeny.

12. Punyak vastu—Here the land is depressed between Ishanya (NE) and east and elevated between Naishritya (SW) and west. This land is fruitful and auspicious for Dwija only (Brahman, Kshatriya and Vaishya)

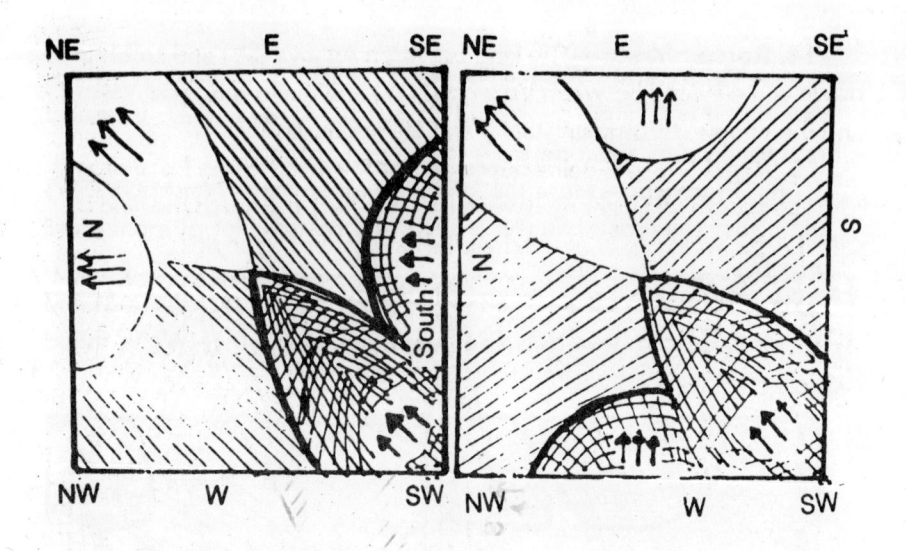

Dirghayu Vastu Land

Punyak Vastu Land

13. Apath Yastu—Being depressed between east and Agneya (SE) and elevated between Vayavya (NW) and west is called Apath vastu. People living here are the ill-affected and attract disease.

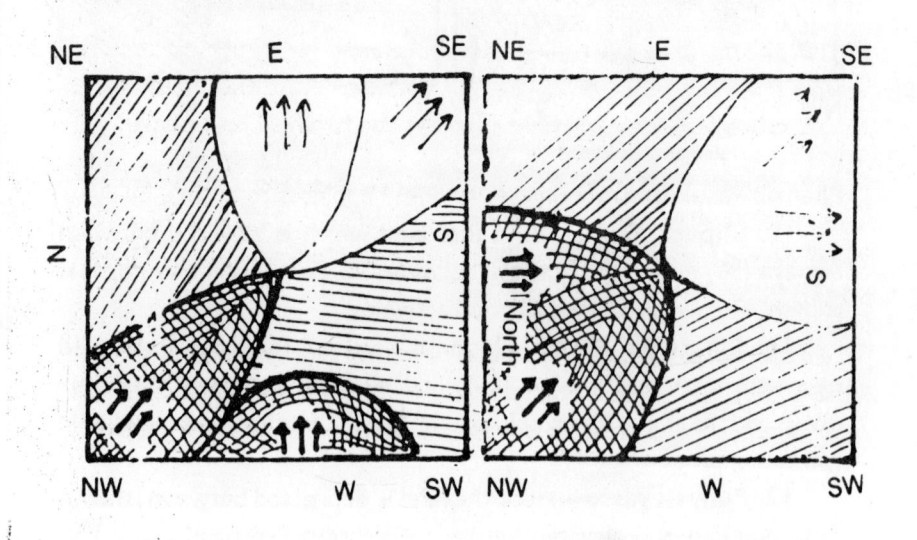

Apath Vastu Land

Rogkar Vastu Land

14. Rogkar Vastu—The land between Agneya (SE) and south is down and elevated between Vayavya (NW) and north is Rogkar Vastu and the people become unhealthy and attract disease.

15. Argal Vastu—Being depressed or lower between Naishritya (SW) and south and higher between Ishanya (NE) and north the land is called Argal which detaches and washes away the bigger sins.

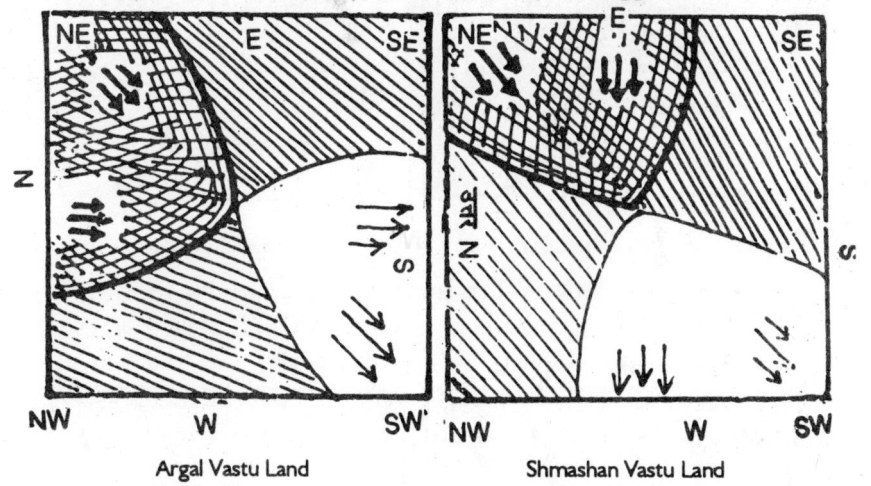

Argal Vastu Land   Shmashan Vastu Land

16. Shmashan Vastu—The land which is higher between Ishanya (NE) and east and depressed between west and Naishritya (SW) is called Shmashan Vastu. It destroys the family of land owner.

17. Shyanek Vastu—It is the plot, having land depressed in Agneya (SE) and higher in Naishritya (SW), Ishanya (NE) and Vayavya (NW). Such plots are cause for destruction and indicate death of land owner.

18. Swamukh Vastu—The land, elevated through Ishanya (NE), Agneya (SE) and west and depressed in Naishritya (SW), is called swamukh. Such land provides poverty and makes the owner a pauper.

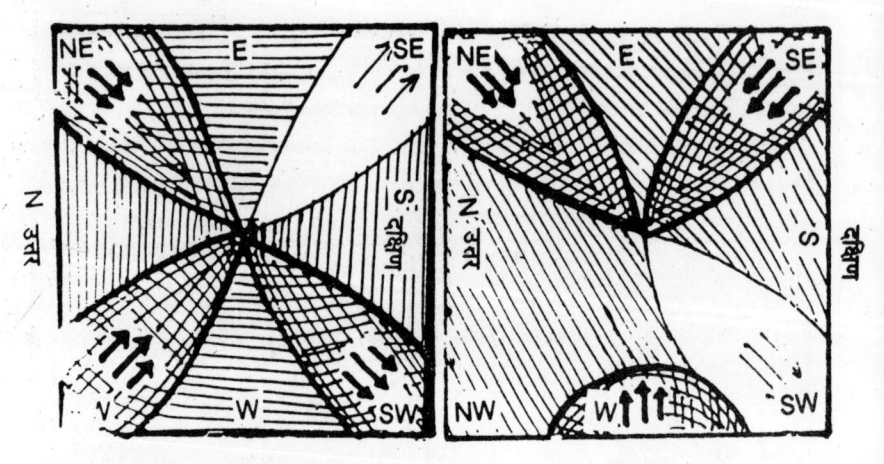

Shyanek Vastu Land

Swamukh Vastu Land

19. Brahma Vastu—The land, higher through Naishritya (SW), Agneya (SE), Ishanya (NE) and lower in Vayavya (NW), is always destructive for the people.

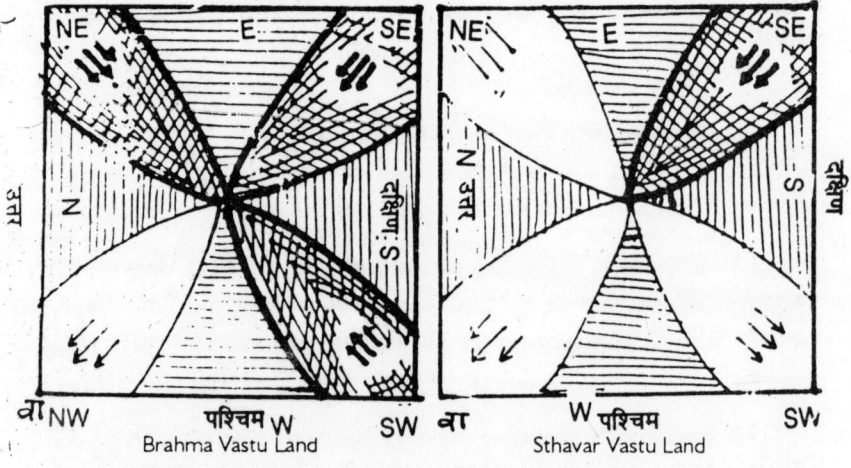

Brahma Vastu Land

Sthavar Vastu Land

20. Sthavar Vastu—Higher in Agneya (SE) and lower through Naishritya (SW), Ishanya (NE) and Vayavya (NW) is called sthavar vastu. Such land is auspicious.

21. Sthandil Vastu—Higher in Naishritya (SW) and down in Agneya (SE) Vayavya (NW) and Ishanya (NE) is called sthandil vastu which is auspicious for each person.

Sthandil Vastu Land　　　　　Shandul Vastu Land

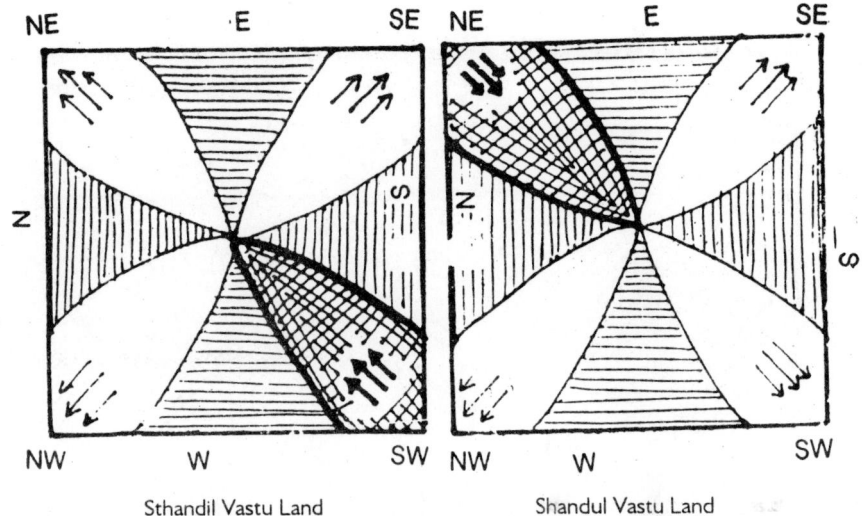

22. Shandul Vastu—elevated through Ishanya (NE) and depressed through Agneya (SE), Naishritya (SW) and Vayavya (NW), this is inauspicious for everyone.

23. Susthan vastu—The land, which is elevated through Naishritya (SW) and Ishanya (NE) and depressed in Vayavya (NW), is called susthan vastu. This land or plot proves favourable to Brahamnas.

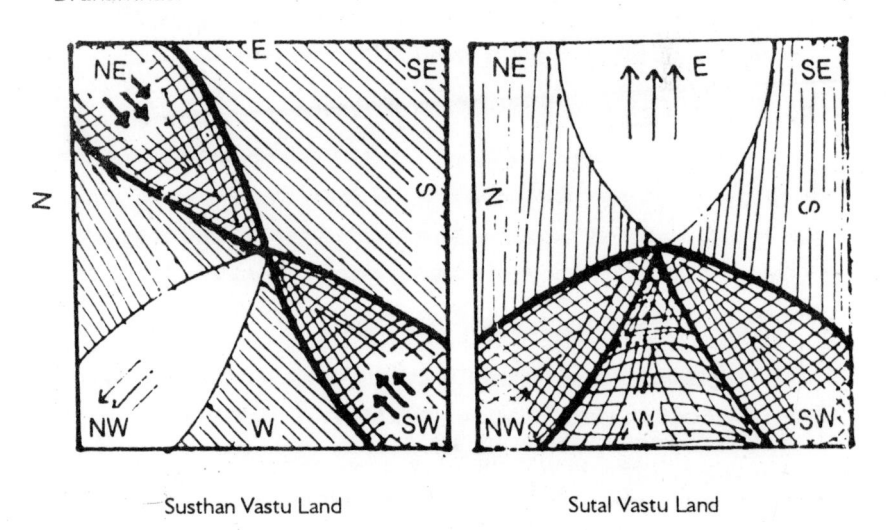

Susthan Vastu Land　　　　　Sutal Vastu Land

24. Sutal Vastu—Depressed in east direction and elevated in Naishritya (NW) Vayavya (SW) and west, is called the land of sutal vastu which is very much favourable to a Kshatriya.

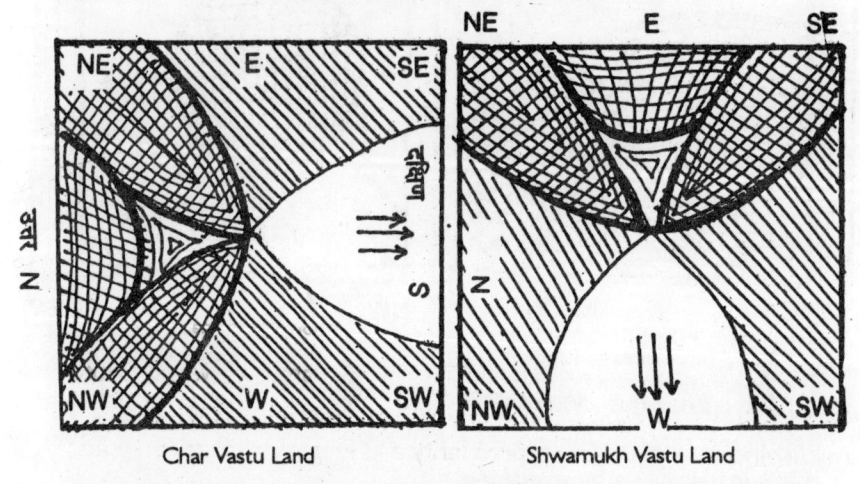

Char Vastu Land   Shwamukh Vastu Land

25. Char Vastu—The land being elevated towards north, Ishanya (NE) and Vayavya (NW) becomes depressed in south, is called char vastu which is extremely good for Vaishya.

26. Shwamukh Vastu—The land, being depressed in western direction possess high land in Ishanya (NE), east and Agneya (SE), falls in shwamukha vastu and this is favourable to shudras.[7]

(B). Test of Land with the Flow of Water

Flood irrigate the land to be examined. If the water flows towards north, the land is good for Brahmana.[8] Eastward flow of water, on the land is favourable to Kshatriya, southward flow on land is good for Vaishya and westword flow of water is best for Shudra.[9]

(C). Test of Land from Land-Surface

The middle and hard plateau is called Pristha (surface) of the land. From this point of view four types of land are discussed:

---
7. बृहत्संहिता, अध्याय 53/श्लोक 91/पृष्ठ 346
8. बृहद् वास्तुमाला, श्लोक 41/पृष्ठ 8
9. बृहद् वास्तुमाला, श्लोक 42-64/पृष्ठ 9-12

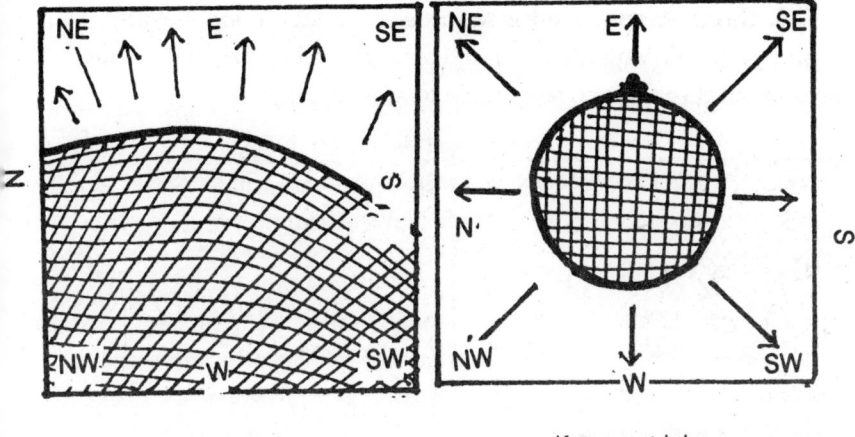

Gajprishth

Koormaprishtha

1. Gajprishth—The land which is elevated towards south Naishritya (SW) west and Vayavya (NW) is called Gajprishth. There is regular increase of property, prosperity and longevity for its residents.

2. Koormaprishtha—The land which is elevated or high in the middle of the plot and is depressed all around is koorma prishtha which is suitable for residence and it gives courage and provides happiness and property.

3. Daitya Prishtha— The land which is high towards Ishanya (NE), east and Agneya (SE) and is lower towards west is called

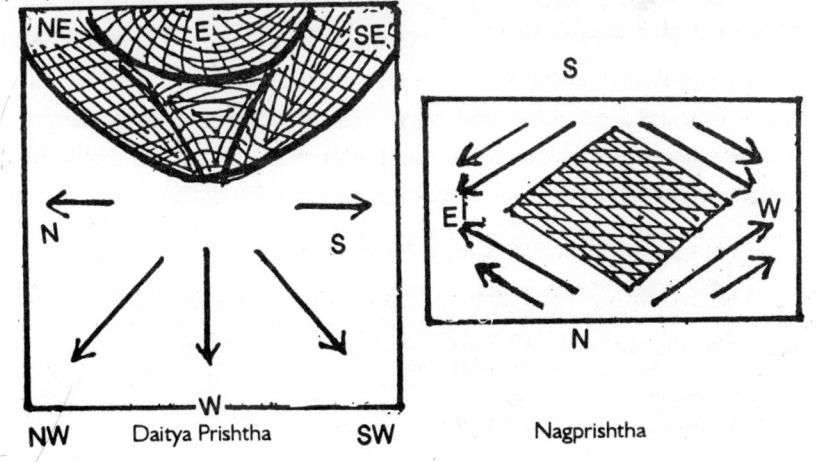

Daitya Prishtha

Nagprishtha

Daityaprishtha. Putting oneself on such land does not provide prosperity and causes loss of wealth and progeny.

4. Nagprishtha—The land, which is lengthy towards east-west and elevated towards south-east is called Nagprishtha. Death is certain of the people living on Nagprishtha land and increases enmity at every step including loss of wife and children.[10]

Shape of Plot

Success in every field (Sarvasiddhi) with rectangular plot, income or wealth with square plot, increase of intelligence and wisdom on circular plot; welfare on throne shaped plot; a pauper on chakrakar (wheel shaped); mourning on odd plot; fear from administration on triangular plot; loss of money on Shaktavar (cart-shaped) land, loss of animals on Dandakar (bar-shaped); loss of animal wealth on shoorpakara (winnowing basket shaped) land pain on the Gav-Vyaghra Bandhan (cow-tiger bondage) and, much fear due to living on Dhanushakar (bow-shaped) land is expected.[11]

Trees as indicators in defect of land

The land with important and worthy roots and lata (creeper), having sweet soil with good smell without holes and burrows gives wealth to land owner.[12] The land having termite and anthill near house creates trouble to the owner of the house. Any deep trench or pit near the house causes disease of thirst, the land of tortoise shape destroys wealth and property.[13]

The land is good and alive if plants, trees and grass grow, otherwise the land should be taken barren and dead. Ashwath (pipal) tree towards east, Utumbur (Gul'ar) towards south, Bar (Banyan) towards west and Pakar towards north of land are supposed to be

---

10. बृहद् वास्तुमाला, श्लोक 82/पृष्ठ 15
11. आयते सिद्ध्यस्सर्वश्चतुरस्रे यनागमः। वृत्तेतु बुद्धिवृद्धिः स्याद्भद्रं भद्रासने भवेत्॥
    चक्रेदारिद्रि त्याहुर्विषमे शोकलक्षणम्। राजभीतिस्त्रिकोणेस्याच्छकटे तु यनक्षय।
    दंडे पशुक्षयं प्राहुः शूर्पे वासे गंवाक्षयः। गोव्याघ्र बंयने पीड़ा यनुः क्षेत्रे भयं महत्॥
                                              —बृहद्वास्तुमालायाम्, श्लोक. 90-92/पृष्ठ 17
12. बृहत्संहिता, अध्याय 53/श्लोक 88/पृष्ठ 345
13. बृहत्संहिता, अध्याय 53/श्लोक 90/पृष्ठ 345

excellent. Opposite to this the trees of Bar, Pakar, pipal and Gular in the direction of east, south, west and north respectively are destructive. These Pipal, Pakar, Bar and Gular if ill-placed, causes fear from fire, madness, injury from arms, and diseases related to abdominal respectively.[14]

Suitability of land for Residence

Maharshi Garg says that if the mind and eyes get satisfaction on seeing the plot, then one should reside there.[15] According to Vasturatna, one should sow crops on the entire plot. A person should live on the land which is fertile for the crops. The barren land should be rejected to a great extent.[16]

In this way we see that many Vastu scientists have determined the parameters and scales for the land-test from Varahmihir till date taday which are helpful elements to make the human life more meaningful and respectful as well.

Rules for a Foundation

The foundation for house to be constructed should be laid after, worship in the Ishanya (NE) corner (NE) followed by laying in other direction from left to right respectively. In the same fashion, raising of pillars should be done decorated with canopy, garland, cloth, burning incense and chandan (sandal).[17]

Making of Outer-Door (Toran)

To avoid bad-omen and to get auspicious results the tradition of making 'Toran' outside every house on the eve of religions activities, Yagyas (Sacrificial act) and ceremonies, has been continuing from Vedic periods. On the occasion of special ceremonies, an arch-door is made

14. बृहद् वास्तुमाला, श्लोक 71-73/पृष्ठ 14
15. मनश्चक्षुषोर्यत्र सन्तोषो जायते भुवि। तस्यां कार्य गृहं सर्वेरिति गर्गादिसम्मतम्॥
—बृहद्वास्तुमालायाम् श्लोक 93/पृष्ठ 18
16. अथवा सर्वधान्यानि वापयेच्च समन्ततः। यत्र नैव प्ररोहन्ति तां प्रयत्नेन वर्जयेत्॥
—बृहद्वास्तुमालायाम् श्लोक 110/पृष्ठ 21
17. उत्तरपूर्वे कोणे कृत्वा पूजां शिलान्यसेत्प्रथमम्। शेषाः प्रदक्षिणेन स्तंभाश्चैव समुत्थाप्या॥
—बृहत्संहिता 53/श्लोक 112

decorated vividly outside the house more often, which is called 'Toran'. This Toran is formed with auspicious tree's branch, leaves and flowers. In practical and oft-quoted language, it is called Bandhanmala or Vandanmala. Varahmihir has mentioned the things to be used to make 'Toran' under proper direction. Toran should be made in Ishanya (NE) which should be 16 hands higher than the trees like (Gular and Arjun) and 10 hands in breadth.[18]

We do not find things of merit discussed in old 'Granthas' like Narada-samhita, Agnipurana, Matasyapurana, Brihat vastumala etc. Many Torans are discussed in 'Tdranvidhanam' chapter of famous grantha named 'Mansaar e.g. Patra toran' Pushp torana, Rattna toran, Chitratoran, Pashantoran, and Kashthatoran etc.[19]

---

18. नगरोत्तरपूर्वदिक्षि प्रशस्तभूमौ प्रशस्तद्रारुमयम्। षोडशहस्तोच्छायं दशविपुलं तोरणं कार्यम्॥
—बृहत्संहिता, अध्याय 44/श्लोक 3/पृष्ठ 248
19. भारतीय स्थापत्य, पृष्ठ 204

Extension of Rajgriha (King's palace)

Varahmihir has mentioned five types of Rajgriha. Extension of 108 hands inside the Rajgriha is best and other four rooms should be made by reducing the length by 8 hands. The quarter should be extended length wise. In the house of the first type the area should be 108 by 137 hands, in the second type it should be 100 by 125 hands, in the third type it should be 92 by 115 hands, in the fourth type this should be 84 by 115 hands and in the fifth type it should be 76 by 95 hands.[20]

Extension of Minister's House (Mantri house)

According to Varahmihir the breadth of house of ministers should be of 60 hands. In other four houses, it should be constructed by reducing it by four hands. The area should by 60X66/12 hands, 56X63 hands, 52X58/12, 48X54 hands, and 44X49/52 hands for the first, second, third, fourth and fifth house respectively.[21]

Extension of Yuvraj-griha (prince-house)

For prince also five types of houses are needed in which the breadth of first house should be of 80 hands and the breadth of rest houses should be reduced by 6 hands each i.e. the breadth of other four houses will be 75, 68, 62 and 56 hands. The length should be the addition of one third of width to the original width i.e. the length should be 106/16, 98/16, 90/16, 82/16 and 74/16.[22]

Extension Of Chief-Astrologer's (Raj-Jyotishi) house

The width of first, second, third, fourth, and fifth room should be 40, 36, 32, 28, and 24 hands respectively. And the length of each will be the addition of one-sixth of its width e.g. 46/6, 42, 36/8, 32/16, 28.[23]

---

20. उत्तममध्राभ्यधिकं हस्तशतं नृपगृहं पृथुत्वेन। अष्टाग्रेणान्येवं पंच सपादानि दैर्घ्येण॥
—बृहत्संहिता, अध्याय 53/श्लोक 4/पृष्ठ 316
21. बृहत्संहिता, अध्याय 53/श्लोक 6/पृष्ठ 318
22. बृहत्संहिता, अध्याय 53/श्लोक 7/पृष्ठ 318
23. बृहत्संहिता, अध्याय 53/श्लोक 10/पृष्ठ 320

Construction of Other Houses

The houses for animals, saints, dhanyagriha (granary), amudhgriha, agnigriha (room for fire), krirha-griha (game room) can be constructed without measurement, i.e. it depends on the aspiration.[24]

The houses for the younger brother of prince and the servants should be half of the extension of house of the Prince. The length of houses should be equal to that of minor and mandadlik king and Chief Kingman (Rajpurush) and breadth should be equal to the difference of the breadth of the King and Ministers' house.[25]

96 types of houses are mentioned in Narad-Samhita but it does not say anything extra about the king's palace.

45 Types of houses are mentioned in Agnipurana, but Rajprasad (king's palace) is not mentioned exclusively. There is no discussion on Rajprasad and Mantrigriha in Gargpurana and Bhavishyapurana. The description of Rajgriha we find in Brihat Vastumala and Vastushastra is infact the reflection of Brihatsamhita. Rajprasad has been classified among nine-classes in Mansaar.

Nature and Number of Mansions

As the sloka in sanskrit says, the high place of temple made for visitors is called 'Prasad' or Mansion.[26] The large house of king is also called prasad according to Halayudh Kosha.[27] The house of Gods and kings which thrills the heart 27 and mind with happiness is also called 'Prasad' according to 'Amarkosa'.[28] Brihatsamhita has described twenty types of 'Prasad'.

1. **Meru Prasad:**—Six 'kona' (angles), 12 plots, different types of windows, four doors in four direction and spread of 20 hands are found in Meru.

2. **Mandar Prasad:**—This posssesses 6 kona (angle), spread

---
24. बृहत्संहिता, अध्याय 53/श्लोक 16/पृष्ठ 322
25. बृहत्संहिता, अध्याय 53/श्लोक 8/पृष्ठ 319
26. संस्कृत हिंदी कोश, शिवराम आप्टे, पृष्ठ 693
27. हलायुध कोश, पृष्ठ 473
28. अमरकोष, द्वितीय काण्ड/पृष्ठ 136

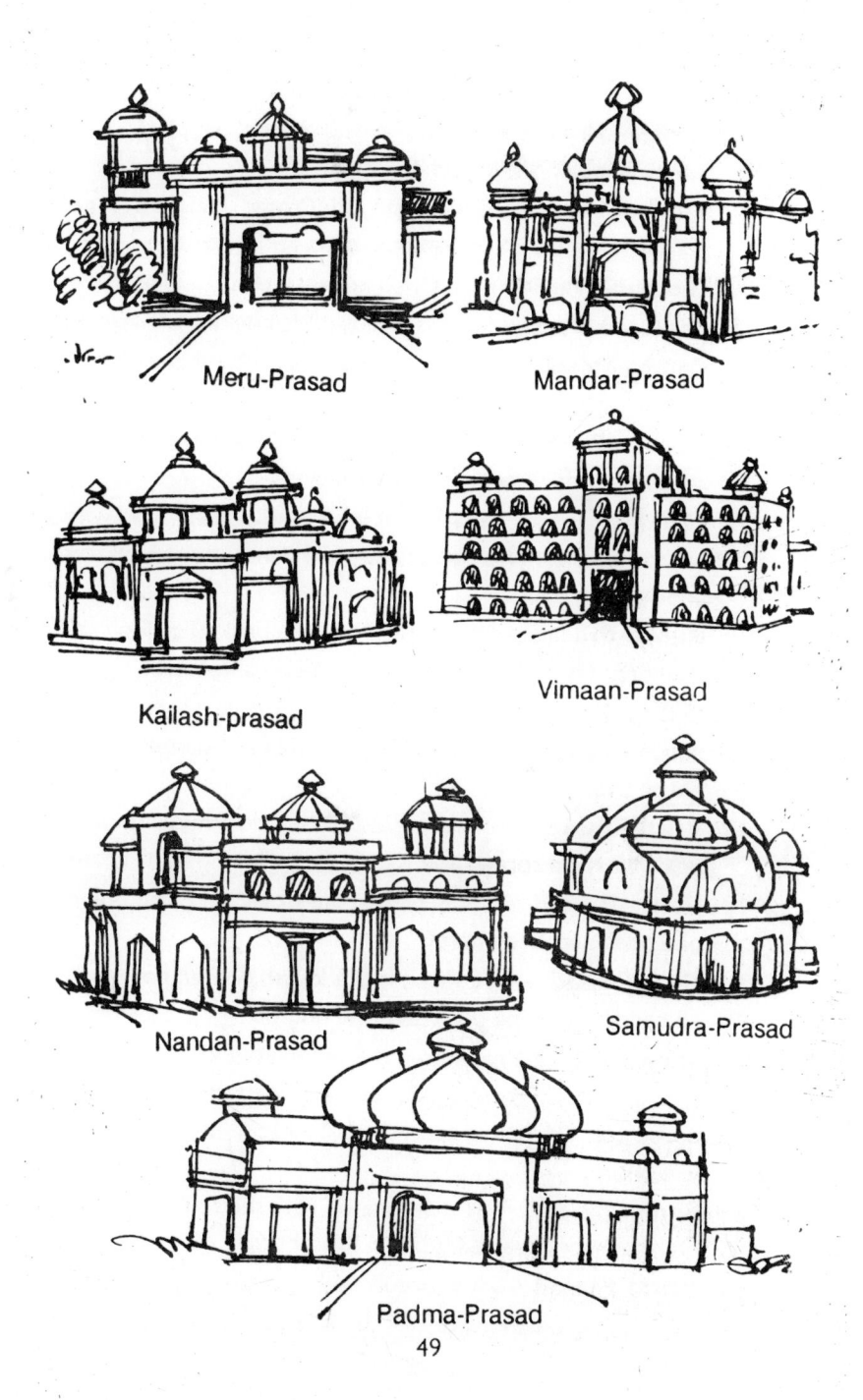

Meru-Prasad

Mandar-Prasad

Kailash-prasad

Vimaan-Prasad

Nandan-Prasad

Samudra-Prasad

Padma-Prasad

upto 30 hands, 10-plots and peaks (shikhar).

3. **Kailash Prasad:**—Spread of 28 hands, 8 plots, 6 kona including peak is found in Kailash.
4. **Yimana-Prasad:**—This type of 'Prasad' possesses grilled window, spread of 21 hands, 8 plots and 6 konas.
5. **Nandan-Prasad** :— It is of 6 konas, 6 plots, 32 hands.
6. **Samudra-Prasad** :— It is circular with peak and of one plot.
7. **Padma Prasad** :— It is of lotus-shape, one peak and one plot.
8. **Garuda Prasad** :— It has the shape of eagle with 24 hands spreads, with 24 peaks and seven plots.
9. **Nandivardhan-Prasad** :— It is just like eagle shaped without tail and feather. This comprises of 24 hands spread, 24 shikhar and seven plots.
10. **Kunjar Prasad** :— Its shape is like the back of a elephant and the spread is 16 hands all around the mula (centre).
11. **Guhraj-Prasad** :— Guhraj Prasad is cave shaped with 16 hands spread and the dice is with three apartments on the house top.
12. **Vrish-Prasad** :— This prasad is of one Bhumi (plot), one peak, 12 hand spread and the shape is like a tree all around.
13. **Hansa-Prasad** :— It is swan-shaped with 12 hand, spread, one peak and one bhumi.
14. **Ghat Prasad** :— It's shape is like kalash (water-pot) and with 12 hands area, one peak and one bhumi.
15. **Sarvtobhadra-Prasad** :— It is associated with four doors in four directions, many peaks, and many apartments above the house top, 26 hands spread, chatushkona (four angled) and five bhumi.
16. **Simha-Prasad** :— It is decorated with the sculptures of Lion, Dwadashapt (twelve fold) and five bhumis.
17. **Vritta Prasad** :— It is circular and it remains dark insides.
18. **Chatushkona-Prasad** :— It is quadrupled (four sided)

Garur-Prasad

Nandivardhan-Prasad

Kunjar-Prasad

Guharaaj-Prasad

Vrish-Prasad

Hans-Prasad

Ghat-Prasad

Sarvato Bhadra-Prasad

Simha-Prasad

Vritta-Prasad

Chatuskon-Prasad

Shoda Shasshri-Prasad

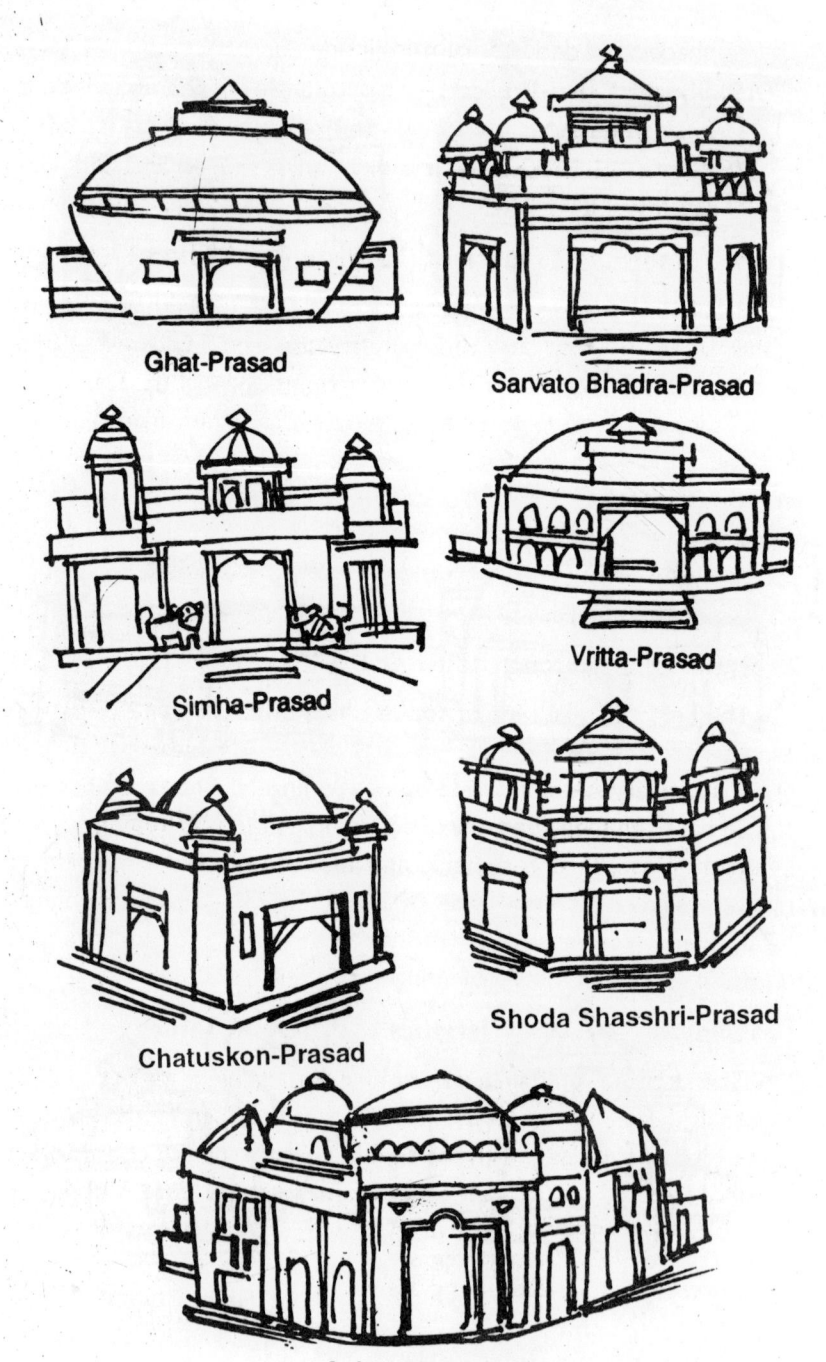

Ashta Shri-Prasad

shaped and darkness remains inside it.

19. Shodsha shri-Prasad :— It is 16 angle shaped and inside it has darkness.

20. Ashtashri-Prasad :— It is eight angle shaped and darkness lies inside it.

Special-Smearing Treatment (Vishista Lep Vidkan)

Heat the green fruit of Tendu, green fruit of kaith, flower of sebhal, seeds of trees, bark of Dhanwan tree mixed with water in a wooden vessel. Heat till the solution becomes one eighth. Then gum from Srivasak (saral) tree; Bole, Guggul, Bhilava, gum from Devdar tree, gum from sarj (sakhua) and wood apple's part is grinded and mixed with the above solution. This smear is called 'Vajralepe.' If this vajralepa were pasted or treated on palace, Mansion, Haveli, roof-projection, sculpture, wall and well then this smear is not wither and be detatched over a long period of time due to its adhesiveness.[29]

Procedure for Making Statue or Figure

The height of a figurine or statue is first divided into 12 parts and each part is again divided into 9 parts. Every part is measured as one finger and every statue is made up of 108 fingers. The face of statue should have the measurement of 12 fingers in breadth and 14 fingers in length. Nose, forehead, neck, apd ears should be of 4 fingers in measurement. Chin should be of 2 fingers. The breadth of head, earsides and ears should be of 8 fingers, two fingers for ears and the length of earside should be of 4 fingers.[30]

(A) Shapes and Characteristics of different statues

The statue of Sri Rama, son of king Dashrath and of Bali, son of Virochan should be 120 fingers tall. The statue of Lord Vishnu should be built of 8 or 4 hands with the sign of 'Srivatsa' on the chest having Kaustuv mani (a special gem or diamond worn by Lord Vishnu). It should be black like the Atsi (flax) flower, smiling face with yellow

---

29. बृहत्संहिता, अध्याय 57/श्लोक 1-4/पृष्ठ 337
30. बृहत्संहिता, अध्याय 58/श्लोक 4-6/पृष्ठ 388

apparel, healthy throat, chest, shoulder, healthy arms, three right hands with sword, mace and chakra (circular weapon) fourth right hand with a pose showing fearlessness and all the four left hands with Dhanush (bow), Dhal (shield), Chakra and Shankha (Conch shell). In the case of chaturbhuj Vishnu, one right hand with fearlessness, 2nd right hand with mace, the left two hand should possess, Shankha and Chakra.[31] Varahmihir has discussed twenty one types of statues in this chapter

Conclusion

Vrihtsamhita is mainly divided into two parts. The first half consists of 52 chapters and from the 53rd chapter onwards starts the 'study of Vastu' and is called the latter half of Vrihtsamhita. Several things on Vastushastra are dealt in this half of Vrihtsamhita. We also find the comparative study of seven great Acharyas (Gurus or teachers) Garg, Manu, Vashishtha, Parashar, Vishvakarma, Nagnajit, and Maya. Due to the ideas of these Acharyas, Vrihtsamhita's importance has increased to a great extent.

96 types of Prasad (Houses) are dealt in Narada Samhita. These houses are mainly of 16 types. These types are increased upto 96 from the door-point of view in all the directions which are Dhruva, Dhanya, Jay Nand, Khar, Karant, Manorath, Sumukh, Durmukh, Krur, Shatru, Swarnprad, Kshaya, Akrand, Vipul and Vijay. But these names are not similar to those names described in Vrihatsamhita.[32]

Vairaj, Pushpak, Kailash, Manik and Trivishtay are five important 'prasads' dealt in Agnipurana. Each having nine types of prasad again.[33] Thus the number goes upto 45 types of prasad characters. We do not find knowledge and material relating to Prasad-character, shapes and classification in Gargpurana, Matasya Purana and Bhavishya purana, nevertheless these puranas have sufficient materials about vastushastra. Other prasad's name which are mentioned in many

---
31. बृहत्संहिता, अध्याय 58/श्लोक 31-35/पृष्ठ 393
32. नारदसंहिता, अध्याय 31/श्लोक 46-47/पृष्ठ 219
33. अग्निपुराण, अध्याय 104/पृष्ठ 189

'Vastu grantha' like Vrihat Vastumala is basically taken from Vrihatsamhita.[34] We find many classifications of Prasad in 98th Atrisamhita of Mansaar but these are infact the 20 types dealt by varahmihir. In this way we find that the research done by Varahmihir was his own, the effect of which was found on vastushastra literature. Among the 20 types of prasads dealt by Varahmihir, Meruprasad's construction rule is dealt. This Meruprasad is probably the Merusthambha in Mehrauli (Delhi) in which the technique by Varahmihir in expressed.

Smearing of special type of liquid on the houses to save it against destruction and deformation is part of Vastushastra. But we do not find anything relating to this anywhere except in Brihatsamhita. We do not find this even in other books of Vastushastra. Even if we find any knowledge relating to this in later books, this was also associated always with Vrihatsamhita or Varahmihir s reference[35] some learned men are of the view that the technique used in this chapter is applied in the Garud stambh (Iron-pillar) of Mehrauli.

We get the maximum knowledge and materials relating to the character, shape and construction of Devpratima (statues) in Bhavishyapurana. According to this a statue of more than 8 fingers height should not be worshiped. A statue of 84 fingers (3 1/2 hands) is associated with prosperity. The statue of Lord Vishnu should be of Nav Tala (4 1/2 hands). The statues of Vasudeva should be of three Tala; Narsimha of five Tala, Hayagriva of 8 Tala, Goddess Durga of Nine Tala, Lakshmi and Saraswati of three tala each and 'sun' God of seven Tala.[36]

Two hundred types of statues have been described with its characteristics and shape in chapters 43 to 55 of Agnipurana in which the shapes of Lord Sri Vishnu is having two hands and four hands and it is said there that Shri Vishnu's mace, Shankha (Conch-shell), padma

---

34. मेरुमंदरकैलाशविमानच्छन्दनन्दनाः। समुद्रपद्मगरुडनन्दिवर्धन कुंजराः॥
—बृहद् वास्तुमाला श्लोक 17-19/पृष्ठ 150
35. गृहरत्नभूषण, भित्ति विचार, पृष्ठ 57
36. भविष्यपुराण, मध्यमपर्व प्रथम भाग, अध्याय 12/पृष्ठ 207

(lotus) and Chakra (wheel) provides salvation and freedom.[37] But we don't find any thing about statue of eight handed Vishnu in Naradsamhita, Matsyapurana, Garg samhita and other old books. Such type of statue may be called Varamihir's own especiality and calibre.

A chaturbhuj-Vishnu (four handed Vishnu) having Abhaya Mudra (pose of fearlessness) in one hand, mace in other right hand, Shankha and Chakra in left hands with Srivatsa sign on chest is found in excavation of Mehrauli. It is obvious from this that this statue had been built under the guidance of Varahmihir and was his own creation and it was set in his temple. This clarifies that this area of Mehrauli having Merustambh not only mentions the activity of Varahmihir but also confirms about his residential place. Complete procedure of laying foundation is given in Agnipurana and the way to establish the four Kallash (water pot) having four rock-cut Nanda, and four angles like Agni (fire), etc.[38] This part became the subject of Karmakanda in course of time and the treatment of worship five cut rocks including sub-cut rocks (Upshila) under 'shilanyas paddhati' (inauguration rules) in Brihad-Vastu-Maala. Shilanyas (inauguration) became the part and parcel of ways of worship (Karmkanda) and way followed for peace (Shaanti Paddhati).[39]

Thus it is an established fact without any argument that Varahmihir was a crafts-man, sculpture, engineer, and Vastukala marmagya (learned of vastu art) of high quality of his time. He was a great teacher and Acharya of this science. From the Vidhan (rule) of constructing, house, road. National highways element (metal) making, element excavation, geological survey, knowledge of age of trees, planting of different types of trees, and the rules of carving wood for statue, it becomes is obvious that he was a great Botanist.

Varahmihir was a perfect architect and a refined sculptor. He carved and helped in carving many types of statue of Sun (surya), Vishnu, Varah, Kamdhenu, Mahavir, Gautam Buddha, Navgraha etc.,

37. अग्निपुराण, अध्याय 48/श्लोक 1-4/पृष्ठ 84
38. अग्निपुराण, श्लोक 5-8/अध्याय 94/पृष्ठ 171
39. बृहद् वास्तुमाला, पृष्ठ 170

gods and demigods. In the precincts of Mehrauli (near Qutubminar), his college used to be run, where twenty-seven departments, e.g. statue department, element department, Botany department, Astronomy dept, geography dept, geology dept, sculpture, architecture dept etc. were established for the students and aspirants. From Pratyaksha (apparent), Anuman (Guess) and Apta (reliable source) it is confirmed that Varahmihir was a perfect Acharya during whose period, Indian old and classical science, attained the pinnacle of glory.

Chapter 4

Laying Foundation for houses

There is a saping 'well begun is half done' i.e. 'if the work is initiated at auspicious moment, then it takes little time to be completed.' Hence the sleeping nature of plot (Bhumishayan) should be considered first of all.

Considering Bhumishayan and Vatsa-Chakra

If Moon Nakshtra (star) falls at 5th, 7th, 9th, 12th, 19th and 26th from the Nakshatra of sun, then the land is sleeping or supta. Digging of land for ponds or house-construction in these Nakshatra, is prohibited. According to the Nakshatra of House-construction's initiation of different chakras like vrish vastu are also examined. Here is mentioned the vrish or vatsa chakra which is mentioned in Rajmartand. The setting up of Nakshatras should be done from the sun's Nakshatra taking the front part of it as Taurus shaped (Vrishabhakar). And then seeing the auspicious moment one should start construction.

Vrish-Chakra

स्थान	मस्तक	अग्रपाद	पृष्ठपाद	पीठ	दक्षिण कोख	वाम कोख	पूंछ	मुख
नक्षत्र	3	४	४	3	४	४	3	3
फल	अग्नि भय	उद्विग्नता	स्थिरता	धन	विजय	निर्धनता	स्वामी नाश	पीड़ा

Place	Head	Beginning part	Last part	Back (peeth)	Right womb	Left womb	Tail	Mouth
Nakshatra	3	4	4	3	4	4	3	3
Result	Fire fear	Anxious and Frightened	Stablity	Wealth	Victory	Poverty	Loss of Owner	Pain

Auspicious Moment to Start Foundation

In Pushya Nakshtra with Jupiter, all the three Uttaras, Rohini, Mrigshira, Shrawan, Ashlesha the house started for construction especially on Thursday is said to be good, providing sons and kingdom. Foundation work done in Ashwini, chitra, Vishakha, Dhanistha, Shatbhisaj, and Ardra especially on Friday is auspicious and provides wealth. Initiation of house construction in Ashwini, Rohini, Poorva Phalgni, Chitra and Hasta especially on Wednesday provides happiness, prosperity and progenies.

गुरुः शुक्रार्कचंद्रेषु स्वोच्चादि बलशालिषु।
गुर्वकेंदुबलं लब्ध्वा गृहारंभ प्रशस्यते॥

Guruh shukrark chandreshu savochchadi balshalishu gurukendubalm labdhwa greharambh Prashshyate

—*Jyotish Tatva Prakash shloka 61/page 421*

When Jupiter, Venus, sun and Moon are exhalted and strong then starting house construction with the help of the power of Jupiter, Sun and Moon, proves auspicious and fruitful.

The Sun in Aries provides reputation, Sun in Taurus increases wealth, cancerian sun is auspicious in leo as it increases happiness from servants, sun in Libra gives happiness, sun in scorpio increases wealth, Sun of capricorn provides property and aquarian sun provides gems, if sun were positioned in above signs at the time of laying the foundation.

Ascendant (Lagna) should be of fixed or dual sign, having benefic planet or aspect of benefic planet at time of laying foundation.

According to Maharishi Parasar, one who worships Vastu in chitra, shatbhisaj, swati, Hasta, Pushya, Punarvasu, Rohini, Revati, Moola, Shrawan Uttaraphalguni, Dhanista, Uttrashada, Uttarabhadrapada,

Ashwini, Mrighshira, and Anuradha Nakshtra gets wealth and prosperity.

वास्तुपूजनमेतेषु नक्षत्रेषु करोति यः।
समाप्नोति नरो लक्ष्मीमिति प्राह पराशरः॥

Vaastu Poojanmeteshu nakshatreshu karoti ya samapnoti naro laxmiimiiti praha Parasharah

If in the horoscope of house under construction, at least three planets amongst jupiter, venus, sun, and moon are either exalted or in their own house; the tenth house having mercury; sun, jupiter, venus and Moon in their own houses are exalted the age of that house to 200 years and Laxmi (prosperity and wealth) resides there for a very long period.

Restricted and Prohibited Notes

1. Do not start construction on Sunday and Tuesday.
2. Avoid foundation or initiation in the ascendance of Aries, Cancer, Libra and Capricorn.
3. Do not start constructing the house if malefics are situated in 3rd, 6th and 11th house of horoscope of the house.
4. If 6th, 8th and 12th houses have benefic planets in the house-horoscope, do not construct.
5. Hasta, Pushya, Revati, Magha, Poorvashada and Moola associated with mars if falls on Tuesday, then work should not be undertaken in that nakshatra, otherwise it gives fear from fire, and theft, and sorrow from son.
6. Poorvabhadrapada, Uttarabhadrapada, Jyeshtha, Anuradha, Swati and Bharni associated with saturn if falls on Saturday the work undertaken such Nakshatras makes the house inauspicious as evil spirit.
7. If Sun is weak, setting or debilitated on the day of house construction, then the owner of the house dies.
8. If Moon is weak, or debilitated on that day then the wife of owner dies.

9. If jupiter becomes weak and debilitated on the day of starting the construction then loss of wealth is inevitable.
10. Do not start constructing a house on Rikta Tithi i.e, 4/9/14 of the Hindi calender.
11. At the time of laying foundation, the Sun of Gemini provides death; Sun of Virgo gives disease, Sun of Saggitarius provides bad results; and Sun of Pisces gives disease and fear.
12. Initiating house construction in Leo ascendant is prohibited
Jyotisha Tatava Prakash /73/425.
13. Do not build new houses when the Sun remains in Gemini, Virgo, Saggitarius and Pisces.

Jyotish Bhaskar

Chapter 5

Entering the House: Griha Pravesh

One thinks about Griha Pravesh (first time entering the house to live in) after construction of house, shop or factory. A wise man considers Griha-pravesh when one wins over enemy, or coming of new wife, or returning back from abroad. Griha-pravesh is of three types-Apurva, Sampurva and Dwandwa.

To enter in a new-house is called **Apurva**. Entering the house after travelling is called **Sampurva**— While entering the house after repairing the worn out is called **'Dwandwa'** Here, discussion about 'Apurva' entrance is especially useful. Entrance (Pravesh) is best in magha, phalguna, vaishakh, jyeshtha month while this is medium in kartika, and margshirsha.

माघफाल्गुनवैशाखज्येष्ठमासेषु शोभनः।
प्रवेशो मध्यमो ज्ञेयः सौम्यकार्तिक मासयोः॥

'Magh Phalguna Vaishakh Jyeshthamaseshu Shobhanah Pravesho Maadhyamo Gyeyah Soumayakartik Maasyo

—*narada*

Pravesh should be completed upto tenth tithi (Dashmi) of krishna paksha (fortnight after full moon) and in shukla paksha (fortnight after new moon) one should enter after the rising of moon. In the case of a repaired house which was damaged in the Dakshinayan month (sun moving in the southern course) is auspicious. Generally the setting (dooming) of Jupiter and venus are considered everywhere except for the repaired house.

It is auspicious and a good sign to enter in the Nakshtra of all the three 'Uttara' Anuradha, Rohini, Mrigshira, Chitra, Revati, Dhanishtha, Shatbhisaj, Pushya, Ashwani and Hasta.

Grih-pravesh is favourable and auspicious when the position of moon and Nakshtra are congenial with Lagna shuddhi (rectified ascendant) of planets including the benefic Tithi and day.

If the sun remains in five bhavas from the 8th, in the horoscope of a house facing east, sun in the five bhavas from 5th bhava in house facing south, sun the 11th bhavas in house facing west ward and sun in five bhavas from 5th house in house facing north, are called Vaama Ravi (or opposite sun) which is very neccessary, in the case of Griha-pravesh. In the Kumbha chakra (aquarius wheel) five Nakshatra, from the Nakshatra of sun, is malefic and bad, again 8 Nakshtra from there are good and favourable. 8 Nakshtra again after this are unfavourable, and from there again 6 Nakshtra are auspicious. From 6th to 13th and 22nd to 27th Nakshtra, from sun's Nakshtra are among auspicious kumbha chakra.

If the old house is destroyed or burnt with fire and again it is built with mud, and lime, then enter the house in swati, pushya, Dhanishtha, shatbhisaj in the month of Kartik, shrawan, and Margshirsha. Here, one should not think much about setting of planets or Nakshatra.

At the moment of entrance. the Yajman (owner) should enter with a pot filled with water, flower, Deepa (lamp), Durvadal (auspicious-grass), leaf of mango tree, in both the hands and should worship a virgin (unmarried girl), Pandit (Brahman, who chants mantras), going left to right around a cow before the entrance. The Brahman should read vedas with the blowing of shankha and pleasant songs in praise of God. The brahman carrying Kalash (auspicious pot) should be ahead followed by the Yajman' family-member, according to an 'Acharya'. Five unmarried girls should move ahead, each with a 'Kalasha' followed by the owner (Yajman), with family-members. This system, is in vogue in maximum parts of India..

Chapter 6

Hindrance in Free Movement : Air Sun-rays, Dwar-Vedha

Dwar-Vedha

Dwar-vedha means to restrict or block the path of wind and sun-rays. This is based in a way on extremely developed and matured tradition of frontal view of a house. The things which can be hinderances in the free movement of air and sun-rays to the house and the people in it house is called Dwar-Vedha in Vastushastra. 'Vedha' is a technical term which is very large in connotation. It is not only related to the house directly but also concerned with the objects lying near or adjacent to house.

We find a general Vedha-classification in vastushastra. These Sapta-vedha are Talvedha, Kona Vedha, Talu Vedha, Kalavedha, Stambh vedha, Tula Vedha, and Dwar-vedha. In this chapter we are concerned with Dwar-vedha only we shall discuss the other vedhas in the following chapters. In Dwar Vedha, faulty constructed doors are prohibited, at every cost. If the door is perforated or shadowed by chatwar (a quadrangular place or a place where several ways meet), Rathya (highway, host of chariots), Dhwaja, tree, mud, drainage, well, Devta. then it is considered as unfavourable and destructive. It is a difficult situation for adopting corrective measures. Hence it is advised to shift the door away for favourable results. The object providing shade to the front door can be remedied only if a vacant space double the height of the house is left. All the books on Architecture (shilip g aranthas) have accepted unanimously that 'The vedha does not cast its adverse effect when vacant space double the height of the house is left.' When the object is providing vedhaka (which is falling in front of door), in such condition if vacant space double than the height of house is left, the vedha is subsided. In this way, all the shilp Granthas (architectural book) have accepted this law unanimously that **'The Vedha does not remain or it vanishes if double space than the height of the house'** (i.e, from door to vedha) is left vacant.

Nevertheless Dwar-vedha are of several types, old classical writers have confirmed 8 types of Dwar-vedha—

1. Do not make door in the middle and meeting-place of a house.
2. Do not make a door on the rear portion of a house if the a house is not multistoreyed.
3. There should not be any chariot-path crossing well, pond, gutter, corner of other house, big trees, pole, peg for the animals, garbage before the main gate or door of the house. These are mentioned from the safety and cleanliness point of view.
4. There should not exist mud or flowing water infront of door. Regular water in front of house will accumulate and increase mud which will weaken the foundation. Hence these also form Dwar-vedha.
5. Killa-Vedha —There should not be any peg to tie the animal (cow, goat or other animals). This is called kila-vedha.
6. Swar-Vedha—The sound which arises during opening or closing of the door is called swarvedha which is a bad omen (inauspicious).
7. Koop Vedha—If well, man-hole, and water-reservoir, are in front of the house or shadow of house falls on the well, then it is koop vedha which should be avoided.
8. Brahm-Vedha —If oil-grinding machine or factory exists in front of house then it is called brahm

vedha. This is a sign of trouble and pain.
9. If the door of the house is wave shaped with high and low architecture, that is also called Dwarvedha. Dwarvedha is faulty if there is high wall, compound wall, big block of building. This is a big impediment towards the prosperity and progress of the house owner. (see the fig 1)

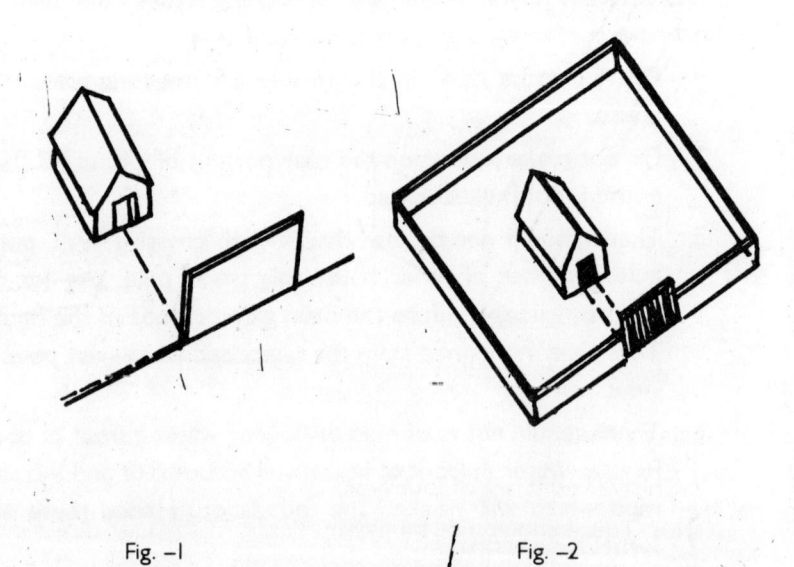

Fig. –1   Fig. –2

In fig 2 you will observe that the compound wall of the factory is away but the substitute gate (secondary gate) is bigger than the main gate and is even higher than the compound wall. Such a construction proves unlucky for the progress and fortune-making of the house owner. Such faults do cause havoc to the whole factory and industry. Hence it should be borne in mind, that the secondary gate (door of compound and wall) should not be higher than compound wall and the main gate. Observe the figure 3 arid 4. There should not be the wall of other house in front of any one's residence. This blocks the progress of house-owner.

Kona-Vedha

In fig. 4 the corner of one house is just in front of the other house. This also is a fault under vastu. The people living in such houses generally do not get favourable results. This is mainly called Kona-Vedha. There should not be vedha on any house from the corner of the other house.

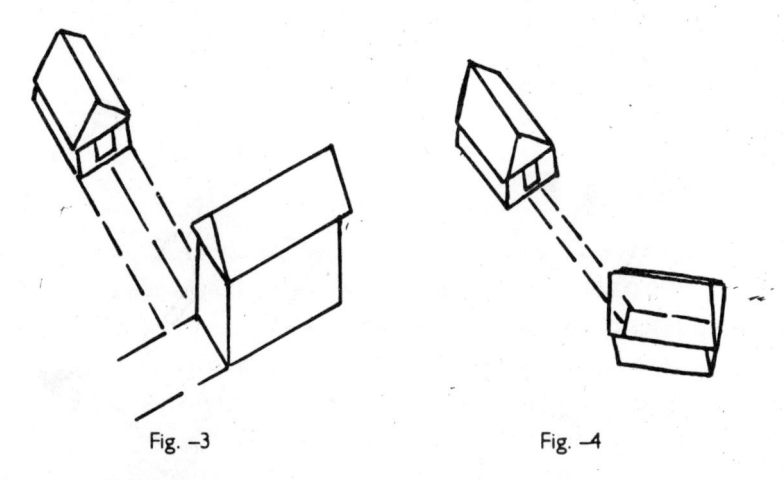

Fig. –3   Fig. –4

Chhaya-Vedha

Chhaya vedha are of four types

1. There should not be any mountain in the east direction of a village. The shadow of mountain should not fall on the village at the time of sun-rise. The village should be established away from or out of the shadow of the mountian.
2. In the same fashion, the shadow of a big tree should not fall on the house. The shadow will not fall on the house if it is distant from the house. In such a case, even if the tree falls on the house it does not harm the house.
3. The shadow of any temple should not fall on the house. This is called chhaya vedha (obstruction by shadow) since there is always crowd in the temple. On the occasion of festivals the crowd is much bigger, Hence the open space around the

Fig. –5   Fig. –6

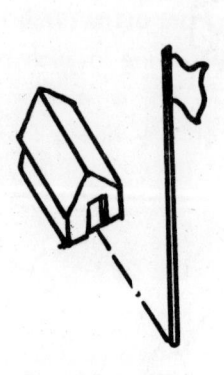

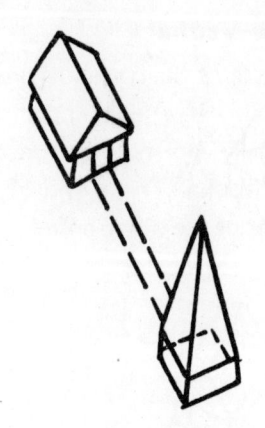

temple is necessary. One should not canstruct a house upto the point where the shadow of the flag (Dhwaja) reaches. The rules made by old Acharyas has reality. See the fig 5. A flag was waving just before a hotel, having shadow of the flag. This shadow proved inauspicious for the hotel owner. He suffered from a serious disease. When I removed that flag under Vastu nidan (Treatment in Vastu) the medicine taken by him showed their effect and he became healthy.

Observe fig 6, A monument was built in remembrance of soldiers. The house in front of this was deserted due to death of all members of a family. Hence it is wise to be away from or to escape from chhaya-vedha. There should not be any pole, dome or monuments in front of the house. 4. It should be also kept in mind that the shadow of one's house should not fall on any.well. This is also inauspicious.

Vriksha-Vedha (Obstruction by trees)

When a big tree is in front of a door, then it is called 'Vriksha-Vedha'. With increase in age the growth of tree also increases. Such trees, while falling cause damage to the house.

1. The foundation of houses becomes weak due to the trees

Fig. –7   Fig. –8

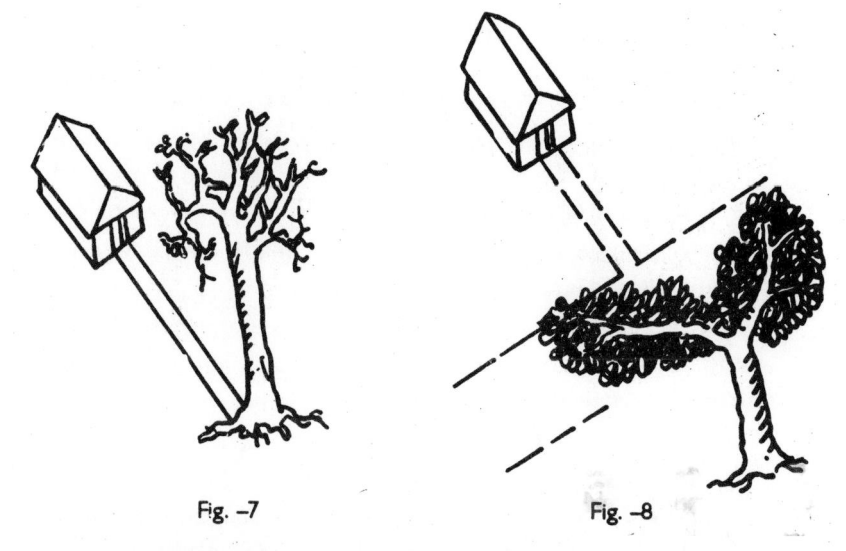

nearby and the walls also get cracks.
2. Different types of animals, birds, dried leaves etc. inhabiting the trees are objects of harm to the people in the building.
3. If a dried up or leafless tree is present just in front of door, then it is inauspicious. The shadow of tree should not fall on the house. Vriksha Vedha is not auspicious. see fig. 7.

Fig. –9   Fig. –10

4. If any horrible tree with two branches is just before the house or on trans-road, then also, it is inauspicious. see fig 8
5. Due to cyclones, typhoons and heavy rain, the big tree create horrible noise. Big & tall trees attract the cloud towards itself which causes lightening. Due to this the house owner or the people living around it can meet with death. Hence Vriksha Vedha should not exist.
6. See the fig. 9 the house is between two trees and in the fig. 10, the house is surrounded by big trees. For a hermit, Sanyasi, Yogi or sadhus such a situation is suitable but for the worldly or social people such a house is not considered to be auspicious.
7. The shadow of tree should not fall, more than one prahar (3 hours) on a house, mansion factory etc. Albeit shadow remaining for one prahar is also inauspicious

वर्जयेत् पुर्वतोश्वत्थं, प्लक्षं दक्षिणतस्तथा।
न्यग्रोधं पश्चिमेभागे, उत्तरे चाप्युदुम्बम्॥
अश्वत्थे तुभयं बयात प्लक्षे ब्रूयाप्तरूयवम्।
न्यग्रोधे राजतः पीडा नेत्रात्रय मुदुम्बरे॥

'Varjyet Purvatoshwatham plaksham dakshinasthata
Nayagrodham paschimebhage uttre chapyudumbam
Ashwathe tubhyam bayat plakshe bruyatruyavam
nayagrodh rajatah peeda netratreye mudambre

8. To plant bad and prohibited trees on the door and around the house is called Vriksha vedha. For example: Udumbur tree (a wild fig tree) in east, Bat vriksha (a banyan tree) in the south direction and Nyogrodh tree in the west should never exist.
9. Trees bearing fruits, milk (viscous white liquid) and thorn near house are always inauspicious. This is the version of shastras. Thorny trees always give, tr ouble, and there is danger of theft due to fruit bearing trees. Perhaps, thinking these aspects, Rishi's (hermits) have compiled such restrictions.

Planning of Plantation in Modern Houses

10. Banana, champa flower, chameli flower, patal (pink coloured) flower and other flowers, with good smell and beautiful trees, are auspicious.
11. According to shastras, Barh-tree (banyan) in the east, Gular in the south, Pipal in the west and Pakad in the north are auspicious. Observe the fig 11. But don't plant trees in the middle of plot.

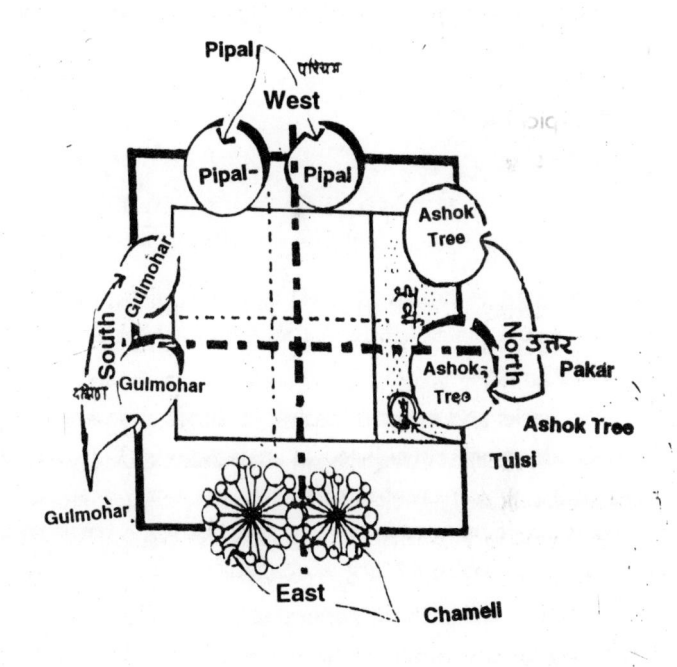

Fig. –11

12. The wise persons agree to planting Tulsi plant (Basil) in the open place of a house. Tulsi-plant is a herb like nectar (amrit). It can be planted anywhere in the house.

Marg-Vedha (Obstruction in the path)

If any factory or industry comprises of a pond on its one side and ditch on the other side where garbage is burnt or fire is present then

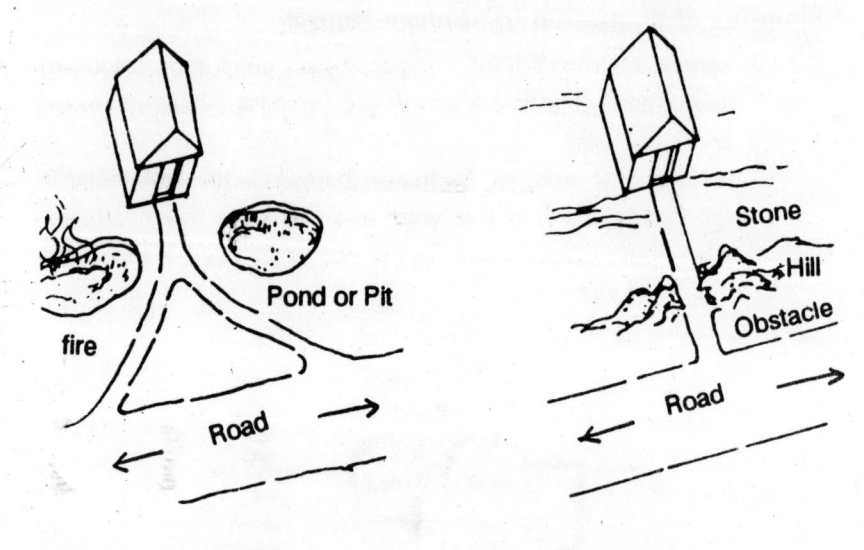

Fig. –12   Fig. –13

it is a bad sign. A house situated on three directional ways meeting point, is more inauspicious in the eyes of Vastushastra. These are called Marg vedha.

Hills, rocks and other undesirable th!ngs and obstacles in front of entrance door are considered as inauspicious. This is also a type of Marg-Vedha which creates obstacles on every step for the house owner. A Single path, to enter into two houses, is troublesome for the residents. This is also a Marg-vedha fault.

Similarly, if the path for general use runs inside the compound wall of the field for the people living in the house is also a part of the faults of Marga vedha. It results in worry and pain, ultimately.

The pond just in front of the door of the house is inauspicious. If the pond is triangular in shape then it is more inauspicious, even if this pond is on the opposite side of the road. Observe the fig 14. The triangular shaped pond and ditches are supposed to be inauspicious near the main gate of the house. The compound wall higher than the factory, Industry or shop also falls in the category of 'Bhawan Vedha' (obstruction of house). Observe fig 15. Capitalist or industrialists

Road

Triangular Pond
Fig. –14

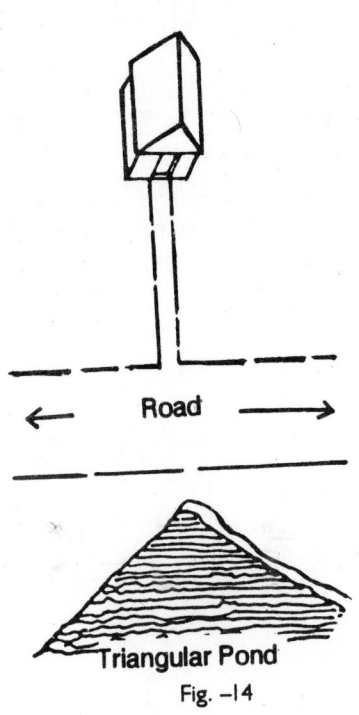

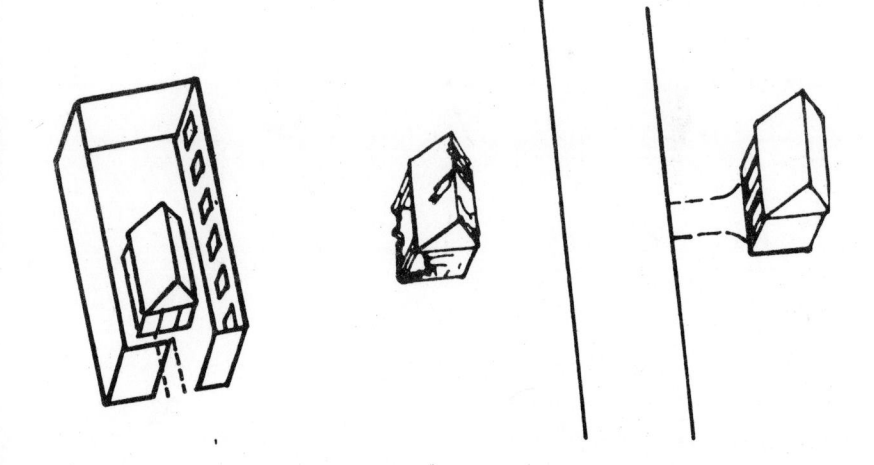

Fig. –15

Fig. –16

should observe these points carefully in relation to their prosperity.

The existing broken and demolished house, Khandhar (very old broken dirty house with no residents or remaining part of old house are not a good sign. By looking and seeing such houses daily, a person goes to the nether world and his industry, service and business suffer from irrepairable loss.

☐

Chapter 7

Entrance Gate : Pravesh-Dwar

Samrangan Sutradhar gives an elaborate description of Dwar (door). 'Door' is an important part in Indian architecture. The Sutra Granthas contain detailed analysis about this subject. First of all we should think briefly about the part of doors. Door is called by various names like entrance, exit etc. The wooden part and the lintel above the door frame (chokhat) is called 'Udumber'. Under this Udumber or lintel is made the door. The open part or vacant portion between both the wall is called 'Dahliz' (Door-sill) or Dehli. It is also called Kapatashraya or support for the panel of doors. Other constituents of door or Pallas (panel of door) is called 'Dwar paksha', Kapatput, Paksha, Vidhan Varan and Dwar Samvaran and a pair of doorpane is called 'Kapatyugal'. The third part of dooi is 'Kalika' or 'Argala' (bolt) which closes both the panels of the door. It has got three names 'Argalasuchi' (if its size is big), Pa, idha (bolt of fort's door, bolt of town door) and phulih which is called 'Gajavaran'. Besides these 'Phalak' (dice-board), Jal (net), Toran (ornamented doors) Lion, Karn (handle of the vessel or ear) etc. components are also supposed to be part of door in ancient art.

Seven important parts deserve to be described under the constituents of door-frame which are Pedyapind-Chatushtaya, Udumber, Dwar-Shakha, Rup Shakha, Khalwa Shakha, 'Bhahyamandala' and Bhar Shakha. We can tell about Udumber.

Shakha is concerned with site frames'. Some of its definitional names are Devi, Nandini, Sundari, Priyanana and Bhadra.

In this context the description of temples, town-doors or huge door (Mahadwar) and Pakshdwar is not intended (Nevertheless gate and door both are Dwar). Hence it is necessary to give attention to ornaments, and Vedha (obstruction or perforation) as well as the length, breadth, height and the situation of doors suitable to houses.

Dwar-Praman (Door-Measurement)

It is a general rule, that the height of the door, should be double the breadth. In fact, this is a very scientific measurement but, one should take care that, the width should be four feet or a minimum of three and half feet. Now a days the doors of one panel instead of a pair of panels can't be of this measurement. The ancient Acharyas were very farsighted, hence, they had fixed the height thrice of the width of door, in Vishwa Karmprakash and Vrihatsamhita. In 'Samrangan' the direction given, about the height of the door is more scientific. The 'extension of door' is imagined according to the house. For example, if the extension of the house is 18 hands then the door's size will be of 18 fingers, the width will be half lhe height. Since door is classified as—Large, medium and small gyeshtha, Madhyam and Kanishtha), hence the height and width will differ accordingly. It is a rule, that the more the height of house the more will be height of door ' (see 24 Dwarpitha Bhittirnanadik also) '. 'Samrangan' believes in height being double the width'.

Place of Door (Dwar-sthiti)

Where should a door be posited for different directions is a matter of discussion in Dwar-sthiti. Where a door should not be opened, for that, following rules are especially mentioned. Where as regulations (vidhan) are concerned, following Sloka in Sanskrit is enough to deal.

पूर्वद्वारं तु माहेंद्रं प्रशस्तं सर्वकामदम्।
गह्क्षतं तु विहितं दक्षिणेन शुभावहम्।

गंधवमथवा तत्र कर्तव्यं श्रेयसे सदा।
पश्चिमेन प्रशस्तं स्यात् पुष्पदंतं जयावहम्।
भल्लाट्मुत्तरे द्वारं प्रशस्तं स्याद् गृहेक्षितुः।

**Poorvadwaram Tu mahendram prashashtam sarvkamdam
grahkshtam tu vihitam dakshinen shubavaham
gandarvamathva tatra kartavoyam shreyesey sada
pashchimein prashastam syat pushpdantam Jayavaham
bhallatmutre dwaram prashastum syad Griheshitu.**

Four prominent categories of door are mentioned in Samrangan—Utsang, Hinbahu, Poornabahu, and Pratakshaya. Among these Utsang will be called, the doors found in same region or direction of Vastu or house and these are supposed to be auspicious. Hinbahu (Lesser hand) is condemned as it means literally in which the house falls on the left from Vastu- entrance (entry point of plot). Hence such residence is dispensible. Where the house remains, on the right of Vastu pravesh (entrance of door) then, it is called Poornabahu which is propounder of complete Siddhis (accomplishment). Where the entrance of Vastudwar is attatched to the portier part of the house then it will be called Pratyakshaya. Entrance (from right to left) entrance is established, and this is also inauspicious. It has already been mentioned in the case of Dwarsthiti that Door should be never in the middle. This is the speciality of 'Secular Planning'.

मध्ये द्वारं न कर्तव्यं मनुजानां कथंचन।
मध्ये द्वारे कृते तत्र कुलनाशः प्रजायते॥

**Madhye Dwaram na kartavyam manujanam kathamchana
madhye dware krete tatra kulnash Prajayate.**

The door on the upper floors, should be in accordance to the door on the ground floor, as already mentioned.

Characteristics of door

The characteristics of doors are related to the construction of door, its suitable covering etc. and the firm and tender wood used as well as its shape etc. Hence we find collection of all these characteristics in Samarangan Sutras which are as following:—

It should be well placed, syrnmetrical, beautiful, Swadravyojit, Riju, Swakiya-Digbhagshila, Not veiy small (Na-Harshwa), Not very high (Na-Atyuch), Not very less (Na-Alpa), Not very crooked (Na-Kubja), Not very outside (Apindit, Na-Bahirgat), Not very weak (Na- Adhmat, Na-Krish), Not on the middle (Na-Madhyagat), Not inside the heart (Na-Antar-Kukshik), Not very sprouted or enlarged (Na-Vidwat), Not very concised (Na-Sankchhipt).

Dwar-Dosha (Fault of Door)

Dwardosha is opposite to Dwar-Guna, e.g. weak (Krish), deshaped (Vikrit), very high (Atyuchh), sound producing (Karkal), loose (Shithil), copious (Prithu), crooked (Vakra), enlarged, stretched-out (Uttaan), thick ahead (Sthulagra), middle or heart part very small (Harshwa-Kukshik), Self moving (Swapad chalit), small (Harshwa), Lesser colour (Hinvarna), extremity of nose (Mukhanat), stretching out on lateral side (Parshwagra), deprived of sutramarga (Sutramarga Bhrast). It is observed in Samrangansutra (48, 75-78) that, door producing sound on being closed are worthless. If the door is closing on its own then it is considered inauspicious.

Dwar-Bhusha (Ornamentation of Door)

It is very old custom to decorate the doors with an picture. In all the ancient and old houses an especially temples one can see doors decorated with pictures. Simple and undecorated doors are prohibited. Hence we find enormous material on Dwar-bhusha in architectural-books like Brihatsanhita, and Matasyapurana. It is also mentioned in Samrangan but it is to be realised that decoration of doors has got special importance on the doors of temples. The decorations used in temple are not necessary for the houses for residing. This is elaborated and made clear in the chapter Aprayojya-Prayojya of Samrangan Sutradhara, The subject of decoration and composition is much needed in architecture. Not only the door is suitable for decoration but also the wall, meeting place, caves, rooms of Gods, shasya (sleeping place), panjar (cage, enclosure), Asan (sitting place), Yan (cart), Bhand (vessel of mud), Alankar (ornaments), chhatra-Pataka (Umbrelia flag), deserve to be decorated.

Following pictures are praise worthy on the door (specially on house door):

(i) *Kula-devata (Family God):*—But its size should not be larger than one hand length.

(ii) *Two-gate Keepers (Dwarpata):*—It should be ornamented, with Vetrakhand (part of cane) and Khadag (sword), beautiful figures having queer dresses with ornaments.

(iii) *Dhatri (Establisher or possesser):*—It should be short and crooked familiar with Samkhya and followed by vidushak (jester) and Kanchukiyon (armours).

(iv) *Shankha and Padanidhi:*—Gems and gold coins emerging from the mouth.

(v) *Ashtmangala:*—who is being sprinkled with water by elephants and is with its garland of Shankha and Matasya between the Dwar-Mandal.

(vi) *Laxmi:*—She should be Padmasna, (lotus posture) Padmhasta (with lotus flower) and self ornamented.

(vii) *Savatsaa Dhenu (Cow with calf):*—It should be ornamented with clean garlands.

Some Important Directions:

1. Doors should be above the door of ground floor in multistorey building.
2. Do not make doors above wall and wall over door.
3. The doors of each ladder-floor should be at same place. If there is problem in doing so, then the ladder and its doors should be in Pradaxin (from left to right) serial, Don't keep doors in the middle of house or Pada (position).

4. If the house is multistoreyed even then the doors on the front side and the back-side should not be face to face so that one can't see the reardoor from the front door. Don't keep doors on both sides of the house (Samrangan Sutradhar 39.44.59)
5. Where a door exists already, one should not open another door near this existing door by breaking the wall. Actually, at the place of door the strength house is least, hence, if second door is made adjacent to it, then the strength of the house will further be weakened.
6. The wooden part of the door should be solid and strong and it should not be infected by the termite. The wood of Saagwan (Teak) is very strong. The joints in the case of mango tree wood, will. be warped soon and termite and insects will destroy it. One should use same wood in every door as far as possible.
7. Door should be made and fixed in the wall properly, and should be rectangular, i.e. every angle should be right angled and all the facing sides, should be parallel. Door should be upright and should not be lean or be warped. The frame or door should not be fired in just middle of the thickness of wall but it should be little outside from the middle. Its height and breadth should be same allover.
8. Shisham, Rohini, Shak, Sriparna, Chandan, Saral, Ashok, Mahua, Sarj, Neem, Patang, Arjun, Lodh, Khair, Shal,'Sindhuk, Vijaysaar, Nagkesar's wood can be used for building purposes.
9. But Bahera, Pipal, Bargad, Pakad, Gular, Kantak, Kaith, Rogi and the wood from the burnt trees should never be used in the house. These trees have woak wood and not suitable to be nailed, or frame of door or Dharan. The wood of these trees are inauspicious.

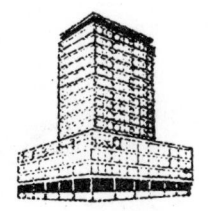

Chapter 8

Commercial Complex

The population is multiplying exponentially in every country of this world now-a-days. The cultivable land is being changed to meet the demands of the increasing population. Hence small places are growing and being transformed into towns and cities. The residential areas are highly congested due to increasing population. The possibility, of new trade and business, is increasing rapidly due to new wants and needs, and new inventions. Industries and factories are also increasing rapidly. For their popularity and sale they need offices amidst dense population of towns. It is increasingly difficult to find shops and offices in the main markets of the town. Hence, big and giant companies have started constructing multistorey buildings and commercial complexes in big towns. Every inch of space is accounted for in commercial complexes. No plot is left vacant. Ground floors are used, for parking vehicles in most cases. Shops and offices are built around the plot. Oblong plots are used for shops. In fact, rules of Vastushastra are not used and followed in commercial complexes to the extent we use for residential purposes. Nevertheless, if we follow the fundamentals of Vastu science for such huge multi storeyed commercial complexes it will be much helpful for business prosperity human life and towards a more meaningful civilization.

In this context we are giving some important rules, by which, the commercial complex can be made more useful and meaningful.

1. A plot square or rectangular and right-angled, on four

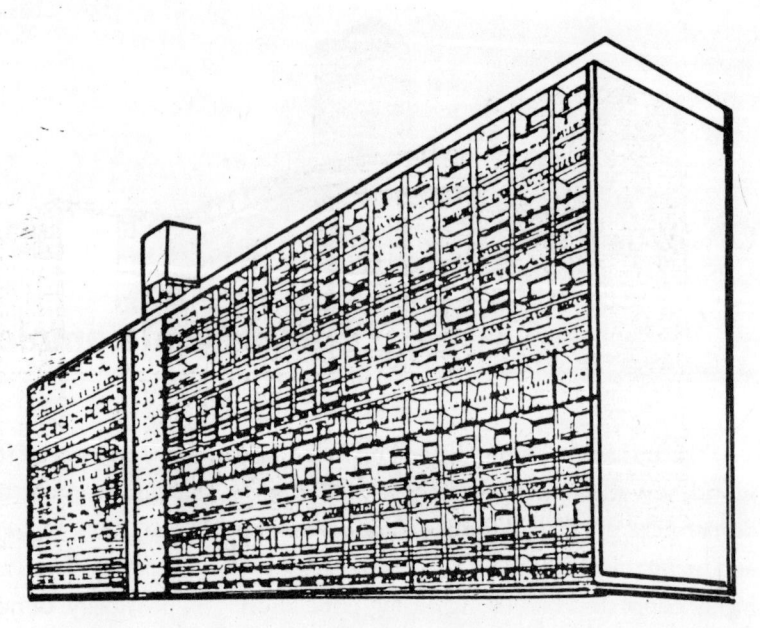

Fig. –1

corners, should be taken into account for construc.tion of a commercial complex. By doing this, the land owner, the businessmen and traders using this, get more benefit.

2. Some space is usually left around the commercial complex and cinema hall. At the time of planning, more space should be left in the East and North directions, comparison to West and South.

3. Lawn and parking space left is best in north-east direction (Ishan) of the commercial complex.

4. The slope of land of a commercial complex should be always in corner (Ishan NE).

5. South-west (Naishrityakona) of commercial complex should always be higher.

6. There should not be big trees and poles around the commercial complex specially in the front side.

7. Borewell should be dug always in the Ishan (NE) of a commercial complex, as it is the most ideal place, otherwise it

Fig. –2

should be in the east.

8. The water tank's construction should be in Ishan (NE), east, north or west direction of the topmost roof of commercial complex. Constructing a tank in Agneykona, south, Vayavya (NW) or middle invites destruction and is inauspicious.
9. Whether it is rain water, or drainage of dirty water, the flow should always be in the north or east direction of the complex.
10. The Gutter hole or tank for dirty water should be in Naishritya (SW) direction.
11. The main gate and main door should be kept in the east or north direction of commercial complex as far as possible.
12. The height of ground floor should be higher than that of the other storeys.
13. Similarly, the height of the entrance door of first floor should be higher than the other doors

of the various storeys.
14. The entrance and exit doors of commercial complexes should be different. This is essential, from the safety and security point of view.
15. Watchmen and Security-Guard should be alert or put on the main gate and exit door. The wall paintings and statues of guards, made on the outside of palace and temples of old age, signify this.
16. Shops and offices are often made around the commercial complex. But it should be taken into account that the sun-rays, moon-rays and fresh air should reach without any obstruction, to each of them.
17. I observed lack of sun-rays, lack of fresh air, in many complexes, in foreign countries. All the halls, offices and shops were air-tight and air-conditioned. The temperature and atmospheric conditions are different there from that of India. If the windows of house or car were opened in the countries like Arab-Emirates, the people will die of scorching Sun and its heat. Hence we should not imitate them completely in India. In foreign countries, the advantage is that electric supply is very good and sufficient, with full voltage. These things can't be applied in India because there is no certainty of regular supply of electricity. In such uncertain conditions, a person can even die, if he is in the lift. The persons working inside air-tight and airconditioned office, are compelled to come out to get fresh oxygen. Otherwise they can suffer due to suffocation, Hence, in India, the builders of commercial complexes should keep in mind that natural light and air should enter the complexes, then only there exists meaning and fruitfulness of Vastu-Science.
18. Maximum rooms should be in the east or north direction. This is a very important aspect to be kept in mind while constructing a complex. The number of offices, rooms and shops in these directions should be more.

19. If bathroom and toilets are attached to each room and office of the complex then keep in mind that toilet should be in Naishritya (SW) kona (south-west).
20. The storeys on the upper floor should be of lesser height in comparison to lower one. If the building is 6 storeyed and the first storey (i.e. ground floor) is of 10 feet (leave the under ground floor) then the second, third, fourth, fifth and sixth floor will be of 9 feet, 8 1/2, 8, 7 1/2 and 7' in height respectively.
21. If store room is also made with office and shop in the complex, then it should be built in the south or west part of the office or room.
22. Ladder or stairs should be in south or west direction. Keep in mind that stairs should not be made in the Ishan (NE) because it is not auspicious.
23. Balcony should be always in north or east direction of the complex.
24. The length and breadth of each room of the complex should be such that breathing can be smooth. There should be proper ventilation and air pipe for the exit of impure air.
25. Whether you make tank on the roof of commercial complex, or arrange the objects for advertisement flags, antena or air pipe, it should not move up and down. All the objects' height be in the same ratio.
26. Always provide lightening conductor if the storeys of the complex go above nine or the height of the complex goes above 45 feet. This is a must so that the complex remain safe from rain cyclone, typhoon, bad weather and lightening.

PRACTICAL CASE STUDY

Case no.1

I am presenting here three practical case studies in the context of commercial complex for my wise readers. First of all see the map of Bhopal Gas Factory. This is triangular in shape. Entrance is in south direction. This is called Yama-dwar which causes death. In Naishritya (SW) or south there are two tubewells. Well in Naishritya (SW) is cause for death.

This Bhopal Carbide Gas Factory is established over an area of 80 bighas (1 bigha= 20 katthas) and employs a large work force. This factory has lot of faults and errors, from Vastu point of view, which you must have noticed at first glance.

Around two thousand people died, on 3rd of December 1984 due to leakage of gas. Life of, around two lakhs of people was affected due to this Gas tragedy. The company had to pay crore of rupees as compensation.

Bhopal gas tragedy is the biggest tragedy witnessed by the people of this world. This company associated with America, at long rectified the error through the help, obtained from the Vastu scientist of India; but due to the triangular shape of the land, this place remains the cause for quarrel and litigation.

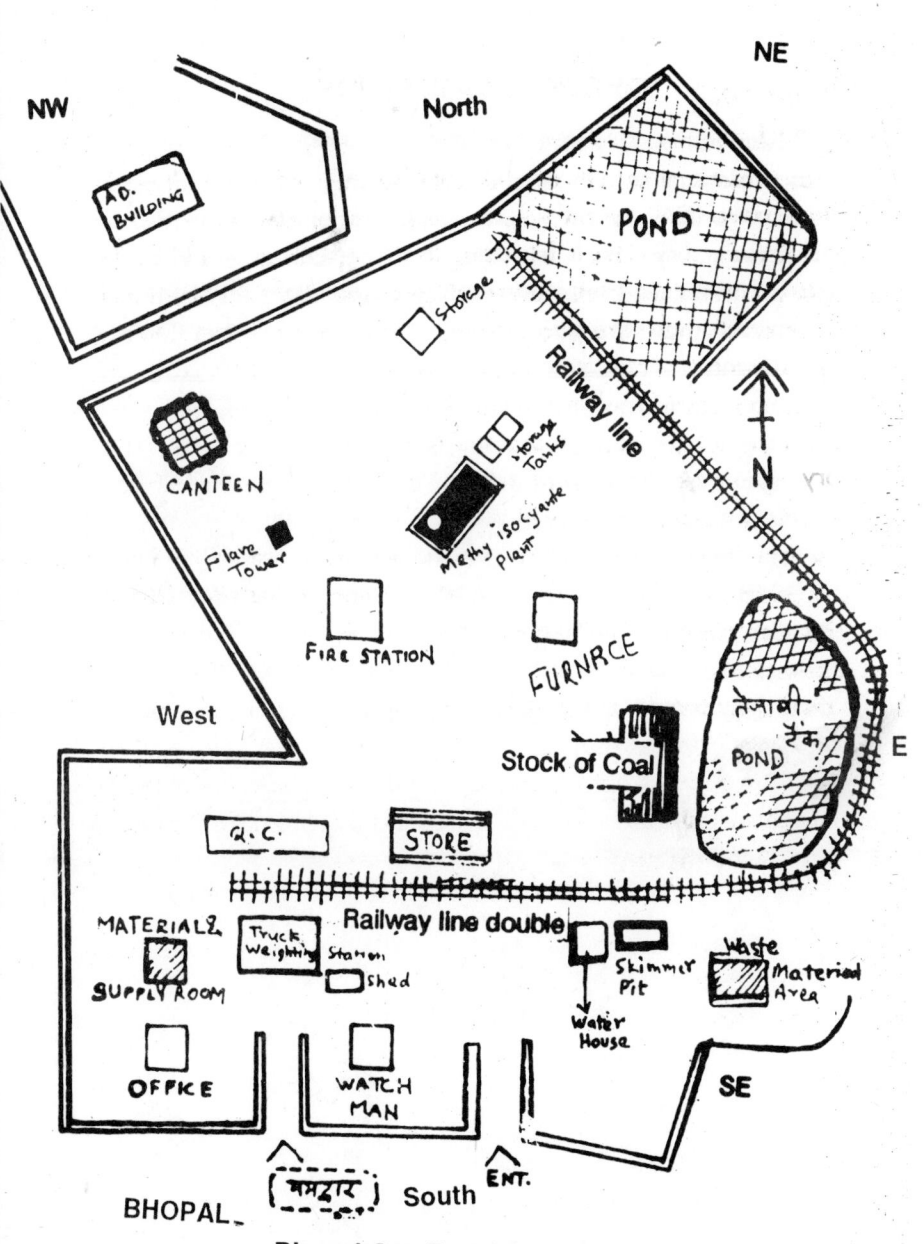

Bhopal Gas Factory-Trianguiar Vaastu

CASE STUDY No.-1

Case No. 2

Second case is related to a famous Indian ice Factory. Its main gate was in west direction, where exists a road. The water source is in Naishritya (SW) which is faulty. Boiler is wrongly posited in south direction. The machines are burnt regularly in the factory. Nevertheless the production was very good and satisfactory but the safety tank was wrongly placed in the Agnikona. The entrance point for the room of Managing director, was wrong. The mixing of water in the tank, above the kitchen and fire, was wrong. The temple, on the Naishritya (SW) kona above the water-reservoir, was also wrong. I changed a bit all the faulty places. Were the name and address is not mentioned due to ethics of secrecy. But with the rectification of the errors the factory started to run full fledged and started earning profit in lakhs. The land of this factory is Kakamukhi (crow-face-shape) hence this type of land is supposed to be very good for industries. The owner of this factory has risen from a very ordinary family. Now they are highly prosperous.

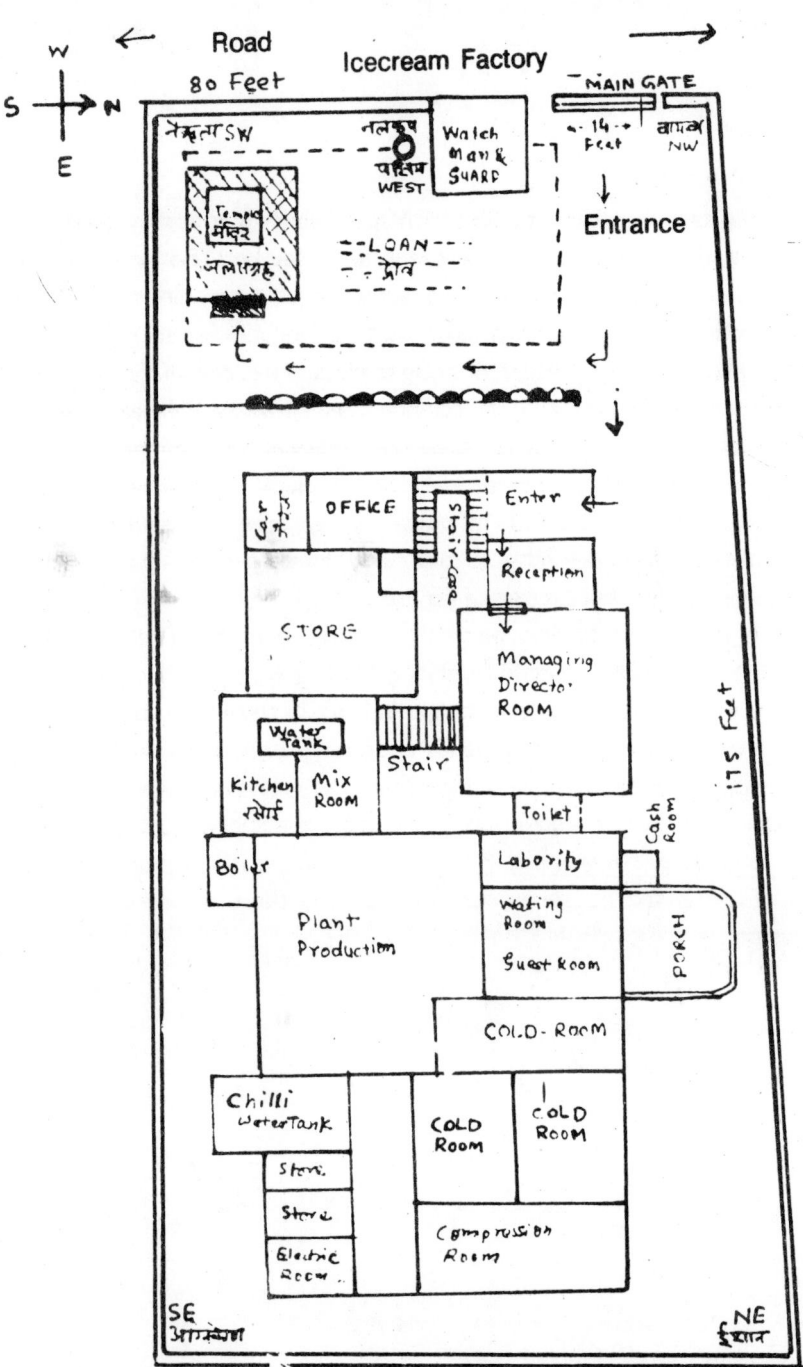

CASE STUDY No. – 2

Case No. 3

This case is related to Shastri Nagar which is a costly place in Jodhpur city. Name and address are kept secret. This is again in triangular shape of four sides, in which the length in east direction is 90 feet and in west direction the length is 42.6 feet. Open field or plot is not available in Shastri Nagar. But due to cheap rate, one of the person known to me bought it: Vastu science says 'Trikone Kalahakalham'. And this happened. There is regular quarrel among the family members. Daily they quarrel just for the hack of it. The wife is suffering from diseases and the house owner does not feel happy in the house. Yagyapuja (sacrifices) and Grih Shanti (peace in the house) rituals were held, but proved of no use.

My attention was drawn to this case in November 1995. There was a beautiful pole, beset in front of the triangular sitting room of the owner. I removed this pole, just right in front of the sitting room. The Vedha (obstruction) due to pole for the sitting room was effecting the decisions been taken in the sitting room. The worship room in house was also not well posited, hence the Gods were angry. House owner was a great social worker. I changed the places slightly at five-six points. Now the house owner is happy and there is peace in the house.

CASE STUDY No.-3

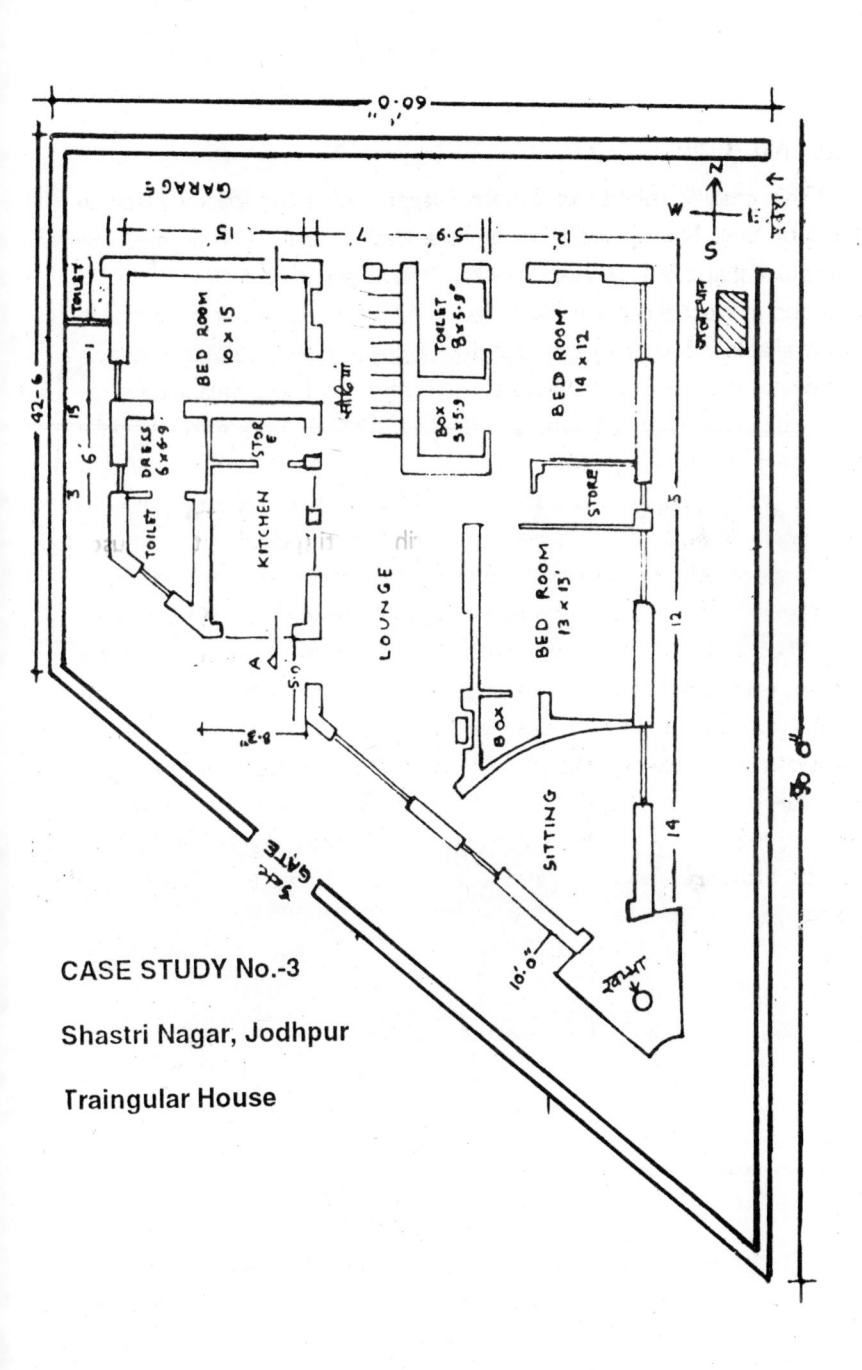

Shastri Nagar, Jodhpur

Traingular House

Technique of Complex Construction

The first formula in the technique of constructing a complex is that the height of complex should be correct. This cement factory was situated on the National Highway and was running well.

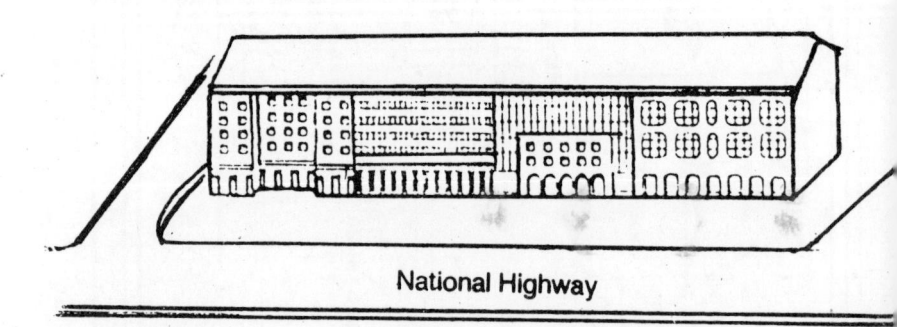

National Highway

The factory owner constructed two 'minars' (minarets) of unequal height without consulting any Vastu scientist.

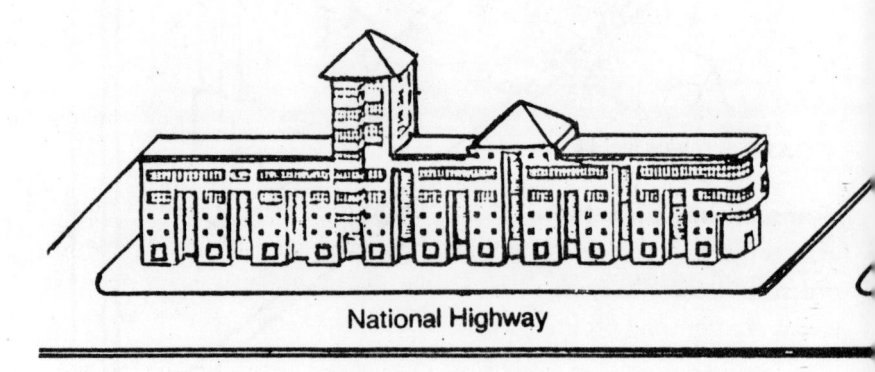

National Highway

Soon after factory started to run in loss and was closed after two years of this new construction. Hence it should be kept in mind that there should not be any construction of unrelated height on the roof.

Commercial Complex should be of equal height

A Vastu scientist and a house builder should keep in mind whether a commercial complex, or a multistorey building for dual purpose is to be built height of all the flats should be same. From the picture it is

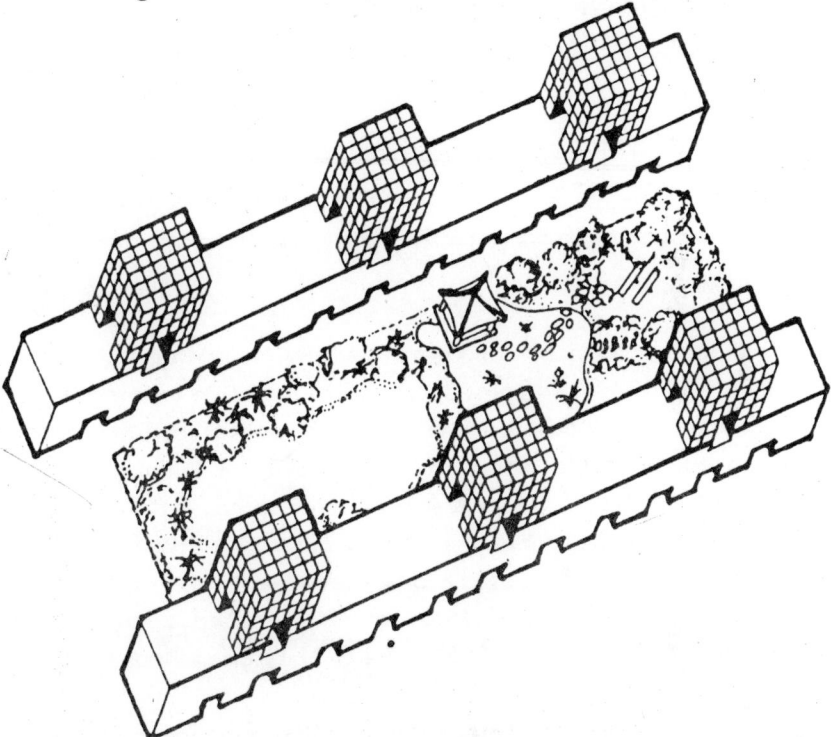

clear that such buildings look marvellous due to equilibrium of bricks, iron, cement and beam and the entrance of light and air. The magnetic pressure creates a balanced situation. People living in such houses remain healthy and prosperous.

While travelling in New York, I have seen a plaza on fifth avenue and the 6 storeyed commercial complex situated on the Rock Feller Centre which are very good examples from Vastu point of view. They never have had any mishaps in the building though it is a fifty years old construction. All the people living in it are happy, prosperous and healthy.

Chapter 9

Effect of Direction on Houses Falling on Roadside

If some people by congregating at any place want to make a colony, then they leave some space before the house for movement. But houses are not built at a time on both the sides of road. Somebody constructs his house before the road is laid out. After this other people construct their houses leaving some space on the road side which makes the previous one's house (adjacent to road) ahead or protruding towards the road i.e. previous houses 'Ahata' (open space) piercing into the road. Under these haphazard conditions of construction the houses affected due to Marg Prahaar (path-hit) on both sides.

Marg Prahaar is good in some cases and bad in some cases about which knowledge is necessary.

1. Houses facing East; if cross the Path then it is affected by Marg Prahaar in north, Ishan and south Agneya. It gives good results to the owner.
2. Houses facing South; if cross the line of path then, Marg Prahaar affects it in east Agneya (SE) and west Naishritya. (SW) Both are like the pierce of javilin giving bad results.
3. House facing West; if crosses the path-line then Marg Prahaar is from north Vayavya (NW) and south Naishritya. (SW) Both are inauspicious.

4. Houses facing North; if cross the line then Marg Prahaar is from east Ishan and west Vayavya direction. This is good and auspicious.

The house-owner, constructing a house with door facing east-north should try to make the house crossing the actual path-line. Such people will be more happy and prosperous than t e other of that vicinity. The more is the line covered by house, the more will be success. This intrusion will have to keep in mind other characters of Vastu also and not of Marg-Prahaar.

If the owner commits a mistake in constructing the house with west-south the door facing crossing the actual path-line, then he will have to face trouble.

How to Select the Place

Before constructing complexes, it will be fruitful to choose the plot after suggestion of a practical Vastu scientist. The selection of Chatushkona (four angled) right-angled, Dirgha Chatushkona (enlarged four angled) will be fruitful from every point. Large land provides prosperity, but it should not be cut in any direction.

Buy additional land, falling in the east or north direction of the house or plot. Even if the land is costly in Ishan direction, one should not hesitate in buying it.

The high and low land effect is reflected in our life. Low land in east, and north direction will provide property. If the land is high in west and south direction, then it will provide enormous wealth during the life. People living on such lands, perform their work smoothly. Always prefer a large plot as far as possible. One can make a home and establish many storeys at such places.

On parallel lines it will be beneficial to choose the plot with road in east-west direction. When a land is suitable to its direction, then the constructed house is also suitable. The land opposite to this should also be tried to made suitable, according to the direction. Hence, if that plot is not according to the indicated direction, then the house should be constructed, according to the adjacent houses and the adjoining road.

The land will have to be chosen on parallel or straight road as indicator of the direction. The road making Ishan (NE) in front will change the plans undertaken. The prosperity of life will be proportional to the height of level in west and south directions.

Triangular shaped land should be avoided as far possible.

As it is not possible to change the character of natural land, similarly no one can change the faults of natural defective land. It is impossible to change the situation if mountains are in eastern north direction and ponds and rivers in lower part of west- south. Similarly to change the path crossing the Ishan (NE) is not possible. A small and congested land between two big and large plots, is of no use. Making houses, at such places is to invite troubles in life.

Protruding land in Vayavya (NW), Naishritya (SW) and Agneya (SE) should never be selected.

If the vacant space, in south-west of the house is larger than north-east, then former should be reduced by constructing wall or open road in Naishritya (SW) direction, by fencing the space for horticulture or it should be sold out.

The path, emerging from your house, should make you move towards east or north. This will be auspicious. If this path leads you to east Agneya or Naishritya (SW) then it will prove painful and troublesome.

Do not choose lower land towards Naishritya (SW) direction. One should take care of this that the water flowing from neighbours house or rain water, should not flow in your land. People at such places do not lead even an ordinary life. When we think about enlarging or reducing of housing-land then west Vayavya (NW) can be protruding or larger but the angle or quarter from Naishritya (SW) to Vayavya (NW) should not be protruding. It should be exactly at 90°. Projected Vayavya is pleasant only from land point of view but if the western Vayavya (NW) of house is protruding then it will be Vastu fault because of Western Vayavya being heavy and the Naishritya (NW) being light and it becomes powerless.

Similarly south Agneya should be protruding only for the land but not for the house. If south-Agneya is protruding ('Agret') then due to its heaviness, Naishritya becomes light and results in loss of its power. It is said that the land can be reduced in the east Agneya part of land but not in the east-Agneya of house. If this happens in the construction then Agneya place will be increased more than the Ishan place infront of the house. Hence an increased Agneya is a cause for Vastu faults.

Similarly north Vayavya of land can be reduced. But the north Vayavya of the house should not be decreased. This will result in an increase of Vayavya which will be more than Ishan quarter's vacant place and the good effect will be decreased.

Errors relating to Vastu, can be rectified. Hence be cautious while selecting the land before construction of house. This will avoid any trouble in future.

How to take the riglst decision relating to 'Kona' (Angles)

The joint of two sides or direction is called corner or 'Vidik'. During house construction the verification of right situation of corner is absolutely essential. With a small fault, the corner in any direction of Naishritya, Agneya, Vayavya and Ishan can either increase or decrease. A slight mistake and the house owner will have to bear its bad result lifelong. Hence each corner should be laid out properly according to Vastu.

Whether the corner flank from the corner is right or not should be verified properly by the mason. First of all the measurement of land should be fixed in four directions then corners will have to be laid out in suggested and directed ways.

If the direction fixed is west, then fix a peg in Naishritya (SW) and from there draw a line with thread tightly drawn towards north with western boundary and towards east with boundary of south. Make a mark near 3 feet in north direction from the corner of the peg. Similarly mark at the four feet measurement towards east with southern boundary. Join these two points, the measurement should be five feet. If this measurement is more than 5 feet then southern Agneya (SE) is protruding. If it is less, then southern Naishritya (SW) is increased. Decision have to be taken here. If it is exactly 5 feet then the Naishritya (SW) corner is laid out properly.

If the pointed direction is towards south, then fix the peg in Agneya direction and mark the point, 3 feet towards west from southern boundary, 4 feet towards north from eastern boundary. The line, joining these points, should be exactly 5 feet. If it is less than 5 feet, then east and Agneya will be protruding. And if greater than 5, then east Ishana is increased. On being exactly 5 feet, the Agneya Angle should be taken as correct.

If the pointed direction is east then fix the peg in Ishan corner. And mark the point at 3 feet towards south from eastern boundary and at 4 feet towards west from northern boundary. The line, joining these two points, should be 5 feet. If it is less than 5, then North Ishan has increased, if it is more than 5 then North Vayavya (NW) is increased. Hence the angle will have to be corrected there, to get 5 feet diagonal.

If the pointed direction is north, then fix the peg in Vayavya (NW). Mark the points at 3 feet towards east, from north boundary and at 4 feet towards south in west direction. The line, joining these two points should be exactly 5 feet. If it is more than 5 feet, then it is increased towards west Naishritya (SW) and if less than 5 feet then West Vayavya (NW) is increased.

The measurement of land and room, with Chatushkona (four angled) and Dirgha Chatushkona (big four angled), should be done from the measurement of Naishritya (SW) to Ishan (NE) and Vayavya (NW) to Agneya (SE). This decides whether both the measurements are equal or not. In this way, in every case, the angle or corner's measurements will have to be made perfect, from plot-decision to foundation, and from foundation to wall construction.

☐

Chapter 10

Vastu and Business Setup

वास्तुशास्त्रेण संबंधें गहनों व्यवसायिनाम्।
व्यवसायोन्नतेर्मूलं वास्तुशास्त्रं विचारयेत्।।
Vaastushastren sambandhe gahano vayvsayinam
Vayavsayonntermulam Vastushastram Vicharyet

Vastushastra is a very thoughtful and deep subject and has close relationship with the life of a common man. It is not only related to residential house but, also, it has got close relation with business and trade. The root of success in business is Vastu science. Hence knowledge of subjects related to Vastu Shastra should be imbibed before setting up of shop, office, 'Gaddi' (sitting place), show room, mill, factory, industry etc.Sometimes we do not get the result of our labour due to a slight mistake. Mature business men also give up. j Hence knowledge of Vastu subject helps in getting over the crisis in man.

A shrewd businessman should think about shop, office etc. the basics of a business-set-up. For obtaining profits, one should examine the good and bad points of the shop before it is set up from the view point of Vastushastra also. If the shop or office is facing east then it is healthy and profitable from business point of view. If the shop is facing west then there is rise and fall in business. shops facing North increase property and wealth; it provides recognition to the establishment and brightens its name. If the shop is facing south then problem arises during lean period and progress in business is slow. Shops facing east and north should be prefered as far as possible. Wisdom lies in this. Sometime we find exceptions. If in the horoscope of a person the planet 'Rahu' is 'Karaka' then shops facing south provide ample of profits and the shop runs well and smoothly. It is true that if the shops and foundations are facing south, then the place for office should be fixed in different directions.

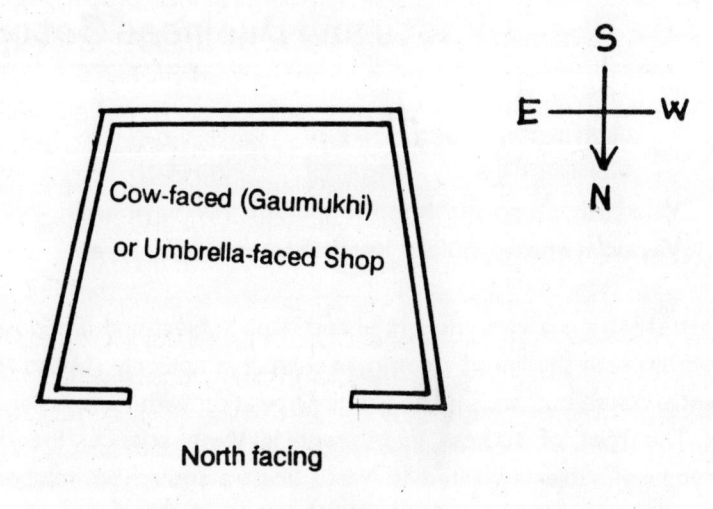

Cow-faced (Gaumukhi) or Umbrella-faced Shop

North facing

Fig. –1

In big towns, shops or offices are facing all sides hence the south direction can never be left completely. Shops are in all directions and the place for business can be attained only at big cost and by giving extra money. We have observed that maximum shops face south in big cities and metropolis. In such cases one should think about his Gaddi (sitting place), chair and counter in the shop. One's sitting place (revolving chairs) should be fixed according to rules. That means south facing 'Aasan' (sitting place) should not face towards south. During weak planet's period, the person may incur even heavy loss.

The businessmen and traders should sit facing north or facing east in his Pratishthan (establishment like shop or office). Sitting facing west and south leads to a situation where a person is confronted with loss in business or faces obstacles at every step. All round development is restricted. Hence it is very important that 'Aasan' or 'Gaddi' should be fixed stricly according to correct direction.

Exceptions—

If Rahu and Venus planets are strong at the time of native's birth, then he will be successful sitting in south direction. Sitting place facing south has also proved good and 'karaka' for such natives.

The land of shop and office should be examined properly. One should think, as detailed in the book in chapter 3, If the shape of the shop or office is 'Chhajmukhi' enlarged on the front and narrow on the rear part, then such shops are not auspicious. It is also called 'Gaumukhi' shop. Simhamukhi (face like lion) shops are excellent from profit point of view, some people call it Kakamukhi (face like crow) also. If the volume is larger then it is auspicious. A proportionate or symmetrical volume for the shops is also considered auspicious.

Shops or hotels, in triangular or crooked shape are not auspicious i.e. triad and three cornered shape is said to be painful and damaging. Similarly the existence of ditch (dirt and garbage) in the front of shop and offices is not supposed to be auspicious. In such condition rectification through possible ways are desired. Ditch does not mean

Simhamukhi (face like Lion) or Kakmukhi (face like crow) shop

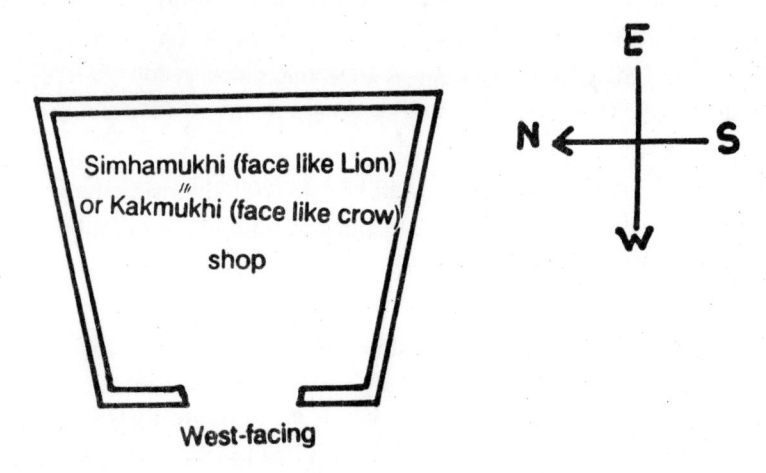

West-facing

Fig. –2

the drainage of the road. Though the drainage of the road is also a type of 'Vedha' which obstructs the movement of people.

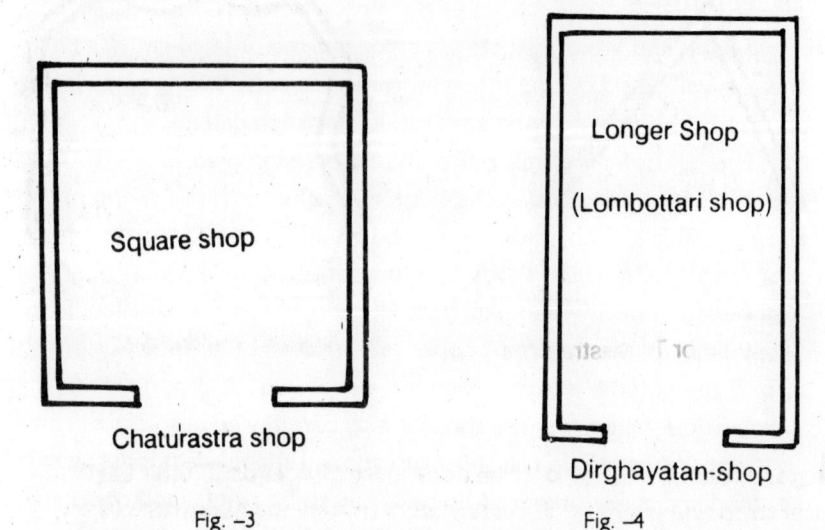

Square shop

Chaturastra shop

Fig. –3

Longer Shop

(Lombottari shop)

Dirghayatan-shop

Fig. –4

If the hotel, Industry, shop, office, 'Gaddi' or business centre is not auspicious from Vastu point of view; or it is out of shape or the sides are crooked and construction is unbalanced or any type of perversion is found, then the 'Shri Yantra' should be set up under the ground (Garbh griha) or foundation or at a suitable place under the advice of a practical Vastu specialist so as to create a sort of auspiciousness to the premises.

As far as possible, crookedness should not exist inside the shop. In such a condition the shopkeeper and the business man find no rest, peace, obstacles assume any form and the wealth increase is not upto the expectation.

There should not be any type of obstacles, frames (Dahlij) flange or high objects (like stone or piled up object). If the obstacle (frames) is there, then it should be even. It should not have slopes or crookedness, otherwise Laxmi (wealth) will not be stable and it will not multiply.

The auspicious timing (Muhurta) for laying foundation of hotels,

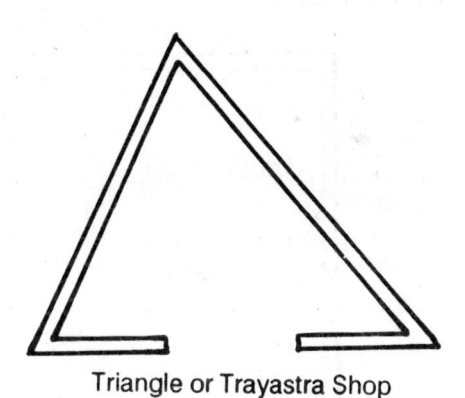

Triangle or Trayastra Shop   Vikala or multiangled Shop

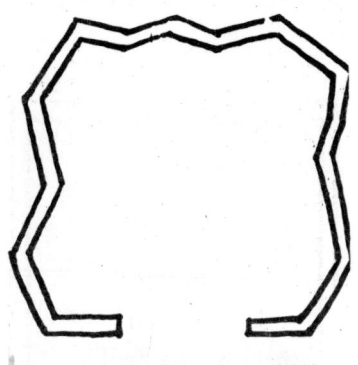

Fig. –5   Fig. –6

shops, business offices should be done in fixed ascendant (Sthir Lagna). After brooding over and discussing about moon and Nakshatra (stars) and finding splendid time (Muhurta), with the assistance of Jyotisha Charya (astrologer) and Vastu scientist, the work should be started. If there is haste, or any unavoidable condition then the 'Muhurta' should be performed during the excellent position of moon, Pushya Nakshatra's day, in libra (Tula) or auspicious ascendant.

The courtyard of business centres like hotel, shop, business offices should be neat, clean, firm and pleasant, otherwise suspicion, about wealth loss is seen. Floor should not be odd or uneven or with much as it obstructs the business.

After fixating of 'Muhurta', only business work in hotel, shop, offices, or 'Gaddi' should be started. Initiation should be done in a pleasant mood with family and friends. 'Muhurta' performed during the first half of the day is auspicious. During sun-set or in the night 'muhurta' for business and trading, should not be held.

First of all, one should meditate, then invoke and worship Lord Shri. Ganapati with 'Ridhi' and Sidhi, after remembering your family God, native place God with clear mind, voice and Karma. The idol of

Fig. –7

Shri Ganesha should be installed on the right of shop, office 'Gaddi' or sitting place. In case of want of the space, Shri Ganesha should be set with Goddess Laxmi, towards the head of 'Gaddi' (Aasan).

The land, from where the hotel, shop, office and Gaddi are fixed, should be rectified and revoked so that the impure land could be pure. The troubles and obstacles coming up can be kept away and peace can exist there; otherwise the mind does not rest at peace even after success due to hard labour. Hence worship of land should be done under the guidance of 'Vedagya Vidwan' (learned of Vedas) Brahman.

All things for sitting i.e., 'Gaddi', furniture, counter should be bought new at the time of auspicious muhurta. White and yellow clothes should only be used. The bed-sheet, cover of bolster and cushion should be of cloth of white colour. Goddess Laxmi is attracted from the light or rays of planet Venus. Hence give attention towards white shiny or silvery colour because white is a symbol of purity and does attract.

At the time of 'muhurta', new items of stationary, ledger books as per requirement should be purchased and worshipped with faith, by the business man. These are the necessary tools for business. The 'balance' (Tula) for weighing should be also worshiped, with proper procedure especially for business men deling in kirana.

Hotel, shop and business centres at the time of 'muhurta' should be decorated with Patra-Pushpa (leaves and flowers), including the stretching of cloth, tents and cloth-decoration. There should be arrangement of Vadya-Vrinda (auspicious music and songs) for pleasant auspicious sound. The centre and shop should be decorated.

One should worship with proper arrangements near the shop, office, etc. after sitting in the right direction near the door, 'Swastik' should be marked with Gandh', (odour), Pushp (flower), Patra (leaves,) Akshat (unhusked grain). This 'Swastik' mark is symbol of Ridhi (prosperity) and Sidhi (success). Instead of vermellion colour 'swastik', saffron coloured 'swastik' should be used so that business tends towards stability and development. 'Swastik' is sign of good luck and it has got the power of attraction. It should be kept in mind that swastik should not be with reverse hands otherwise the results will be opposite. Hence understanding the scientific secret hidden in the 'swastik' is necessary (Chapter 11).

Taking ones shop, Gaddi, office, and foundation as Laxmi-Swarupa, (like goddess Lakshmi) the businessman with full devotion should say "Hey Vipani! You are the greatest Dhatri (mother or nourisher) and greatest to bring us up! You bring prosperity and wealth! you provide physical and materialistic pleasure! Hey Devi! Make my business reputed! Hey Devi! grant fame and name always in my house and let the prosperity continue to increase! Hey Vipani! I bow before you with respect and I regard you." This prayer should be performed in shop, Gaddi, mill, factory and industrial offices.

The lord of wealth is 'Kuber' and its symbol is treasure (treasure box, safe, locker,bag). Hence worshipping Him with regard proves fruitful and pleasant. The treasure remains filled all the time i.e. there is permanent increase in treasure.

Kuber is swami (owner) of permanent prosperity and also the lord of north direction. The north direction is supposed to be excellent for auspicious and business work. Hence one should beg and worship lord Kubera with 'Kuber-mantra' facing north for the gain of wealth and prosperity.

There should be embossed or marked the sign of 'Swastik' on the things holding money i.e. bag, purse, locker or almirah, pass book or cheque book. Five Kanwalgatte (a type of spices) and five unbroken turmeric should be kept together. This has scientific importance on account of its presence, the treasure box or the place of keeping money does not remain empty. One should pray to demigod of business with Dab (auspicious grass), Akshat, Gandh, Pushpa etc. for the presence of goddess Laxmi forever. Goddess Mahalaxmi becomes pleasant with Haridra (Turmeric).

महालक्ष्मि! नमस्तुभ्यं प्रसन्ना भव मंगले।
स्वर्णवित्तादिरूपेण विपण्यां त्वं चिरं वस॥

Mahalaxmi! Namastubhya prasanna bhav mangle Swaranvittadeirupene vipannayam ttavem chiram vas.

Every business man should pray to shri Mahalaxmi Goddess with folded hands "Goddess Mahalaxmi! Lot of Namaskar (respect) to you! O Mangale! benefactor Goddess! Be happy with me and pour your grace. Provide us gold and money in our shop and give blessings to run my business for ever! So this business could run with perennial increase and with maximum gain through your grace."

As far as possible awakened shriyantra should be formed and kept in business office and in front of this 'Shri Yantra' one should recite the 'Shri Sukta' and 'Kanakdhara stotra' (recitation in praise of god). Then Goddess Laxmi rests there permanently.

Chapter 11

Scientific Secret of Swastik

We find the presence of 'Swastik sign' first of all in Vastu and all religious practices and activities. Not only the Hindus, but all the religion of the world, have accepted this sign which is most auspicious and pure. Why is it like this? What is speciality in this Swastik sign after all? What is its scientific ground? Is it enamoured to think of it in this scientific age? Let us give thought to the subject.

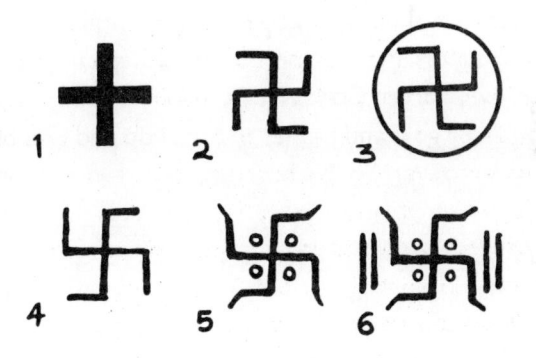

1. Electronic Theory

In Mathematics the + sign as in fig 1 is supposed to be positive. According to science the meeting point, of two negatives of different power, is called positive which is the cause for the birth of new power.

Hence Apbhransh (the fallen and broken shape), of Swastik sign, is symbol of power and prosperity.

2. The Holy Cross of Christians.

The swastik, used in fig 1 is extremely pious + sign (cross) for the christians. This cross + is infact the brief transformation of the idol of Lord Ganesha. The head of elephant is joined as head with the body of chopped up Ganesha. Hence Lord Ganesha is also famous as Gajvadan, Gajanan, Karimukh, Ibhasya etc. In this situation this is clear that the word, 'cross', is also the perverted or diluted form of word 'Kari + Asya' which means the face of the elephant. The word 'christ' of christianity also seems to be the result of summation of 3 words Kar + Asya + Ishta, which means persons who accept and take Shri Ganesha the lord with elephant face, their 'Ishtadeva' (the beloved god to be worshiped). Some people will obviously argue about the formation of Swastik from cross, but it is their suspicion only. Because Swastik sign has been existing for thousands of years before Christ. The four hands of swastik sign, in four directions, present and indicate auspicious things and happenings. Pious thinking puts off the worries and other troubles. This is why, red cross (Swastik) has been accepted and used, as the sign of health gain and consolation, in every health, centre and hospital of the world.

3. The Swastik sign of fig. 2 and 3 are in vogue in maximum countries. This is supposed to be a symbol of victory and auspicious in western countries. The four doors in it represent the four directions and are supposed to be source of enshrining Ridhi-Sidhi. The national flag of Germany under Hitler possessed this embossed sign. When swastik was turned down-right, then it became the main cause for the defeat of Hitler during global-war of 1939-45.

4. Symbol of Evidence (Presence)

In Jain Dharma and Pali language, this is associated with the name 'Sakshi' (eye-witness). On going to the derivation of word from roots this means 'Sakshiyo Karmah' i.e., which is present as evidence in every pious and auspicious work.

The 'Apbhransha' or diluted and broken pronunciation of 'Sakshiyon' was later distorted, as' Sakhiyon or sakiyon in course of time and is now used at many places in colloquial languages.

5. Swastik means Fortune.

The word 'Swastik' is made up of 'Su' (prefix) and the element 'Us'. 'Su' means good, beneficial, excellent, lucky and 'Us' means existence, or presence. Hence the meaning of Swastik is existence or presence of luck and benefit, presence of auspicious atmosphere. Where 'Shri' (bliss) is present, beauty is present, Punsavad (male child domination) is present; fraternity, happiness and prosperity is present; aesthetic sense and beauty of life is present, there exists the sense of 'Swastik'. In Swastik symbol is hidden the essence of world development. Swastik sign is the symbol of ancient religious fortune for the development of human beings.

'Samapti Kamah Mangalam Achharet'. According to Patanjal Yoga Shastra, to complete any work smoothly, it has been a very old custom to write 'Mangalacharan' (auspicious), but the self-composition of beautiful auspicious poems is not possible for common people. The 'Rishis' had created the 'Swastik sign' for such work whose formation is sufficient to complete the work without obstacles. It is mentioned in 'Amar-Kosha' 'Swastikah Sarwato Ridha'. Swastik means to make human life blissful through fragrance from all the directions in every way. The essence of 'Vasudev Kutumbakamp' (Whole earth is my family) is present in swastik.

Swastik is a sign of peace, prosperity and fortune. Many ladies perform Swastik Vrat (fasting) during 'Chaturmasya' (four months). There is no fear, of widowhood on worshipping daily in the temple by making Swastik with 'Ashtadal' (eight flanks). Such a story is described in padmpurana.

This is the reason, to keep friendly and beloved throughout life the couple during marriage, is shown 'Swastik'. The infant is made to sleep on the cloth, with Swastik sign, on the 6th day from birth. This leads the infant to get a Swastik field in his life. Newly married girls, in Shrimali Brahmana family use 'Oran' (a type of cloth) with 'Swastik'. Swastik sign is painted with beautiful colour on every door of houses in Gujarat. The philosophy behind this, is that all the things—rain, cloth and prosperity when dawn in the house, will lead to being pious. and the guest, arriving in their house come with good news.

6. Swastik—Symbol of Lord Shiva's power

The upright (vertical) line indicates the Swambhoo (self-birth) Jyotirling (lusturous phallus). This Shiva phallus is the root cause for the birth of world. The horizontal line of swastik represent the stretch and extension of world. With the addition of Shiva and power, this creation has been extended. Hence the root philosophy of this Swastik sign is also acceptable.

7. Swastik is symbol of lord Vishnu and bliss

The four sides of Swastik are the four hands of Lord Vishnu. Lord Vishnu nourishes the four directions with four hands in Swastik shape. The middle point of Swastik, which is the place of Nabhikamal (navel like lotus) of Lord Vishnu, is the place of Brahma. The image of universe the creation of the (Shristi) is reflected in this sentimental symbol. Swasti is symbol of 'Shri' (bliss). This 'Shri' is the symbolic sign of Lord Vishnu and the Goddess of wealth Laxmi. In Fig. No. 5, Swastik is made for Laxmi Upasana (worship), Shrikamana (desire for bliss).

8. Symbol of Ganapati (Lord Ganesha)

Swastik sign is the symbolic form of compound shape of Ganapati. 'Tantricism', cult of Mahayan sect of Buddha religion (Buddhism) has accepted the worship of 'Swastik' in symbolic form of 'Vinayak' (Lord Ganesha). It is worshiped as 'Haremb' in Nepal. The people of Greece worship Ganesha by name of 'Orenus'. Orenus has got importance in their ancient books. Sri Ganeshji is called 'Laxashindhu vadan' according to Hindu religious books, which takes an extremely deep red vermillion colour like lac (red dye). It also shows that 'Orenus' of

Greek which is of orange and red colour can, in fact, be the worship of Swastik-shaped-Ganapati. Swastik is called Sogsadaag in Bhot language, Maha-Piyenney in Burmese, Twotkharun khagan in Mangolian, Prahkenij in Combodia, Kuad-shi-Tiyenu in Chinese and Kangiyer in Japanese.

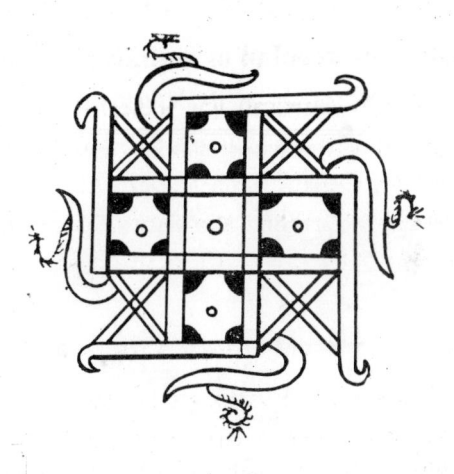

The founder of intellect and most revered, among Gods in Egypt, is called 'Acton'. This symbol is made in cross-shape with 'Kumkum' (saffron colour). It is possible that the word 'Acton' is also the 'apabhransa' (distorted form) or synonym of Shri Ganesha as 'Ekdanta'. Hence in Hindureligion in Dipawali festival, in book-keeping and accounts, the worship of Laxmi is performed alongwith the worship of Swastik as in fig 6. When we imagine this, in the sense of Ganesha, Ridhi-Sidhi is written in symbolic form by two lines on both the sides. Many people write Labh-Shubh (Ridhi-Sidhi) on both sides, as Ridhi is for gain and Sidhi is for luck. There is no dearth of wealth if Ganesha in Swastik form invoked and worshipped in Hindu ancient tradition.

9. Swastikasan (Sitting place of Swastik)

'Swastik', made in fig. 4 and 7 is introduced for sitting place for auspicious work. Swastikasan is made (as in fig. 7) on the altar of sacrifice (yajna) by Shrimali Brahman and this swastikasan is made on Thali (plate), with 'Tandul' (betel leaf) and saffron, Kumkum, (vermillion) to invoke and ignite fire (Agni). This is not made as a representative of Ganesha, but only in the form for Aasan (sitting place).

10. Swastik is the position of Saptarshi (Major ushra-stars) in palo Dhruva-Parikarma (Circumbulating):—

In addition to all these pastulations, Swastik sign has relationship with astronomy. Swastik is the root sign of 'Saptarshi' (collection of 7 stars), in eternal movement. We recite Swasti, before starting any auspicious work.

स्वस्ति न इंद्रो वृद्धश्रवाः, स्वस्ति नः पूषा विश्ववेदाः।
स्वस्तिनस्ताक्ष्र्यो अरीष्टनेमिः स्वस्ति नो बृहस्पतिर्दधातु॥

Swasti Na Indro Vadshrava Swasti Na Pusha Vishawvedah Swastinastaksharyo Arishtanemi Swasti No Vrihapatirdadhatu

—*Yajurveda 25/16*

This 'mantra' (hymn) is so much famous that the learned use this as a bliss during 'Tilak' (mark made with sandal paste on forehead). The literal meaning of 'Mantra' is—Let the biggest named and famed Indra, propitiate and give blessings to us, Let the Pusha Dev the God of Knowledge of universe give us blessings, Let the Garud the God with arms to destroy the losses, save us and let the Brihaspati consolidate blessings on us.

1. 'Chitra' is the nakshtra (star), falling in the middle of 27 nakshtras whose owner is Indra, in the 'Taitriya' branch. That is indicated in this hymn. In the hymn the word 'Vridhshrava' adjective is used due to its shape of stars.

2. Just on the paralleled half of 'Chitra' at 180, lies the nakshatra 'Revati' whose god is ' Pusha'. Being the last member of Nakshatra sphere, 'Vishvedah' (with all the knowledge) is

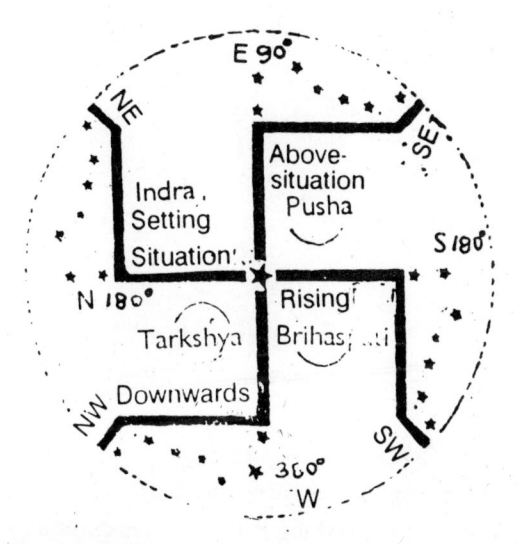

used in this hymn.
3. Shravana Nakshatra with 3 stars is at Chathurthansa (90°) from the middle. 'Tarkshayam' word is associated with this hymn. The lord of Shrawan Nakshatra is Lord Vishnu and Tarkshya (Garud-eagle) is the vehicle of Vishnu.
4. Pushya Nakshatra lies at a distance of chaturthansa, i.e. 90°, from Revati whose lord is Jupiter. This is used in the fourth part of this hymn.

In this way total universe is divided, among Pushya, Chitra, Shrawan and Revati (of 90-90°) with four parallel parts. And it has been prayed — "O Gods of all the four directions! Be blissful to us". Four points signify the lords of four directions. The seers have propounded, in this hymn, the science of nakshatra in a few words, the simplicity of which adds beauty to this.

To give place and prominence to Swastik means to obtain the blessings of Seven seers Marichi, Arundhiti, with Vashishtha, Angira, Atri, Pultsya, Pulah and Krit, by invoking them, before performing any auspicious work. This is why in Vastushastra, Swastik has great importance.

Chapter 12

Eradicate Vastu-faults.

It is necessary for a business man to have acumen for his business progress through his simple and harmonic behaviour. He should not be so much flexible that everything is lost, or his conduct should not be so harsh that people think a lot before meeting him and they have no access to him. Behaviour and conduct is the root of success in business. Wealth increases through conduct, and fame pervades all around which provides a lot of happiness.

Good conduct is the cause for happiness in the world, is the basis of business. Hence, the soft-spoken and loving behaviour is expected from businessmen, A businessman should conduct himself in such a fashion, that consumers could be attracted to him.

Traders and businessman are the important organs of society. They are wealthy, prosperous and every sect of society has hope and expectation from them. Needy people go to them with hope. Hence traders should behave softly with the needy and should not turn them out. Nevertheless, beggary is a blot and curse for a society and it should be eradicated, they should be treated softly and should not be chided and ill-treated. Sometimes, curse of the beggar, too, is associated with angry planets during lean period.

Following is the 'Sidha Bisaa Yantra' (an accomplished amulet) with power in which 'Nirvana Mantra' (hymn for freedom) of Goddess Jagdamba is included. The bad intentions and the evil eyes do not harm, if it is kept or made on the frame of the door. Curse and evil-thinking do not effect it. This is a shield for the shop in a way. It should be kept in the shop, after awakening or establishing soul inside the pure element.

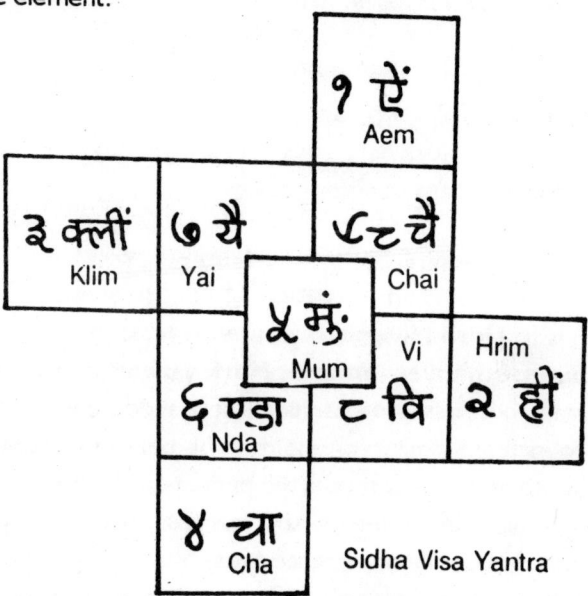

		१ ऐं Aem		
३ क्लीं Klim	७ यै Yai		८ चै Chai	
		५ मुं Mum	Vi	Hrim
		६ ण्डा Nda	ट वि	२ ह्रीं
		४ चा Cha		

Sidha Visa Yantra

The idol of Shri Ganesha should be installed in the shop. Do not keep Ganesha's idol facing south. The Ganesha for worship should be placed in the Gallaa (treasury box)

'Kuladevata' and 'Ishtadevata' should be installed in his shop, 'Gaddi' and offices and they must hang the picture of the teacher (Guru) who inspired them. The business man should pray daily to 'Kuladevata' and 'Ishtadevata', at the time of opening the shop. Then worship the founded God and Goddess in the shop with flowers, garland, scented fumigates and 'Deeps' (lamps).

The traders should give honour and regard to God during worship with thought, voice and action. Soul should possess pious thought. This increases the business and empowers the will-power.

This life is not for the self only but is dedicated to the whole universe and to, both living and non-living beings. Hence, businessman should spend, some part of his income earned from business, for religious activities. He should donate some part of his income to public work and human-service. By doing so, one gets self-satisfaction and increases name and fame and Ridhi-Sidhi in business continues.

One should spend, either sixth part or tenth part of income in religious work. This will keep adding to the income and development of business. Religious work here does not relate to any community but it indicates to the welfare of human; beings.

दृष्टिदोषनिवारार्थ विपणेद्वारस्तम्भयो:।
जम्बीरं स्थापयेत् सम्यक् मरीचीद्वयसंयुतम्॥

Drishti Dosh Nivararth vipanedwarastambhyo jambiram sthapyet samayak Marichidway sanyutam

Sometimes business progress is all of a sudden and prosperity continues to increase. This progress can't be borne by many people out of jealousy and rivalry. It makes the person dull Sometimes due to lack of preception and evil-eyes the business becomes dull. This obstacle is called Nazar Dosha. Hence every businessman should hang a lemon with seven green chillis pierced in one thread outside the shop, office or Pratisthan on Saturday. Lemon and chilli should be hung at such a place which can attract everyone's eyes.

व्यापारे संभवेद् हानि: कृते यत्ने निरन्तरम्।
इन्द्राणीयन्त्रमास्थाप्यं विधिवद् वास्तुविद्-धृतम्॥

Vyapara sambhaved hani krite yatne nirantram indraniyantramasthapyam vidhivad vaastuvid Dhritam

This Indrani Yantra is given the human shape of 'Bisa-mantra'. It is said 'Jiske paas Ho Bisa, Uska Kya Karega Jagdisha' i.e. who possess Bisa, even Jagdish can't harm him.

Even in the case of business being balanced with various efforts it is still running in loss, the businessman should find 'Indrani Yantra' with the help of Vastu scientist to save against losses.

चौरी संजायते भूयश्चा ग्निदाहो थवा भवते।
स्थाप्य तत् वास्तुविद्-सिद्धं भौमयन्त्रं विधानत:॥

Business related Indrani Yantra

**Chouri sanjaayte bhushcha agnedaho thava bhavte
stapya tat vastuvidh-sidham bhomyantram Vidhantah**

    If pilferages and theft is going on in the shop or offices, either by consumer or employees then, 'Bhoum Yantra' should be founded with proper rules and regulations after discussing with Vastu scientist about the place. If there is doubt and fear of fire then set 'Bhoumyantra' in the land. It should be established in east-north corner or east direction by digging 2 feet deep from the floor level in a proper way.

    If there is no feeling of interest in the shop, no increase in the treasure, no saving, even after regular income, then put idol of God Ganesha on the front and rear side of frame of main entrance door. Nectar is found in the front and poverty in the back of Lord Ganesha. Ganesha is found only on the front side in many a business man's house. This idol causes welfare of the people or consumer coming and not the house owner, because one cannot see the Ganesha inside the house. Hence this is my special experience that put Ganapati on both sides whether it is shop or house and then see the miracle. If 'shweta' (white) Ganesha, with Shriyantra in silver (coin sized), is fixed on the frame of door then the good result is accelerated. The grace of Laxmi and Ganesha both are effective on that house or shop. The learned reader, if he finds difficulty in getting Yantras, can communicate with the writer without any hesitation.

If retrograde sun is creating Vedha (perforation) on shop, office and Gaddi or sun be debilitated, at the time of foundation, then the shop only proves quarrel and worry. When businessman too is affected by debilitated sun, then pain and trouble continue even after gain in business and the native suffers from self-grief.

The shop's face may not be in right direction, and public turmoil (movement, violence, turmoil by antisocial elements), and fire, burning, loot etc. are creating destruction In this condition 'Yamkilak Yantra' should be founded to solve the 'Kala-dosha' problem (time-fault).

राजकीय विपत्तिश्चेत् कदाचिद् विपणौ पतेत्।
सूर्ययंत्रं तु संस्थाप्यं सर्वविघ्न-निवारकम्॥

Rajkiya Vipatishchyate kadachite vipanou patet
Suryayantram tu sansthapyam sarvavighan-Nivarakam

'Surya Yantra' should be installed in case of problem created by government body, or any type of administrative trouble. Recitation of 'Shri Laxmi Sahastranam' should be done if peace does not exist even after regular income in business, quarrel continues, and unrest continues among the partners.

□

Chapter 13

The Importance of Directions in Constructing a House

The effect of vedha is not only limited to doors, but it can cast its bad effects on any part of the house. Hence it is emphasized in book of Indian Architecture to live aloof and keep distance from this vedha. The particular directions relating to the residence in each part of a house are given. Some examples will suffice to describe it.

If the floor of the house is not even (i.e. both high and low); ditch of water, well or path of other house lie in front of door, then it is called 'Tala Vedha' (floor obstruction). It is Kona vedha (obstacles due to corner) if all the corners are not equal. If the back portion of the part is low and high, then it is 'Taala vedha'. If the middle of upper frame of door gets back then it is 'Shirvedha'. If a pole is in the heart of house or fire or water place is found in the middle then it is called 'Hridya-Shalya' (heart impediments) or 'Sthambh Vedha'. If the back of house, is lower and upper part is uneven and unbalanced it is called 'Tula Vedha'. All these Vedha show their own bad results and an explanation is not neccessary.

Just after Vedha comes 'Bhang'. It has been discussed in four chapters of 'Samrangan' (see A-42,43,46,47). Perhaps such a description of 'Bhang-fault' is not available elsewhere. 'Bhang' is related to different parts and sub-parts of house construction. Description of all the 'Bhangs' here, is useless hence one or two bad results have been described elaborately, with illustrations which are sufficient. 'Toran-Bhang' is especially described here. 'Granthas' (books) say that 'Toran-bhang' directs the 'Rashtra-bhang'. Similarly description about other 'bhangs' are given. One full chapter is written on 'Dwar-Bhang'.

In the house-error described in 'samrangan' Kapot-Dosh (pigeon fault) is a peculiar error. If anyhow this error enters the house, then it proves very inauspicious. The book has assumed pigeon as 'Kaalmurti' Papmulakarandak, 'Vihanga-pasad' Krishnachari and Vihangam has divided pigeon into four classes—Sweta (white), Vichitra Kanth, (queer-throat), Vichitra (queer), and Krishnak (black). On entering of a pigeon in the house, the bad consequences are not restricted only with simple worship, but the house owner is directed to give gifts to priests and Brahmanas in proportion of its property—one fourth, or two fourth or three fourth or the whole property. This suggestion in present age civilization, is not understandable, but as it been said by the great Seers and hermits it must have had significance in days of yore to be mentioned in Granthas. We had discussed a lot on the error of house, which has more importance from religious point of view but architectural importance is less. But we find ample articles and things, in these books on different subjects, indicating error from art point of view. Those errors among art and architecture and composition are condensed here, especially which is either related to door-composition (Pat-vinyaas) or disobeying the rules of facing-directions, emotionless (Bhavananghinata), Aprashastcheya (faulty) or wrong material-mix up. I have indicated large number of house abodes in which. we can find faulty placings, through long-short extension. Similar.ly, the proclamation of some house errors can be done with faulty houses, due to unexpected and undesired composition of some part e.g.

1. Griha-Sanghatt— Placing of two abodes in the same wall.
2. Valit-Chalit, Bhrant and Visutra (face rising or going out) are called Mukhvinishkrant. Prishthanishkant (back going out), Dir Murh (confused about direction) and Karnhin (earless).

3. Khadak—Anya Prishthasthil Dwar
4. Vikokila-Pratyang Vishal Griha.
5. Saachhatra—Bahyodak.
6. Sakshak Ubhyodak.
7. Saparikram—Saavishyaya.
8. Saprabh—Mukh, Prishtha, single terrace in front of door.
9. Hinbahu—De, Dwarprabheda(sub division of door).
10. Pratyakshay—De, Dwarprabhed.
11. Bhinna deha —De, Dwarprabhed.
12. Sanchhipt —'Yathanaram, Chunaayi is done briefly all around.
13. Nridangakriti—Anta Sanchhipta (piled and extended in the middle).
14. Mridu Madhya —Addyant (soft in the middle, starting and last portion.)

Due to improper placement of a terrace, in front of the door, we find error in houses. The abode should not be lower than the terrace (Alinda) for example. If there is only one 'Alinda' is to be made, it should be in front of the house or in the side portion of south, otherwise the fault is inevitable. Similarly 'Hal Kalind' is the special category of Alinda, whose improper design is supposed to be faulty. Hence, there are many House-errors like this, for example Bhitti Dosha (fault in wall), Stambh-Dosha (fault of pole), Tula-dosha (fault of equilibrium) Dwardosha (fault of door) etc. Marmapidan (suffering mortally) is also a big fault among house-errors. Marmapidan is related to Vastu-faults which is indicated in previous chapters. Hence at the end following house-errors are briefly listed

1. Uch-Chhadya.
2. Chhidragarbha.
3. Bhramit
4. Hinamadhya
5. Vamit-Mukha
6. Nashta Sutra
7. Shalyavidh

8. Shiroguru
9. Bhrashta lindakshobh
10. Vishamasth
11. Tulatul
12. Anyonya Dravya viddh
13. Kupadpravibhajit
14. Hinabhittika
15. Hin-Uttmang
16. Vinashta
17. Stambhbhittik
18. Bhinnashal
19. Tyavat Kanth
20. Nishkand
21. Manavarjit
22. Vikrit

Layout Plan Twin-House

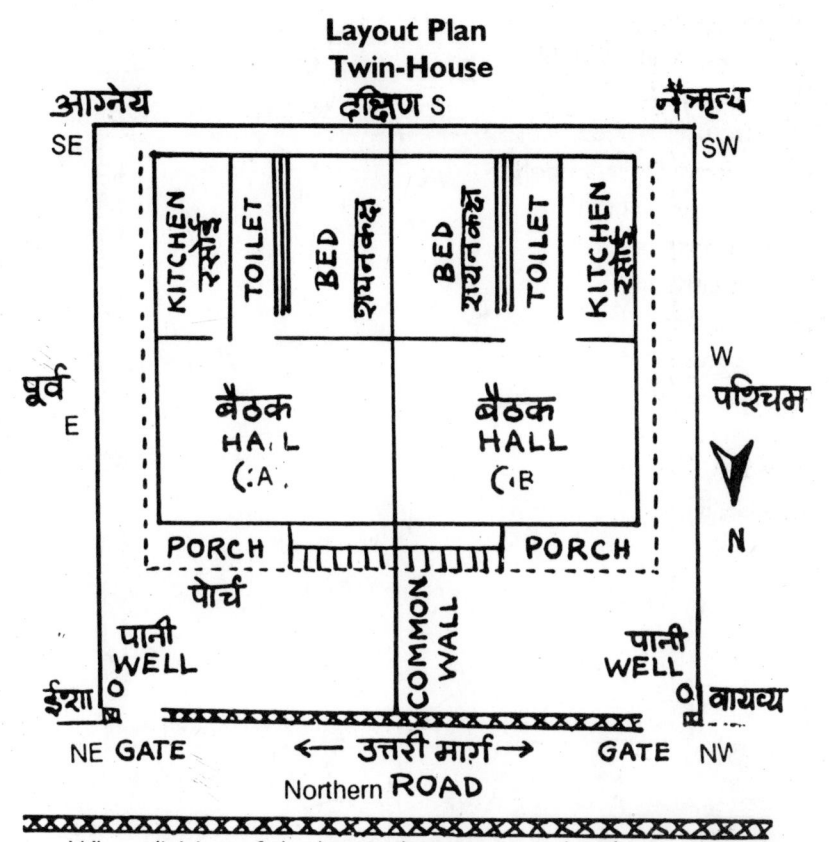

When division of the house, between two brothers, takes place usually a common wall is drawn in the middle of the house, which is wrong. This is called a twin-house or when two friends buy a plot jointly and construct twin-houses as indicated in the plan above. In this twin-house one partner prospers and the other is sometimes not so well off.

From the plan above one will understand that the abode of owner of part (A) is congenial to Vastu but part (B) is just opposite.

Precaution

Whether the house be joint or a associated colony, each part should be according to Vastu.

Auspicious-Inauspicious approach to house facing east
Dir.—East, Lord—Brahma/Indra, Ayudh—Yajra
I. Shubhashubh approach to east direction

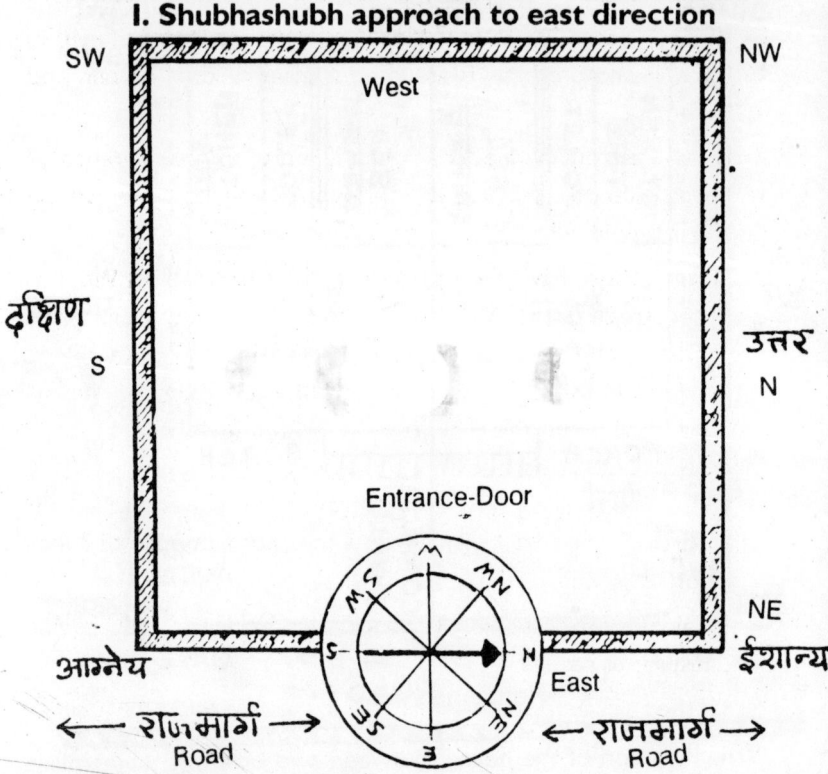

The auspicious-inauspicious results of east-direction is applicable to the male child only. The house, with open space in the east and north direction, is progressive from the health and economy point of view. This is truth based on experience. Each and every part of Vastushastra has not reached the point to be proved by machines but it has been studied on experimental basis. Under such conditions, it is very difficult to convey that the real cause behind this or that situation is perfect. Please observe the houses which have no vacant space in north and east, and the houses which have open space in west and south and read the people living in, you will know the result yourself. It is a truism that the Japanese, are the first to observe sunrise in the world, and they are dominating the entire world in many spheres. With this illustration we can clearly understand the effect of sun-rays.

1. If open space left in east direction is more, then increase in wealth and progeny, is assumed a male child, is certain and effective.

2. In the eastern part of the house if room, or the 'Veranda' is constructed or falls lower, the people residing there will be healthy with all round prosperity and wealth.

3. If the house, having a main gate in the eastern direction, has open space in the north, the Ishan (NE) present in northern line is fruitful. Even if the 'Ishan' (NE) of that house is reduced and the house constructed in a southern direction, is having faults and error, the house-owner will get beneficial results. If the adjacent house-owner constructs anything on the compound wall, in the east direction, then construct a four feet high wall of 4 inch width at a minimum distance of 3 inch from that wall.

4. Main door in east and other doors also facing east will provide auspicious results.

5. If the main gate is in east direction after constructing a house on the entire plot and there is no open space in north'cfirection and the inner construction of house is according to Vastu Shastra, then the result will be auspicious. The less the height of wall in the east of house, the more will be the name and fame of the house-owner. If one joins the eastern part of the land with the house, then the house owner will live longer and gain health.

6. If floor is lower in the direction of east than the floor of central-room of house, peace and fortune will exist.

7. The Veranda in the east should be made sloping. With this the person will enjoy health and fame. People who desire to construct R.C.C. block, should make a balcony of at least, two feet in east-north. This will ensure open-space in the

east-north of house.
8. If the water used in the house flows towards east then it will be suitable for good health of the men of that house.
9. The wall in east direction should be of short height, in comparison to that of western boundary wall. It will be helpful for the progeny.
10. Well and water tank in east direction is auspicious.

Bad-results

1. If the land in the east is high, the house owner will be poor, and the progeny will be unhealthy and dull mind.
2. Without leaving space, if construction is done by joining boundary, there will be dearth of male-child or the child will be handicapped.
3. Poverty, litigation, fear from thief and fire will disrupt the life if main gate of east or other gate is facing SE (Agneya).
4. Disturbance, economic loss will be there and the house-owner will be indebted, if the floor in the east is higher than the Grih Garbha (the room in the center).
5. The person is trapped by vhrious diseases and passes away in early age if the house is made adjacent to east and leaving space in the west.
6. There will be loss of property and progeny, if garbage, piles of stones and heaps of soils are present in the east.
7. Eye problem, paralysis and other diseases affect the person, if there is no open space in the east and the sloping of the veranda is downwards west.
8. If the house owner rents his house, the owner should live at the higher level and the lower, level should be given to tenants. If the tenants vacate the portion, then other tenants should immediately be allotted that portion. If tenants do not come, then the owner himself should shift to that portion or use it; Otherwise, the place falling in the north, being carrier of weight, will create problems of a complex nature.

9. The compound wall should not be high for the house facing east. The main door of the house should be seen from the road otherwise bad result will happen. Loss of progeny is seen if the boundary wall, in the east, is higher than the boundary wall in the west.
10. The owner of the house and the tenants will have to face the ill-effects if the house has not been built as per Vastu-principles.

Layout Plan of an ideal Two Bed-room house situated on road on the east

Ideal house of Two Bed-room on eastern road

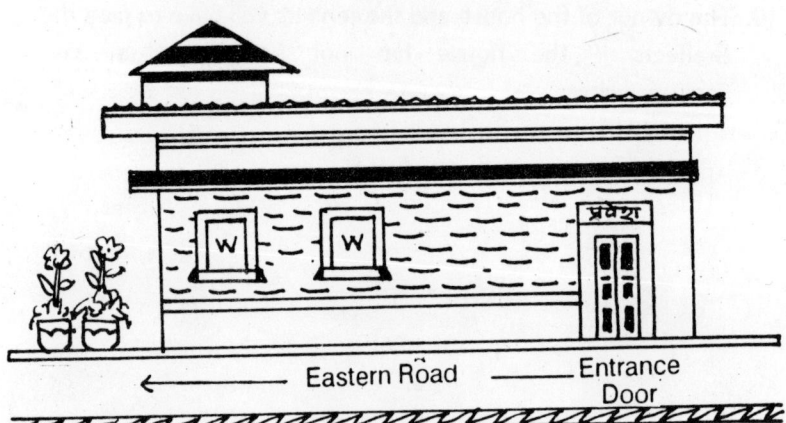

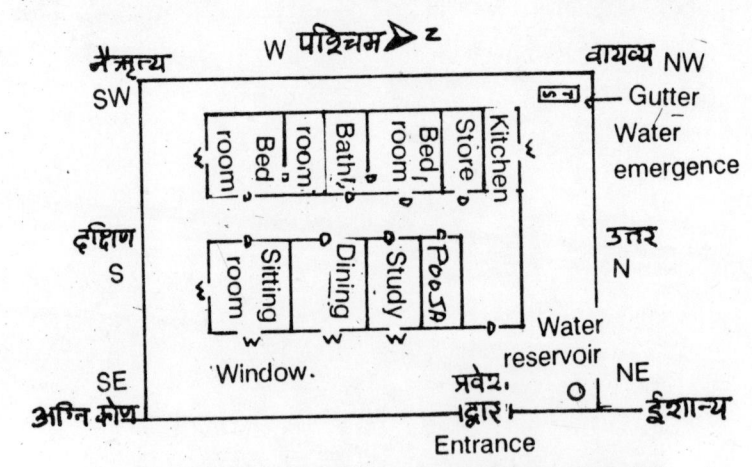

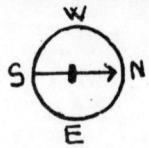

SAMPURAN VASTUSHASTRA

Analysis of an Ideal house of Two bed-rooms house on eastern road

1.	Main Entrance door	Ishanya (N—E)	Very good
2.	Kitchen	Vayavya (N—W)	Medium
3.	Master Bed room	Naishritya (S—W)	Good
4.	Second bed room	Vayavya (N—W)	Medium
5.	Worship room	Ishanya (N—E)	Excellent
6.	Dining hall and sitting room	Ageneya (S—E)	Very good
7.	Well and water reservoir	Ishanya (N—E)	Very good
8.	Store room (collection of goods), Almirahs (treasury)	Vayavya (N—W)	Good
9.	Toilet, bathroom	Naishritya (S—W)	Good
10.	Study room	Ishanya (N—E)	Excellent
11.	Sewage Gutter	Vayavya (N—W)	Good

12. Total doors in house = 12
13. Total windows in house = 6

Auspicious-Inauspicious decision about House Facing West

Dir.—West, Lord—Varuna, Ayudh—Pash

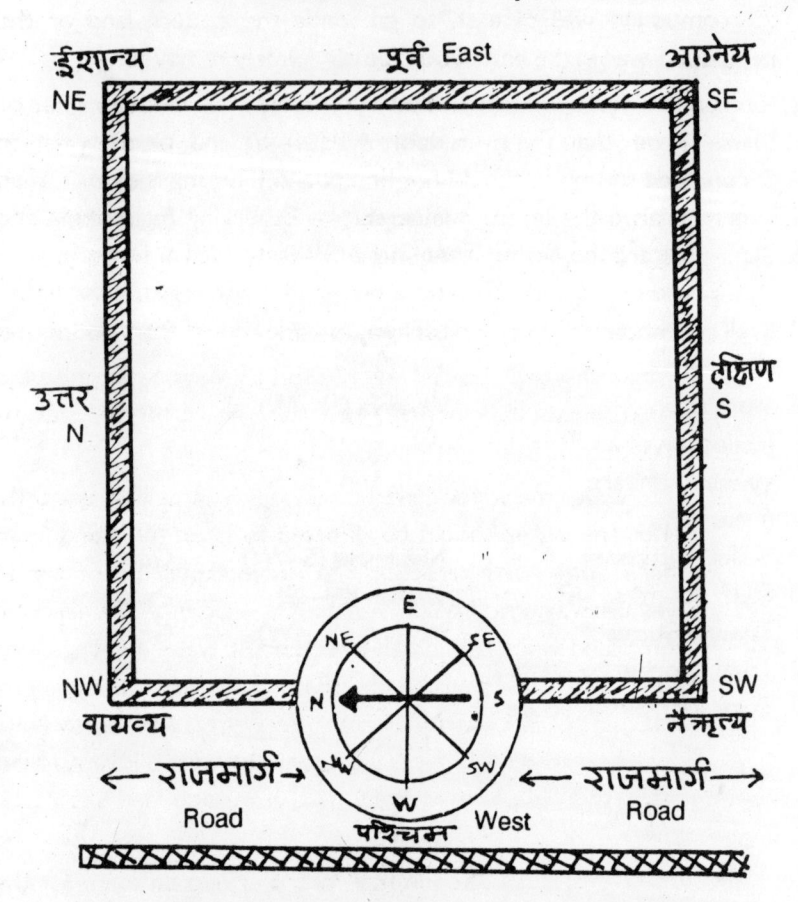

2. Shubhashubh Decision about Western part

The auspicious or inauspicious result of west facing house will affect the male child of owner. If the house is facing west, then buy the vacant place in the north and put a high gate in northern compound wall. In the western Vayavya (NW) of newly bought land, make one more gate. If the present house is struck by the western Vayavya (NW) path then the land, in the north should not be bought. If it is bought, then the western Vayavya path 'Prahaar' (strike) will become Naishritya (SW) path 'Prahaar' and it will give bad results. If in such houses, the land in the east is bought, a gate should be opened through the compound wall of east, to go inside the eastern land or the compound-wall in the east should be completely removed.

1. The compound wall of a house facing west can be higher or lower than the main door. A house or land, on the western side of house, should not be bought. If buying is a must, then change the house ownnership to others by registration and vacate the house. Then buy that western part. Demolish the old house and construct a new one. Then register the house and land in your name. Then only one should enter the house.

2. If the rain-water flow of western part is not possible toward the east direction then all the water should be managed to flow outside from Ishan (NE).

3. Sometimes the water can't be drained towards east or north. Then the water should be directed to Ishan (NE) and from there along north direction the water should be ousted in western Vayavya (NW). The result will be more beneficial if some land was left in north direction for water-flowing along north compound wall and constructing another wall along one side and the land is made suitable to allow the water to flow. If water is flowing towards west then the west is lower, to get rid of this fault, the western part of outside land should be lower

4. If iron-grill is not fixed in the Veranda made on west, for the house facing west, then it becomes necessary to make a sloping Verandah in the east of the house.

5. If Veranda is necessary in the west then it should also be in the east.

6. If grill or wall is not present in north-south of Veranda, and main gate is in west and Veranda in the front portion then construct wall in north-south direction at least 3 feet high

which permeates movement in east-west direction. In such a condition Vayavya (NW) and Naishritya (SW) will have no movement.

7. The slab of portico, in western side will have to be constructed without pillars, because pillars will touch the ground. Then this construction will be lower than the house. Hence portico should be made, by extending the slab of house. If pillars are necessary, then the flooring of portico should not be lower than the heart of house (Garbh-griha).

Good Results

1. If the road is adjacent to a house in the west, then house should be constructed, facing west, then one will get all types of auspicious results. If land of other people or sewage is there, beside the house owners land in western part, then construct a compound wall and construct house, at a distance of 2-3 feet away from it.
2. Garbage, stones etc. in western part provide good result.
3. Main door on western side and other door facing only west has good results.
4. If sloping floor towards west is not present and house is constructed with high wall in front side then it is auspicious.
5. If floor of west is higher than the heart of house (sthal-Garbh), then fame, recognition and economic gain is expected.
6. The low-land in west, incurs economic losses. Disease may also affect. But platform (Chabutara) should not exist in west Vayavya (NW).
7. If the floor of Grih Garbha (heart-room) is higher than the floor of sub-rooms in west then gain of name and fame is expected.
8. If the wall of Garbha and compound wall is higher in the west then good results occur.
9. Big trees, planted in the west, provide good results.

Bad Results

1. If the courtyard, land inside compound wall and the western part of Veranda is low then it will bring defame and loss of property. If the eastern vacant place is larger than the open place of west then loss of male child likely.
2. If the floor of hut, rooms, parn-shalayen (room of leaves) in the west is lower than the floor of Garbh Sthal of house, then it brings defame and economic loss.
3. If the door, present in west, is facing SW (Naishritya) then prolonged diseases, unnatural death and economic loss is possible. If door of western part is facing NW (Vayavya), then there will be increase in court-litigation'and loss of money. If the floor of platform on west is lower than the 'Garbh Griha' it brings economic loss and poor health.
4. If the water of western part or rain water exits through western part, then the man becomes victim of chronic diseases. Naishritya (SW)-fault will be effective due to Godavari for Kodand Ram sitting in Bhadrachal, and due to Krishna river for Nrisingh of Vedaachal. Due to this Naishritya fault there was not much contribution, even after their name and fame.

Ideal Plan of a
Two bedrooms house on Western Road

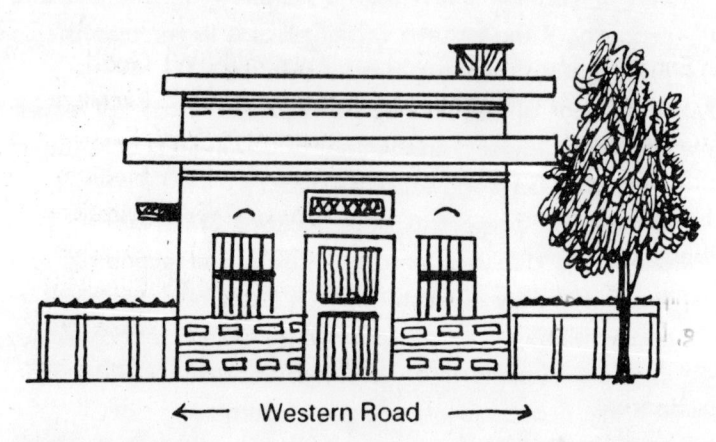

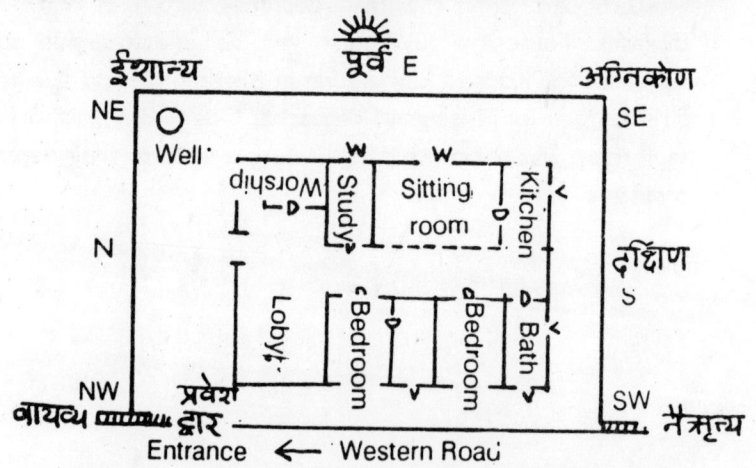

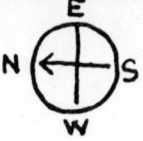

Analysis of Ideal House of Two bed-rooms on westroad

1. Main Entrance door,   Vayavya (N-W)   Good
2. Well, water resources, Tank, boring Ishanya (N-E) Excellent
3. Master bedroom   Naishritya (S-W) Excellent
4. Second Bedroom   Vayavya (N-W)   Medium
5. Big hall, Dining room   Agneya (S-E)   Excellent
6. Kitchen   Agneya (S-E)   Excellent
7. Worship, Meditation room   Ishanhya (N-E) Excellent
8. Sitting, Drawing room   Agneya (S-E)   Excellent
9. Lobby   North   Very good
10. Total doors 9
11. Total Windows 4
12. Ventilators 4

Auspicious-Inauspicious results of House facing North
Dir.—North, Lord—Kuber, Ayudh (weapon)—Mace

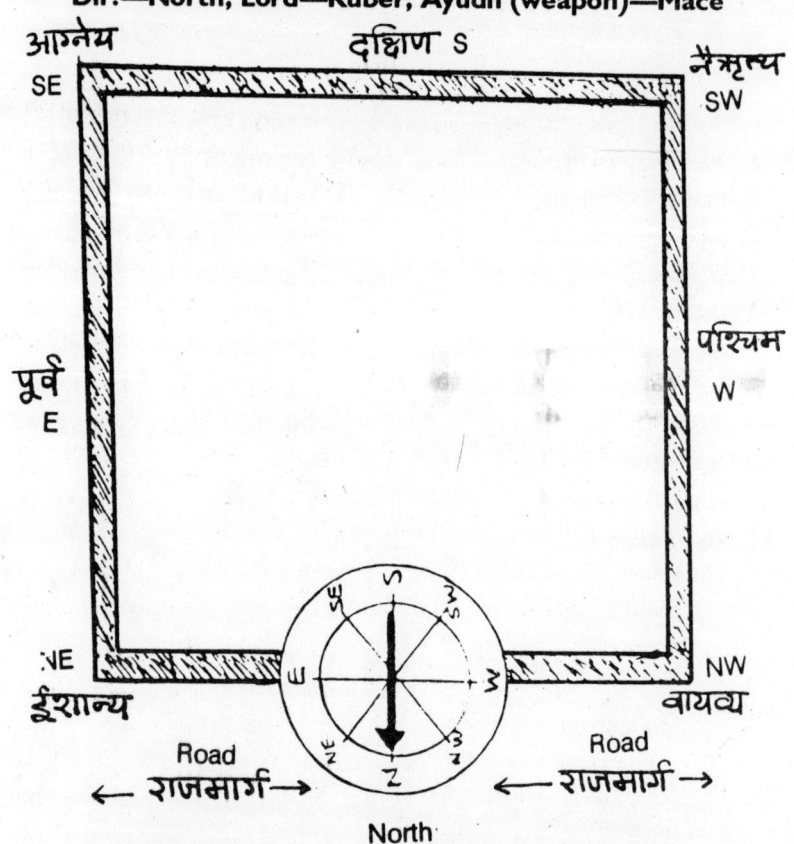

आग्नेय SE — दक्षिण S — नैऋत्य SW
पूर्व E — पश्चिम W
ईशान्य NE — North — वायव्य NW
Road ← राजमार्ग → — Road ← राजमार्ग →

3. Auspicious-Inauspicious result of northern Part

1. Auspicious-inauspicious results of north portion affect the ladies and wealth.

2. The level of floor should be lower, while constructing a house in the north part. This should not be applied only on to the base level but also, to the other floors. Lower level, in the north, will be fruitful on every storey. If the veranda is lower than these northern room floor level, then it is again good.

3. If there is no open place in the east of a house facing north

then the Ishana (NE) on the eastern side will be auspicious. Even if the Ishan (NE) is short, the room of the west or room on the west of previous, room on the western path may be auspicious.

4. For the house facing north, the compound wall constructed should be such that the door can be seen from outside. Hence, construct the compound wall after the house is complete in all respects.

5. The owner of the house, if wants to rent his house he should reside on the higher portion of the house and lower portion should be given to tenants. If tenants are not available then he himself should use that portion, including the previous one. Otherwise the front portion will be vacant in the east of owner part and will be heavier which will create problem. Kitchen should not be in north direction.

6. House construction should cover the whole plot and road should be in north direction with door opening in north itself. Even if open space is not left in the east the house should be according to Vastu. This proves to be auspicious.

7. The Veranda in south should be higher than the sloping Veranda in the north. If one likes to put R.C.C. slab for house construction then build it in east-north. Construct necessarily a balcony of minimum 2 feet. In this way there will remain a vacant place in east north. If south-west does not have open space, it is not harmful. If the neighbour constructs anything on the compound wall, then a wall 4 feet high with a width of 4 inch should be erected, at 3 inch distance at least.

Good Results

1. If the level of land, vacant space inside the rooms and the northern part of the veranda, is lower then wealth will increase and ladies will get happiness and satisfaction.

2. If the open space in north is more than that in the south, then the house acquires all types of happiness and riches.

3. If rain water passing along north portion, flows through Ishan (NE) then one gets all types of auspicious results.
4. If rain water, flowing through the door of north portion becomes north-facing then the result is good. Brilliant students will come up and the house will be prosperous with happiness and peace.
5. Economic progress and name and fame are expected if floor of the platform in northern direction, is lower than that of the 'Grih-garbh'.
6. The ladies' will be in good health with longer life span if sloping veranda is constructed in the north.
7. The vacant place in the north should be mingled with ours after buying it even at higher cost. This provides all riches.
8. If open space or enclosure is left in the north of boundary wall of the house, it provides prosperity of all types as well as happiness and satisfaction.

Bad Results

1. The family property ruins and ladies will be unhealthy if north direction is protruding high.
2. If no open space is in the north; and house is flanked with the boundary and the south portion has a vacant space then that house becomes property of others and it will be deserted.
3. Loss of wealth is seen if north direction has useless things, heap of cow-dung, piled up object and garbage.
4. Fear from thief and fire will continue if door of the northern portion is Vayavya (NW) facing.
5. More expenditure, quarrel, lack of peace, debt burden will be seen if the floor in the north is higher than the Griha Garbha.

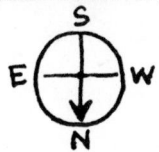

Ideal Two bedrooms house of on Northern Road

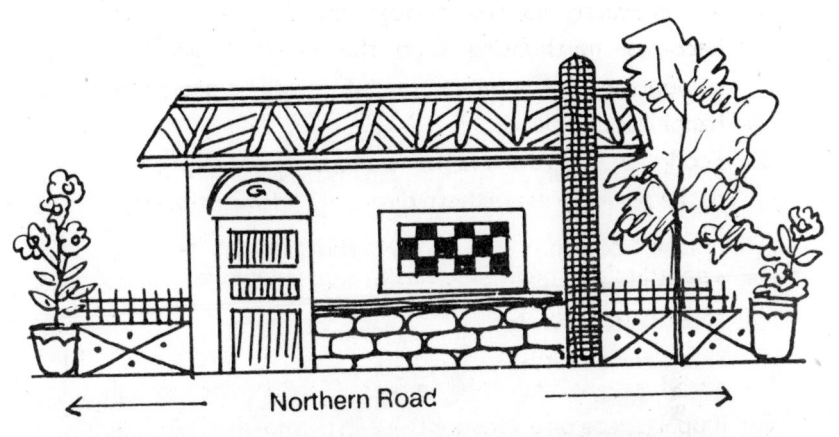

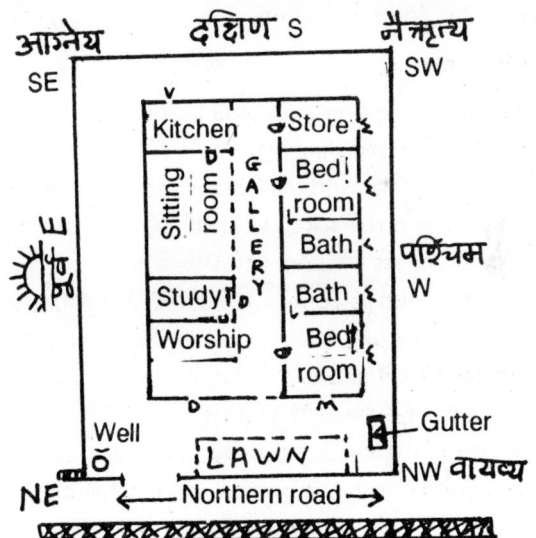

Analysis of an Ideal Two bedrooms house on Northern Road

1. Entrance door	Ishanya (N-E)	Very good
2. Lawn	North (N)	Very good
3. Water reservoir, Well and Tank	Ishanya (N-E)	Excellent
4. Master bed room	Naishritya (S-W)	Excellent
5. Second bed room	Vayavya (N-W)	Medium
6. Water-exit, Sewage, septic-tank, Gutter	Vayavya (N-W)	Excellent
7. Study room	Ishanya (N-E)	Excellent
8. Worship room and Meditation room	Ishanya (N-E)	Excellent
9. Bath room (Toilet)	Naishritya (S-W)	Very good
10. Second bath room (Toilet)	Vayavya (N-W)	Very good
11. Big hall, Drawing room and Dining hall	Agneya (S-E)	Very good
12. Kitchen	Agneya	Excellent
13. Open place, Lobby	Ishanya or North (N-E)	Excellent

14. Total doors 10
15. Total windows 5
16. Ventilators 2

Auspicious-Inauspicious result of house facing South
Dir.—South, Lord—Yama, Ayudh—Dand

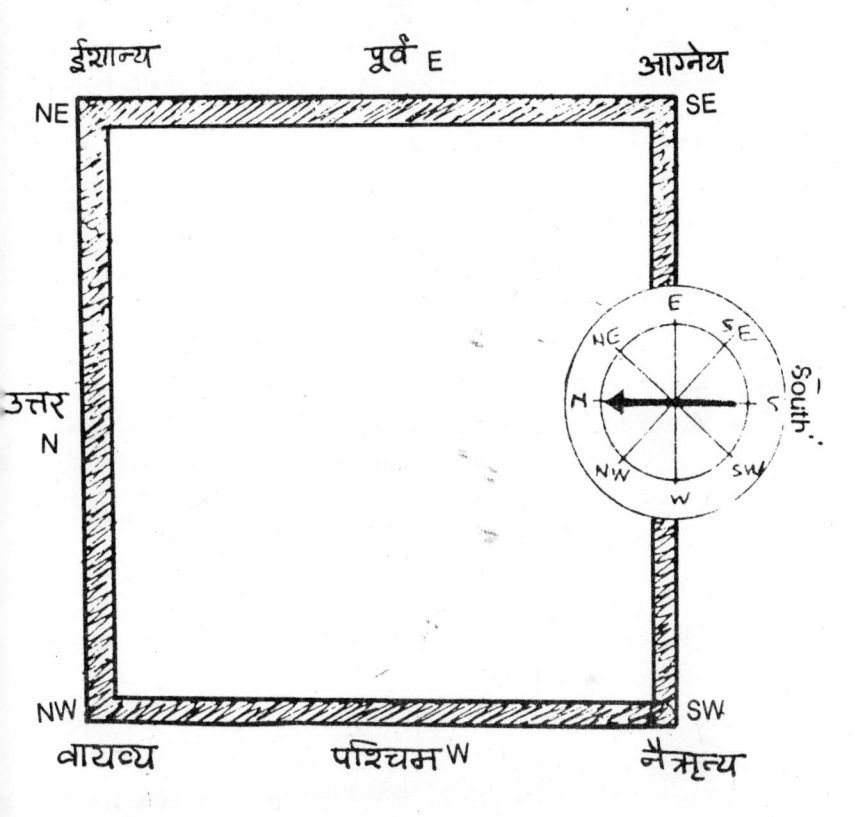

ईशान्य NE — पूर्व E — आग्नेय SE
उत्तर N — South (arrow pointing) —
वायव्य NW — पश्चिम W — नैऋत्य SW

4. South Portion—Auspicious-Inauspicious Assessment

The good and bad result of south portion affects the ladies. Due to bad results the house constructor has to face economic problems.

If an iron-grill does not cover the Veranda in the south of house facing south, it is necessary to construct Veranda in the north direction. If, it is not possible, then open door after making the fence of iron-rods in the south. The boundary wall, in the south, can be of less height in comparison to the main door of the house. To construct a house with a boundary in south is fruitful. But if a market is not situated towards south, then only boundary wall should be constructed. If it is necessary to buy the land or house in west or south of one's existing house or land, then the house should be vacated first of all after changing it in other's name. Then, buy that western or southern land and demolish the house. Start constructing the house from west or south and complete it. Change the name to yours and then only perform Griha Pravesh Yajna.

If one's house is facing south and the open space of north direction is bought then it can be added to his house by breaking down the wall in the north, or by fixing gate at height in that boundary wall one can enter that bought place. If the east portion of that house is bought then gate should be made at the higher place of eastern boundary wall or the boundary wall of east direction can be demolished completely. Keep one gate in South-Agneya (SE) of that bought place. If this is not done then the present house will be cause for its southern-faults. But in the house which has southern Agneya (SE) path attack (Marg Prahaar), then don't buy the land in the east.

Good Results

1. Natives of the house will be healthy and prosperous if southern portion is high.
2. Useless things kept on such higher south will give good results.
3. House owner will be prosperous, if the door of southern part is only facing south.
4. If road is in the south adjacent to plot then house construction should be done from the boundary of the southern part. It gives good result. If any sewage or land of other person lies in the south adjacent to your plot then first construct boundary-wall, then construct house 3-4 feet away from it.
5. House owner will be prosperous due to the high-level of a room in the southern part.
6. If the floor in southern portion is high in comparison to the 'Griha-Garbha' then health gain and money-gain is there.

7. Water of rooms in south direction, if exits from northern direction, then there are gains and development in the health of ladies.
8. If the water inside the house and rain water is in no position to go outside from north direction, then manage to flow it out via eastern direction. The males living there get good health and fame.
9. If the used water in the house and rain water drains out through south direction in spite of north direction then manage in such a way that, total water exits through Ishanya (NE) and from there it goes out from south along the eastern boundary wall through sewage. The drainage should be kept covered. Otherwise, one more wall should be constructed close to eastern boundary wall, in the direction of east so that water could go outside via Ishanya (NE). Water flowing towards south means south will be low. To eradicate the fault, one more wall should be erected then the fault, arising from the lower southern part outside the fence, will be lessened to some extent.
10. If southern portion is high and cow-dung heap and stone-piles are there, then it proves fruitful from every angle.

Bad-Results

1. The ladies will be unhealthy, and economic loss and sudden death will trap them if southern portion in open space, courtyard of house, all the rooms of house and the veranda, is low.
2. Possibility of economic loss and accidental death increases if a well exists in southern part.
3. Some people assume that the southern part is the home of 'Pishach' (evil-spirit) and house should be constructed after leaving some space. If it is constructed by lessening the southern portion a little bit in comparison to northern part then there will be no fault.

4. If the house wall and boundary wall in the south will not be higher than the north, then it will have big misfortune.
5. If platform (chabootara) in the south is lower than Grih-garbh then there is possibility of more expenditure and poor health.
6. If the door in the south portion is facing SE (Agneya) then g there are possibilities of fear from thieves trouble from fire and litigation relating court.
7. Different diseases, enemy fear and sudden death are possible if southern door is facing NW (Naishritya).
8. Sloping Veranda towards south next to room should not be constructed. This is inauspicious. If one is compelled then the slope of northern Veranda should be more than that of southern side.
9. Slab in the south should be constructed without pillar because due to construction of pillars it will touch the land and constructed pillar will be lower than the constructed house. The root cause for mishappenings is that the southern part is lower'. Hence portico should be built without pillars, on the house's slab. If pillar is inevitable then it's flooring should not be lower than the Garbh-griha.
10. Economic loss, quarrel and disturbances are seen if the southern portion possesses more open space.

Ideal house of
Two bed rooms, situated on the southern road

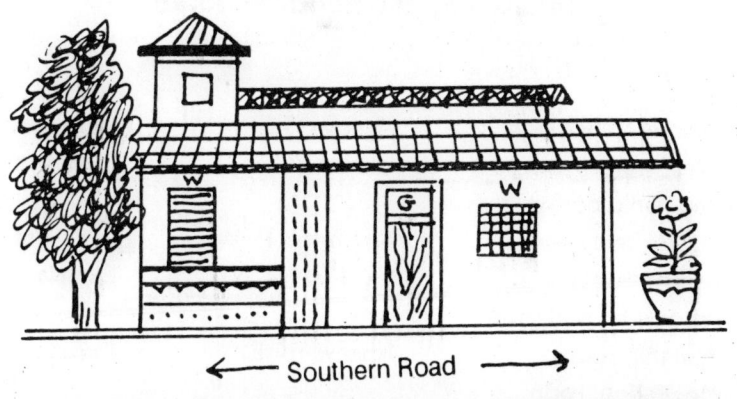

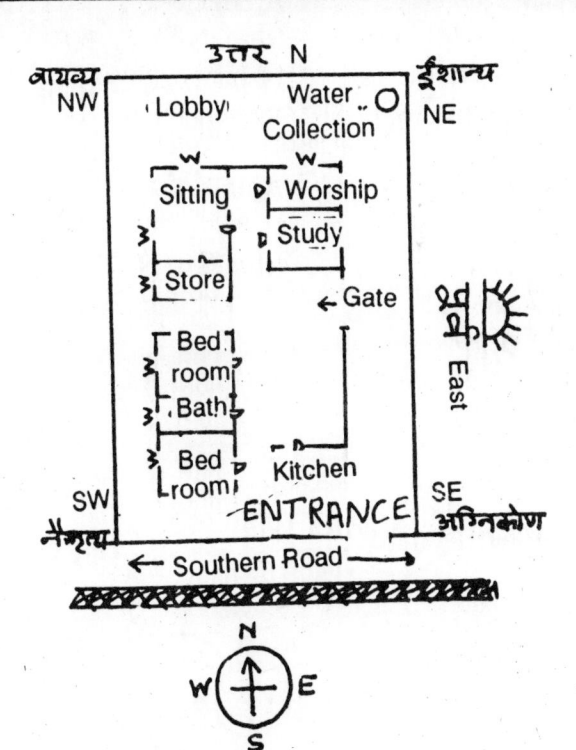

← Southern Road →

वायव्य NW | उत्तर N | ईशान्य NE

Lobby | Water Collection

Sitting | Worship

Study

Store | ← Gate

Bed room
Bath
Bed room | Kitchen

SW नैऋत्य | ENTRANCE | SE अग्निकोण

पूर्व East

← Southern Road →

N / W / E / S

145

Analysis of an Ideal Two bedroom house situated on the Southern Road

1. Main entrance door	Agneya (S-E)	Very good
2. Well, water resources tap, tank, boring	Ishanya (N-E)	Excellent
3. Master bed room	Naishritya (S-W)	Excellent
4. Guest room or Associated bed room	Vayavya (N-W)	Excellent
5. Worship room, Meditation, room,	Ishanya (N-E)	Excellent
6. Kitchen	Agneya (S-E)	Excellent
7. Study-room	Ishan (N-E)	Excellent
8. Bath room, Toilet	Naishritya (S-W)	Very good
9. Toilet attatched to Guest room	Vayavya (N-W)	Excellent
10. Big hall, Drawing room, dinning hall	Agneya (S-E)	Excellent
11. Lobby Lawn	Ishanya or North(N-E)	Excellent
12. Total windows 5		
13. Total doors 9		
14. Ventilators 2		

Auspicious-Inauspicious approach of North East Directional (Ishanya bhimukh) house

Dir.—Ishanya, Lord-Rudra, Ayudh—Trishul

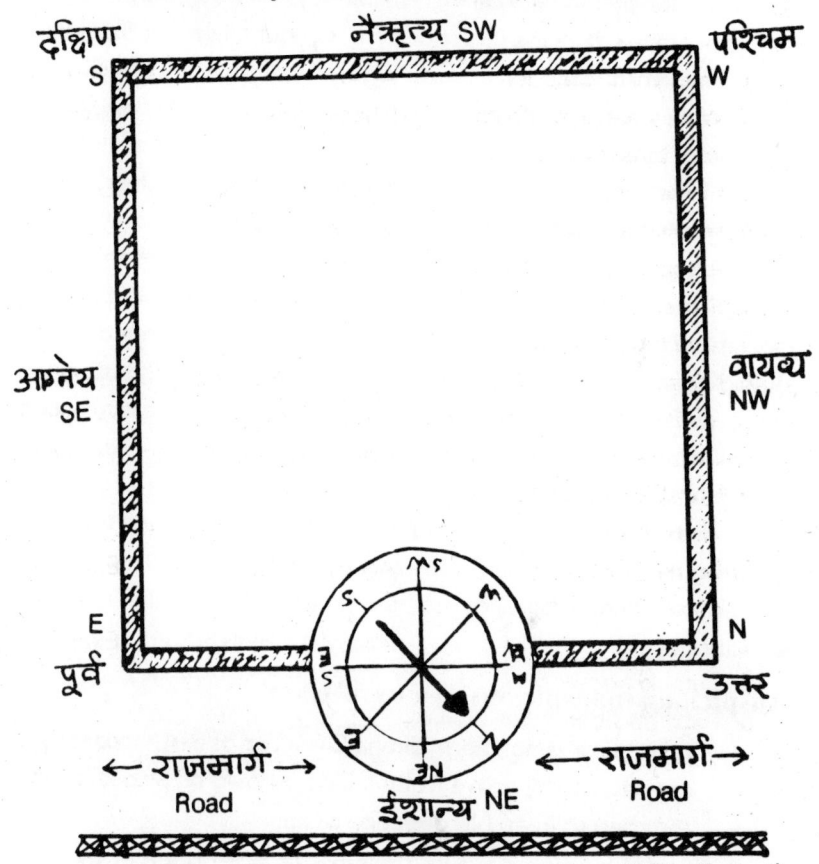

The auspicious and inauspicious result of Ishan (NE) affects the house owner and the male children.

The place on the road of eastern and northern direction is called 'Ishan-block'. It has been proved on the basis of experience that this block is better than any other block. Vastuscientist of ancient period have compared the Ishan block with the Alkapuri town of Kuber. This land is said to provide prosperity-gain, progeny-increase, brilliant progeny and all the good results.

Description of Ishan (NE) Construction

Ishan (NE) is very important amongst the eight directions. Hence house builder should take care of Ishan (NE), from very beginning and should protect it. If all the directions are without any error, from Vastu point, but Ishan does have Vastu-errors, that house can't flourish. Some people get land or house with faulty Ishan easily. If they neglect the fault of Ishan and buy the land, on the merit of other angles, then all their income will be spent on futile things, and they will be penniless. They will possess only labour. Hence, on taking care of Ishan, full safety is assumed. If the land on Ishan (NE) is lower than the eastern road, then the gate should be facing east. But, according to campass, if east looks east Agneya (SE) more than 20 degree then gate should be in east-Ishan (NE) and movement should be from northern Simha Dwar (Lions-door). That house should have an eastern door also. Similarly, if northern road is lower than the eastern road, then main gate should be in the north. But, according to campass, if north is seen north-Vayavya (NW) more than 10 degree, then gate should be constructed in north Ishan (NE) and movement should be through Simha-Dwar (Lion's Gate) of east. Doors should be fixed in the north of that house.

Auspicious-Inauspicious results of Ishan

1. Whether it is northern 'Simha Dwar' or of east, according to campass, it will prove fruitful. Door should be placed in Ishan and tried to keep NE direction open.

2. Some people construct their house, with door in the east, thinking about the main gate in the Ishan (NE). In this way there is possibility of extending Agneya (SE) and lessening of Ishan (NE) in the lawn of the house. It is absolutely necessary to construct the house without shortening the east, north and the Ishan (NE). Ishan can be increased in the entire construction. But every room of house should not be extended for Ishan's extension deliberately.

3. The Ishan (NE) direction will be supposed to be closed, if

entrance door is from west and south direction in the room of Ishan (NE) with no exit-door. Hence door for exit should be kept in east Ishan (NE) of Ishan (NE) room.

4. One should not sell the vacant space of Ishan (NE) or house of Ishan (NE). The rooms of house, in east and north should be protruding more in Ishan (NE) than his house.
5. Mosquito net rod's or any type of things even the brush for floor cleaning, should not be kept in the Ishan (NE) of any room.
6. One should not be satisfied with this as to house or sub-room should be in the Ishan only during well-digging in Ishan (NE). In the east-north lawn or lobby of house only the well should be dug.
7. Portico should not be made in east or north direction of block in Ishan (NE) direction. Due to construction of portico in east, the Ishan (NE) and Agney (SE) is cut. Due to portico, in northern direction Ishan (NE) and Vayavya (NW) is cut. Hence, these are useless. If a suitable portico has to be constructed, portico should be extended up to Ishan (NE) quarter.
8. The boundary-wall, in Ishhn (NE) direction, should not be circular. On the crossing of towns, if the corner of boundaries of each block is made circular, then it is not a matter of much concern. But, the Ishan (NE) portion and the Ishan (NE) block, should never be made or kept circular, at any cost.

Good results of Ishan (NE) place

1. The native will be prosperous, will get wealth and progeny will be very brilliant and dedicated. If the road in the east, and north of Ishan (NE) block were not lessened and the Ishan (NE) direction is extended.
2. If Ishan (NE) corner is right, and more land is vacant in east than west, in the north than the south, and the land lies lower in the east than west and lower in the north than the south, then the people living at such place will lead very happy life for

many generations.

3. If ponds, canals and wells exist near Ishana (NE) direction, then the house will have prosperity and wealth.
4. If 'Marga Prahaar' (path-obstruction) is in the east of the block then the people will be famous. If this 'Prahaar' is in north-Ishan (NE), the native will make enormous wealth.
5. If Ishan (NE) direction is extended towards north only then, they will be rich but of a greedy nature. If Ishan (NE) is stretched, then the coming generations will be fortunate. By its protruding nature, the house people will get good results.
6. The native will be religious and devotee of God as well as rich and famous, if the Ishana (NE) is protruding towards east.
7. If Ishan (NE) portion is lower, having ditch or well, then native will be owner of countless wealth (Ashtavidh property).
8. In the land for house-construction, if the vacant part in the lobby of house or Ishan (NE) in the Veranda are lower then economic prosperity will be gained as well as happiness and fame.
9. Downwards slope, towards east of Ishan (NE) block and downward slope towards north, provide good results to male and female respectively.
10. Buy a high land in the prominity or at a distance in the Ishana (NE) of house and combine these two to look one. Construct hut in Naishritya (SW) of high land. This provides good result, by kicking out the bad effects of Vastu faults. Movement in the hut on higher land than own house will result in good. Buy the land towards Ishan (NE), even at high cost, to join it with land already in possession. This has an auspicious result.
11. Make the water of rooms flow outside through Ishana (NE). If rain water flows out, through Ishana (NE) direction, then the progeny of owner will develop and he will be prosperous.
12. Ishan (NE), protruding in any way, gives very good result. It is said that more the Ishan (NE) is extended, more auspicious is

the result. But, for every hundred feet, extension by one-or two feet is suitable.

Bad Results of Ishan place

1. If the construction is upto demarcation of north, after shortening the length of northern direction of Ishan (NE) block, then the house wife will be susceptible to diseases and can meet with untimely death. Or she will lead a painful life with economic constraints.
2. If construction is done on eastern boundary after shortening the area of eastern direction, the owner and the elder son will meet the above bad results. The generation of that owner will be finished by the third stage.
3. If east and north direction is joined, then life will be monotonous, even after having wealth. He will not be blessed with a child. Even after an adopted son, bad results will be problematic.
4. If the constructed part, in the Ishan (NE) of the block is either covered or removed the consequences will be bad.
5. If the house be at the end of the block and ditch is in the Nairut (SW) then consequences are bad.
6. If the elevated floor (chabootra) is higher than 'Grih-Garbh' in the east-north, in the room of Ishan (NE) or outside, bad consequences are met. The elevated seat, made in east, affects male and if made in north, affects ladies.
7. If northern door is higher than southern door and eastern door is higher than the southern one of this block, then they will get bad consequences.
8. The consequences are bad, even if the gate of the house boundary wall of this block is high in east-north direction.
9. If Ishan (NE) direction of house or boundary wall is shortened then one will not get male child. If child is born, it will be handicapped, mentally retarded and will be short-lived.
10. Even if the Ishan (NE) of boundary wall is okay, but the Ishan

(NE) of house is vanished, the owner of the house will have to perform funeral rites of his son himself.

11. The owner will face bad consequences if the well and ditch (bore) is in other direction, barring Ishana (NE).
12. If any error is in Ishana (NE), child of that house will be handicapped.
13. Economic loss and many troubles with child-loss is met, if Ishan (NE) were high.
14. Destruction of generation with poverty is met, if huts were in Ishan direction, and house is constructed close to east and north.
15. Enmity, lessening of age, and breeding of bad characters are seen if garbage and heap of stones are in the Ishana (NE).
16. Quarrel in the house, and economic loss reckons if kitchen is in Ishana (NE).
17. If toilet is in Ishana (NE), ceased the progress of male-issue then the people, living in, are put to quarrel, bad-character and chronic diseases.
18. Even if the enclosure of the house is constructed according to Vastu, but the road in the east and north is higher than the house floor, the natives of the house will not be able to get good results.
19. If the road, in the eastern direction of Ishan (NE), is turned towards west, instead of eastwards, or the road of north-direction is turned towards south instead of being straight eastwards, or the east and the north, of that land is joined, then total good results will be lost.
20. If Ishan (NE) of the house is faulty, then Naishritya (SW) will certainly be faulty. If Ishan (NE) is high, covered, cut or having lavatory, then Naishritya (SW) will be down, or well may be present over there. Hence, west-south Naishritya (SW) is protruding. If septic tank is there, then Naishritya (SW) will remain open. Similarly, if Naishritya (SW) gets Vastu error, then Ishan (NE) certainly becomes faulty.

Auspicious-Inauspicious approach to Agneyamukhi (SE) house

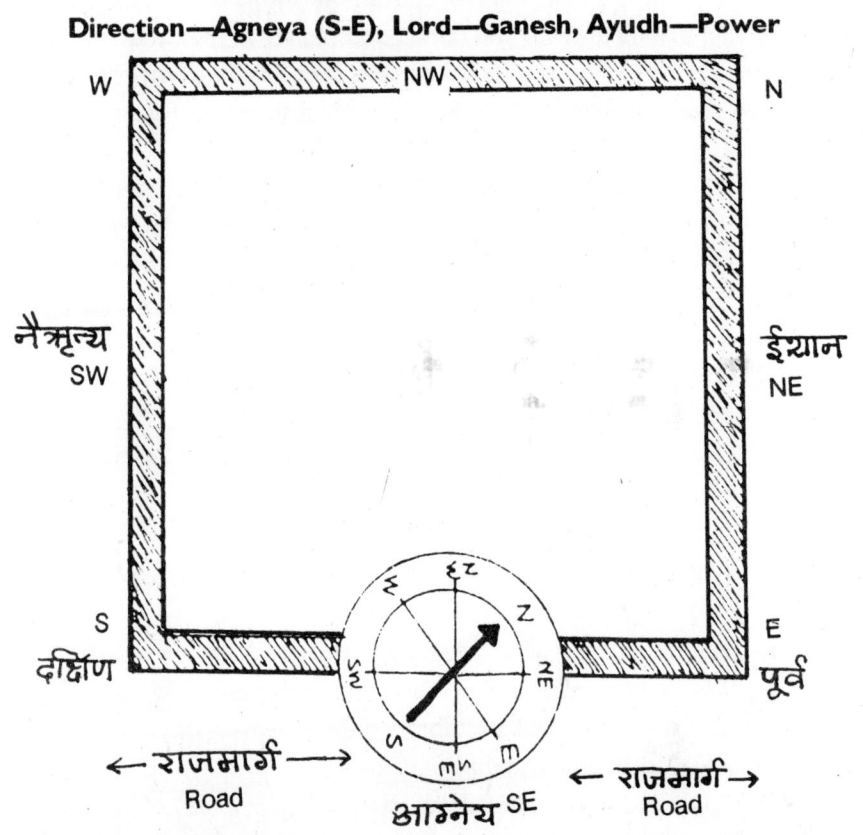

Direction—Agneya (S-E), Lord—Ganesh, Ayudh—Power

The auspicious and inauspicious consequences of Agneya (SE) part will affect ladies, children and especially the second son of that house. Death of ladies from burning, mishappening like suicide, quarrel etc., are the consequences met by the owner.

Construction of Agneya (SE) place

The land of the east and the south by the road side is called Agneya (SE) place. Agneya (SE) possesses less effect of Vastu in comparison to other quarters. Person living in the Agneya (SE) place of village and town bear more pain than those living in other directions.

Agneya (SE) place is the poorest for providing good results. But according to the treaties, the defects can be remedied so that it will not remain behind in giving the same good results as the others do. If the house is to be constructed in Agneya (SE) inspite of other place available then care should be taken according to Vastu. For it to be fruitful.

1. If in the Agneya (SE) direction, southward road is lower than the 'Gali' (narrow passage) of east, then the main door should be opened eastwards. But, according to campass if east looks east-Agneya (SE) by more than 10°, then entrance should be through east-Ishan (NE) door and northern lion's door (Simha Dwar) will have to be made. That house should also have a door eastward.
2. Door can be opened in the south Agneya (SE) part of house.
3. Neem, coconut trees and big trees can be planted, from south Agneya (SE) to Naishritya (SW).
4. Water, used in the house, should not emerge through Agneya (SE) direction.
5. The boundary wall of the Agneya (SE) block can be circular.
6. If electric transformer or boiler has to be set in Agneya (SE) then it will have to be established there, leaving open space of 3 feet from east without touching it,
7. Toilet will have to be constructed, in Agneya (SE) of industry at 3 feet away from the east boundary.

Good Results

1. Nevertheless if the house in Agneya (SE) block be against the Vastu- formula, one can still get good results observing rigidity the following conditions
   (a) The construction in Ishan (NE) side of the house is to reduced for people residing in northern side.
   (b) Keeping lesser space in south than space in North direction.
   (c) Lesser space in west than that in the east.

(d) Construction of doors at elevated places.
(e) Restricting the stretch of corner in Agneya (SE) Naishritya (SW) and Vayavya (NW)
(f) Ishan (NE) direction should be according to vastu formula. It should be lower, if protruding, and the flow of water should be in the right direction.
(g) Marg-prahar (path obstruction) should exist in south-Agneya (SE).
(h) Marg-prahar should also be in eastern Ishan (NE).
1. Nothern direction is lower and the southern be elevated. People living there will flourish.
2. Consequences are good on having lower land in Agneya (SE) place.
3. If entrance door be in south; there should be no vacant place in the west, vacant place remains in north and eastern direction only; well in Ishan (NE); eastern land lower than the western; land in north direction is lower than the south then people residing here prosper a lot.
4. Kitchen in Agneya (SE) direction provides all types of riches.
5. Toilet in Agneya (SE) is good but there should not exist a pit. The pit of latrines should be constructed in the east.

Bad Results

1. For the house, constructed in Agneya (SE) place, if east Agneya (SE) is protruding (Agret), east-south or south-Agneya (SE) angle is protruding, well and pits are in the lower Agneya (SE); house is constructed upto extreme demarcation of lawn, without keeping vacant space in the north, gate is in the south-Naishritya (SW) of boundary wall or gate is in north-Agneya, more vacant space rests in west than that of east, the owner of such houses will have unimagined pain and losses. Court-litigation and fear from thief and fire will be prevalent. Character assasination of male and female will be abundant. Expenditure will be more than the income and due

to extreme indebtedness, the owner will be compelled to sell his house. In the extreme ase house will be the property of a lady, due to no male child. Same fate will be met, in the case of business.

2. If east is 'Marg Prahaar' of Agneya (SE), for the Agneya (SE)-block, then the male will be of perverted-character and lady will administer the house.

3. If south Naishritya (SW) 'Marg Prahaar' is there, then the ladies will be far from happy and some lingering diseases like hysteria will trap them. Sometimes they may tend to commit suicide without any reason.

4. If lion's door be in south and mansion be constructed in the east by making east-north border of this, then the owner will meet death in middle life or will suffer from permanent disease.

5. If southern main gate exists and exit be in east-Agneya (SE), after assuming east-north as border, bad effect will be on second son.

6. Lion's door be in south, and Veranda be made with a downward slope in south having east-north as border, the house-wife will suffer from diseases and will become a widow. Children will be characterless.

7. If door is facing south and house is constructed making the east-north as border, vacant place will lie in west, west is low in comparison to east; well is in the west, then the owner is prone to many incurable diseases, at a young age.

8. If main door be in the east; vacant place in the south, making the north as border and well be in Agneya, the wife will die in an accident.

9. Lion's door be in the east, north be treated as border and assuming road in the east be the border and if elevated place be in Ishan (NE), then owner will meet an unnatural death.

10. If main door be in the east; north-east be treated as border

and vacant place be in west-south, then high tension and enmity will rock the wife and husband and child will be stupid.

11. If main gate be in the east; north is taken as border and vacant place rests in south and it is protruding in Naishritya (SW) then ladies will meet with an accident.

12. If the road, in the east of Agneya (SE) block, ends near the house without going straight ahead northwards, then the person will be dependant.

13. If main door be in east, gate is in one side of Agneya (SE) in the east of boundary wall, Ishan (NE) of the house is cut or chopped off, well is in Vayavya (NW) and sloping veranda westwards in west-Naishritya (SW), lower land in west gate in the south-Naishritya (SW) of boundary wall, then the house owner will commit suicide, even if he is learned.

14. Lion's door in the south, east is treated as border, vacant place as lower ground and well be in the west, and east Agneya (SE) be 'Marg Prahaar', then generation will be destroyed and the wife murders her own husband.

15. If there is no door, in the Agneya (SE) part in the east of house, theft, fire and quarrel continue.

16. If it is protruding, in the east of Agneya (SE) part, then loss of male children results, as well as the house becomes the ladies-property.

17. If Agneya (SE) be protruding only as an angle, then there will be quarrel, as well as the existence of litigation, disease and fear from fire.

18. If Agneya (SE) portion be protruding towards south direction, then quarrel will continue and the ladies will fall ill. If house be in south of land, basic angle be protruding in the form of south-Agneya (SE) Chatush Kona (quadruped angle) then Vastu fault will be defeated.

19. If door does not exist in the east, north and Ishan (NE) of a room then, even west-Vayavya (NW) and south-Agneya (SE)

be elevated, the door should not open at both these places. Keep only one door at one place.

20. If south Agneya (SE) be low, Vayavya (NW) and north be high, the native of the house will be patient and indebted and peace will be snatched.
21. If land remains lower in south Agneya (SE) and elevated in Naishritya, Vayavya (NW) and Ishana, then people will be poor and unhealthy.
22. If Agneya (SE) is elevated, and Naishritya, Vayavya (NW) and Ishan (NE) are lower, then he will be defamed and his generation will be destroyed.
23. Well should not be in Agneya. If it is like this, then it makes the house-wife and child unhealthy; creates skirmishes and loss of second son.
24. If exit door be of east Agneya (SE) then, to deceive other and to be decieved by others, becomes a normal phenomena, and there are bad consequences due to skirmishes between wife and the husband.
25. If Agneya (SE) place rests at low in vacant space in lobby of house, in every room and veranda, then the fear from fire, theft, and enemies will continue to hover on. Agneya (SE) part should be lower than Naishritya (SW) and higher then Vayavya (NW) and Ishan.
26. If lion's door be in south, Veranda be in front part; grill be in the east and west direction of Varamdah; and if wall does not exist, then a wall at least 3 feet high should be erected in east-west direction so that the exit will be towards north-south. In such a condition, there will be no movement or communication in Agneya (SE) and Naishritya (SW) direction.
27. If veranda is in the southern direction of house, having grill in eastern wall, then the wall below grill is at a lower height, due to which eastern-Agneya (SE) becomes protruding. But it should not be like this. The width of wall of grill should be equal to width of wall of house.

28. If veranda is in the south portion of a house, the wall below grill is made of lesser width, at the time of fixing grill in western wall. Due to this western Naishritya (SW) will be protruding. The width of wall below the grill should be equal to the width of wall of house.

Auspicious-Inauspicious Approach to Naishrityaabhimukhi (SW) House :—

Direction—Naishritya, Lord—Kshetrapala, Ayudh—Khadag (sword)

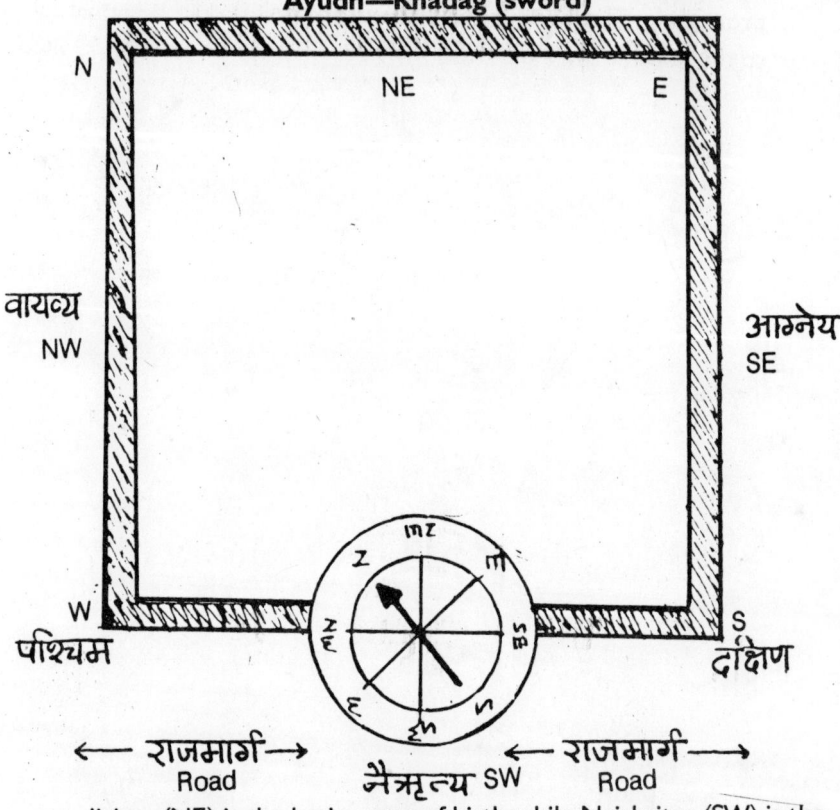

[Diagram showing a square plot with directions marked: N, NE, E at top; वायव्य NW on left, आग्नेय SE on right; W पश्चिम, S दक्षिण at bottom; compass at bottom center; roads (राजमार्ग) on either side of नैऋत्य SW]

'Ishan (NE) is the basic cause of birth while Naishritya (SW) is the cause for death'

The auspicious and inauspicious results of Naishritya (SW) area have effect on the house owner, house wife and eldest son. The inauspicious effect is reflected & faced, due to Naishritya (SW) block in the guise of sudden death, murder, suicide evil spirit and natural affliction.

The land of south Naishritya (SW) road is called Naishritya (SW). If Vastu power is strong, then this may be called better than all the blocks.

Description of Naishritya (SW) Construction

1. In house land or construction, Naishritya (SW) has got equal importance as the Ishan. Ishana and Naishritya (SW) are mutual rivals and in opposite corners. The Naishritya (SW) should be elevated in proportion to the depression in Ishan (NE). Naishritya (SW) should be covered as much the Ishan (NE) is open. As the Ishan (NE) becomes lighter the Naishritya (SW) becomes heavier in that proportion. To what extent Ishan (NE) should be protruding and curved, Naishritya (SW) will be straight in that proportion. Open space should be left around the Naishritya (SW) construction.

2. Generally people are extending the Ishan (NE) in house land, house and room, from a few inches to a few feet and decreasing the Agneya (SE) and Vayavya (NW). Hence, they are caring a damn for 'Naishritya'. Only after Naishritya is O.K., and improving Naishritya, the Ishan (NE) should be made protruding.

3. The meaning of Naishritya (SW) is 'unfortune'. Hence, there should not be any fault relating to Naishritya (SW). Hence, one should be cautious about things constructed in Naishritya (SW) of block, or plot, or room or house.

4. From the height point of view, Naishritya (SW) can be extended or increased more. Main room or sub-rooms should be constructed touching the border of the Naishritya (SW). There should not be well or pit in Naishritya (SW). The room of Naishritya (SW) should be higher. The roof should be high and heavy on that side. The water used, inside the house, should not flow towards 'Naishritya (SW)'.

5. Naishritya (SW) should have concurrence to Ishanya (NE) and if it is free from other vastu-errors then the house will have peace and prosperity. A person may be lucky, but if he is not helped by experience, then luck is of no use. Life is meaningful

when fortune and experience both work. One, who has improved both Ishana (NE) and Naishritya (SW), will share both fortune and success. Western path be lower than the southern one of land in Naishritya (SW) direction, then lion's door will have to be constructed in the south. But according to compass if south looks Agneya (SE) then construct gate in south Agneya (SE) and movement should be through the eastern Lion's door. Presence of northern door for that house is also necessary. Similarly, if the 'gali' in south is lower than the 'gali' in west then Simhadwar (lion's door) has to constructed towards west. But according to compass the gate should be fixed towards 10° Vayavya (NW) from west Vayavya (NW) and movement will be through northern lion's door. It is necessary to have an eastern door for that house.

6. Even if one gets land of Naishritya (SW) direction, without cost or at very cheap rate, it should not be combined with his previous land.

7. The construction of Naishritya (SW) should not be delayed. It may cost life with a small fault. The room in Naishritya, if one has to reconstruct, should be completed immediately. It will not be fruitful to go on travel for the house members during construction work.

8. One should drop the decision of buying land, which possesses large pit, pond, or lower ground in Naishritya (SW) which is difficult to be filled up.

9. Naishritya (SW) part should be elevated for land, house and boundary wall also. Agneya (SE) part should be lower than Naishritya (SW) part, Vayavya (NW) should be lower than Agneya (SE) and Ishan (NE) should be lower than Vayavya (NW). These should be kept in mind, but all the rooms should not be constructed in this way.

10. If close with the land, the road be in south-west direction, then it will be auspicious to construct house making south

west the border. If plot or sewage of another house be in west or south then leaving 2-3 feet open space from the boundary wall one should construct the house.

11. The house and boundary wall will have to be constructed according to the angle of Naishritya (SW).
12. The bed room of house owner should be in Naishritya (SW).
13. If kitchen's construction is possible in Agneya (SE) then it can be made in the Agneya (SE) of the rooms falling in Vayavya (NW) and Naishritya (SW
14. Sloping Veranda in Naishritya (SW) is prohibited.
15. Window should not exist in Naishritya (SW) direction. If window is necessary to be put there then windows should be kept in Ishan (NE) direction too.
16. The pit of latrine should not be in Naishritya (SW). It should be elevated.
17. The boundary of Naishritya (SW) can be constructed angular or circular. But 10° should be constructed inside the baundary wall.

Good Results

1. One gets huge wealth when the land is elevated in south, west or Naishritya (SW) in comparison to other directions.
2. If one wants to construct beautiful house on Naishritya (SW) land then Naishritya (SW) should not be 'Agret' (Stretched) towards road. This should be kept in mind restrict Naishritya (SW) from increasing corner should be made and open space should be left in west-south after digging a well or boring. The owner will get all the riches by constructing Veranda in east north and slope in south-west of house.
3. If big trees are in Naishritya (SW), then these should not be cut. If there is plateau type high land (Tila) in Naishritya (SW), it should be left as it is.
4. Wealth-gain and happiness will come, if Naishritya (SW) part is high.

5. If tall rooms and circular hut is in Naishritya (SW) then good results will be there.
6. Money-gain is there if platform or 'Chabootra' in Naishritya (SW) is higher than house.
7. If cow-dungs heap, piles of stone etc. heavy things are in Naishritya (SW) then health gain and money-gain is expected. Useless things can be kept there.
8. Naishritya (SW), if being covered, is elevated, then all types of happiness will be gained.

Bad Results

1. The corner of Naishritya (SW), at every place should be according to the rooms, otherwise bad consequences are expected.
2. With south Naishritya (SW) 'Marg Prahaar' the ladies of the house will suffer from dreaded diseases. And if well is in Naishritya (SW) then there is possibility of suicide, chronic diseases and death.
3. If west Naishritya (SW) Marg Prahaar exists and well is in Naishritya (SW) then above results will also apply on the male members.
4. 'Agret' should not be with west or close to south or in Naishritya (SW)corner. Extension in south-Naishritya (SW)is for ladies, extension in west Naishritya (SW)is for males, and if both directions of south west Naishritya (SW)are 'Agret' in that corner, then for the male and female both, there is possibility of death, diseases and being of loose character and they will bear enormous pain and losses.
5. If door is for the boundary wall in south-Naishritya (SW) and west Naishritya (SW) or for the houses, then they will be subject to defame, punishment in jail, accidents, and suicide. They will have heart-attack surgery, accident, murder, paralysis and death because this is the place of an enemy.
6. If Naishritya (SW) is down in comparison to Ishan (NE) and well' or pit is there, water flow is from Ishana (NE) to

Naishritya (SW) then enmity will increase and due to stupidity and stubbornness, they will meet bad consequences.

7. For the house in Naishritya, due to sloping Veranda towards south, the female, and due to sloping Veranda towards west the male will suffer from economic constraints and paralysis.

8. The gate in west or in south should be facing unidirectional facing. If gates are in both direction of the house or boundary wall then enmity and indebtedness will mount. But if the door is in north-east then it should be in south-west also.

9. For the house of Naishritya (SW), if open space is more in west-south than east-north and south portion has more open space then the women, and if western part has more space then the male will suffer from health and death in early age and the house will be in the possession of others.

10. For the Naishritya (SW) house, if open space exists in south-west, and north portion does not have open space then by constructing, house by making east-north its border will lead to loss of son and house becomes the property of a lady.

11. In spite of Naishritya (SW) block's Vastu-fault and with above mentioned errors, it has been found auspicious many a time. The truth, behind this, is that if Ishan (NE) vanishes in the Ishan (NE) direction of room among many rooms present in Naishritya (SW) block or the Ishan (NE) is cut-off from that place due to the road of east-north, the people living there will be prosperous from economic point of view but they will be away and far from humanity and good character. If you observe the things relating to murder, or affected by murder, accident in some special condition, you will find the above mentioned faults in such cases.

12. Naishritya (SW) room should be used either as bedroom or store room, but not as bathroom or toilet. If the room of this Naishritya (SW) is lower than the Naishritya (SW) in veranda and other rooms, then loss of wealth, life or diseases are

inevitable.
13. The male-female of the house will suffer from time-curing diseases, if well or pit rests in Naishritya (SW).
14. The female and male will be affected badly, if rain water of Naishritya (SW)passess through the hole in the south and west respectively.
15. Enmity, litigation relating to court and indebtedness are prominent if Naishritya (SW) is 'Agret' (Extended)

Auspicious-Inauspicious Approach to Vayavyamukhi (NW) House

Direction—Vayavya, Lord—'Batuka', Ayudh—'Ankush' (weapon)

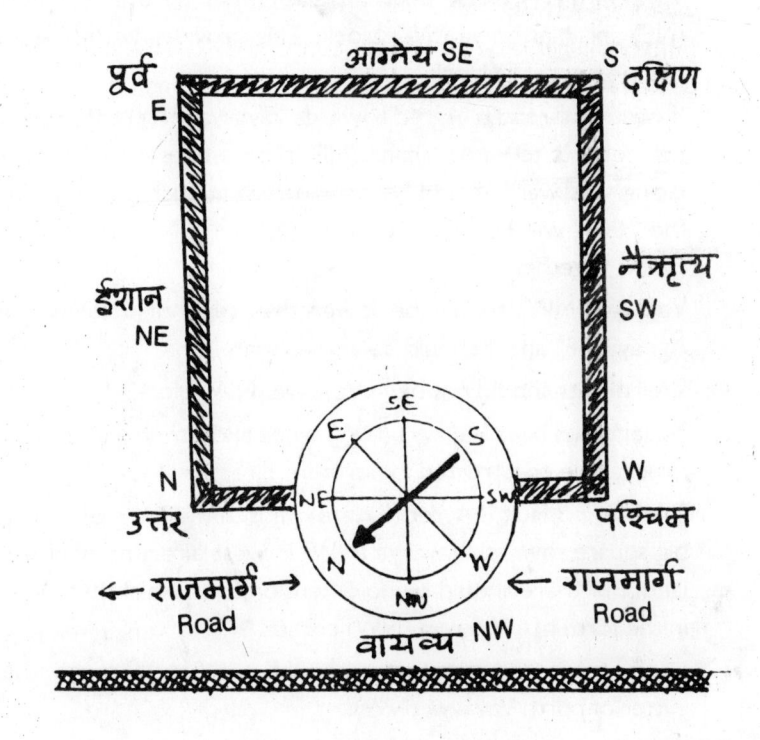

Description of Vayavya (NW) Construction

Vayavya (NW) direction can make the house owner a minister and also can make him a bankrupt. Generally, it is found that owners of such houses are trapped into enmity, litigation, resting on the edge of defeat and victory. The philosopher having no attatchment, passionless families and 'Sanyasis' generally occupy such abodes, where Vayavya (NW) has got Vastu-error.

Neither auspicious nor inauspicious situations remain stable for the owner of this house. The auspicious, and inauspicious consequences are more effective on the house wife and the third son of the family.

1. The place, on the road in west-north direction, is called Vayavya (NW) block. Such a place comes third after Ishana (NE) and Naishritya (SW) block. This provides better result than Agneya (SE) block.

2. If westward road is 'Agret' towards Vayavya (NW) and road in the north is towards Ishana (NE) then a house with a door facing westward should be constructed at such places. Thus the result will be equal to Ishan (NE) and Naishritya (SW) blocks together.

3. Vayavya (NW) should be lower than Naishritya (SW) and Agneya (SE) and it should be above Ishan.

4. Well or pits should not be in Vayavya (NW) block.

5. Toilet could be in Vayavya (NW) block and latrine without pit, tank can be constructed in northern direction.

6. There is no fault if Agret (Extension) is in the form of even a big square towards Vayavya (NW) in west direction of house land. But there should be no extension from Naishritya (SW) in the form of a Vayavya (NW) corner.

7. Used water and rain-water should not flow through the gutter of north Vayavya (NW).

8. If the Vayavya (NW) part of land is underground then it will provide good result. But Vayavya (NW) should not be covered deliberately.

9. Some people have suspicion about the kitchen in Vayavya (NW). If lion's door is in south then it is customary to build kitchen in the Agneya (SE) quarter of the last room in the north. But this will be same as making a kitchen in Ishan (NE) of the whole house. Hence bisect the northern room and make a fire place (Chulha) in the east-Agneya (SE) of Vayavya

(NW) direction.
10. There is a saying by the learned ancients of the old treaties that 'Vayavye Pashumandiram'. On constructing herd-houses in Vayavya (NW) it can be joined with the western wall but not with the northern wall.
11. Firm trees like mango and coconut can be planted and cactus in the pot may be reared in western Vayavya (NW).
12. Flower-plants and cactus in the pot may be reared in western Vayavya (NW).
13. The boundary wall of Vayayya (NW) can be made angular or circular.
14. If westward road of land in Vayavya (NW) is lower than the northern road then a door facing north will have to be constructed there. But according to compass if north sees north-Vayavya (NW) by more than 10° then door in Ishan (NE) should be constructed and movement should be through eastern lion's door. Northern door is necessary for that house.
15. If there exists even small error relating to vastu in Vayavya (NW), it becomes a cause for life long enmity. Hence, if any change has to be made in Vayavya (NW), care should be taken to plan according to the treaties.
16. If communication is from Vayavya (NW) to Agneya (SE) then that place should not be chosen for house construction.

Good Results

1. If the block of Vayavya (NW) direction has 'Marga Prahaar' of west-Vayavya (NW), then people living there will get fame.
2. The course of west Vayavya (NW) of elevated land is very good.
3. If useful heavy things of house is in Vayavya (NW) block, staircase in Naishritya, Naishritya (SW) be lower than Agneya (SE) in Vayavya (NW) quarter and higher than Ishan, then good results will follow.

4. For the house with a door facing west, if open space is more no construction on the boundary wall of east-north; well be in Ishan (NE) and kitchen be in Agneya (SE) then prosperous, brilliant, and judicious people will live there.

Bad Results

1. If there is north Vayavya (NW) Marg Prahaar then the female will not only be unhealthy, but also be forced into wrong habits.
2. If the north Vayavya (NW) is extended, then people will be effected by litigation, theft and fire. There will be lack of male child and peace will not prevail.
3. If Vayavya (NW) corner is lower than Ishan (NE) with well and pits there people will face litigation and disease.
4. When covered in Vayavya (NW) with the north border joined in Vayavya (NW) corner, the house-wife and the third child will face bad consequences.
5. If platform is higher than the Griha-Garbh (heart of the house) in northern direction of this block, then female will be languish and house owner may become indebted.
6. If there is north-door in the Vayavya (NW) block of house, then the house, present in the neighbouring eastern direction, should not be on the rear of this.
7. If fire-place be in the Vayavya (NW) of the Vayavya (NW) quarter then there will be congregation of guests always and the expenditure on fooding will be high. The fire place may be in the Agneya (SE) of Vayavya (NW).
8. If there is a door facing North in the Vayavya (NW) block of house; gate on the depression, then the movement will be in north Vayavya (NW) in lower place. This will lead to suffering from poor results.
9. If a door facing west is there, house is constructed making east north direction as border then persons living in that house will be indebted and the house will be sold in auction.

10. If main door be in north; no vacant place in northern direction, and house is close to other houses; more open space in the south than north, then the house will be centre of many problems and will be dependant on others.

11. If main door be in west, sloping Veranda in the west with eastern border; sloping veranda also on the first floor; then male of the house is attacked by paralysis. Similarly, if house is joined with northern border, and the southern part of veranda has slope on the first floor then females will suffer from paralysis. You will know it, after observing such houses.

12. If main door be in the north and the room and business place has a Naishritya (SW)door in the direction of western door on eastern boundary, then instability will be there and house will seem to go in others hand.

13. If main door be in north and Agneya (SE) Vayavya (NW) be protruding and cut out in Ishan (NE) and Naishritya (SW), then enmity will develop between father-son, wife-husband, brother-bride and mother-in-law, daughter-in-law. They carry mental tension and loss of life may occur.

14. If main door is in the north; eastern-north door be turned or crooked with eastern border, then handicapped children will be born.

15. If Vayavya (NW) corner is protruding or covered, the person will be confused and wander in the country, and may go in for suicide.

16. In some cases it may have good consequences even after having the above mentioned errors. But due to this the Ishan (NE) of northern road of Vayavya (NW) block will go on shortening i.e. if movement be from Vayavya (NW) to Agneya (SE) then Ishan (NE) of the east Ishan's house will be shortened. In such condition people living here, will be prosperous but will be greedy and stupid. They will count money as everything. Generally, female will rule such houses.

17. It is found from observation of the house declared for auction that this happen due to error in Vayavya (NW). These errors are: protruding (Agret) of north-Vayavya; presence of well and pit there; or Vayavya (NW) being higher than Naishritya, or covering of Vayavya.
18. Observations on the house of people affected by fire accident that, in such houses, the measurerment of Agneya (SE) and Vayavya (NW) is greater than the measurement of corners in Naishritya (SW) and Ishana.
19. If Vayavya (NW) is lower than Ishana in the lobby of house or Veranda of house and higher than Naishritya (SW) and Agneya (SE), then number of enemies multiply females from diseases. The house seems to be horrible.
20. If Veranda is in the west of house, then small wall is made with less width, below the grill, when one is going to fix grill towards the wall of north-south. On doing this, north becomes Vayavya (NW) and south becomes Naishritya (SW). Hence small wall should be equal to the width of house-wall.

□

Chapter 14

Pictorial Depiction of Vastu (Shape of Plot)

Shape	Name	Description	Effect
□	Square	Equal on all the sides (Rightangle)	Auspicious, wealth and prosperity
Rectangle (N-S)	Rectangle	Regtangular north-south length (Rightangle)	wealth gain and prosperity
Rectangle (E-W)	Rectangular	East-West Length (Rightangle)	Wealth gain and prosperity
○	Circle	Circular	Auspicious

173

Shape	Description	Effect
Hexagonal	Hexagonal	Destroys calamity and is fortunate
Octagonal	Wheel shaped	Troublesome
Triangle	Triangular	Debt and extreme tension
Cart	Cart shaped	Provides instability
Double and reserved cart	Double and reserved cart shaped	Unstability, Lack of permanent happiness, Inauspicious

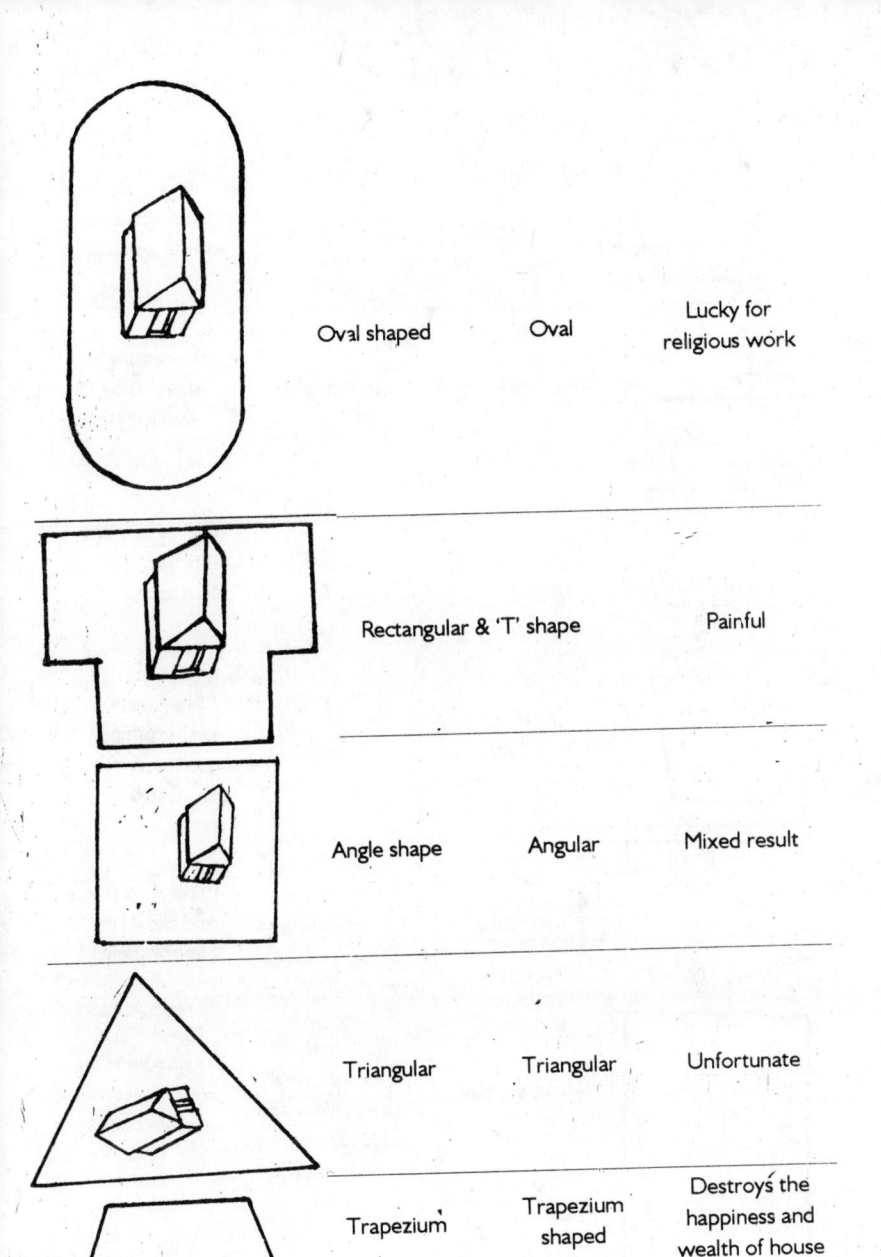

Shape	Type	Result
Oval shaped	Oval	Lucky for religious work
Rectangular & 'T' shape		Painful
Angle shape	Angular	Mixed result
Triangular	Triangular	Unfortunate
Trapezium	Trapezium shaped	Destroys the happiness and wealth of house

Shape	Name	Description	Effect
	Hand-fan	Hand-fan shaped	Makes one poor adds to poverty.
	Bow	Bow shaped	Increasing enemies or enemity
	Semi-circle	Semi circular	Not-favourable, incomplete success
	Tabla	Tabla	Making the owner empty penniless like tabla
	Mridanga	Mridanga shaped	Making empty and penniless like mridanga
	Kakmukhi	Kakmukhi (crow-face) shaped, small size in front and large size on the rear side	The people living are happy and prosperous

ENTRANCE

SAMPURAN VASTUSHASTRA

Result of Acute-Obtuse Quadrangles of Plot

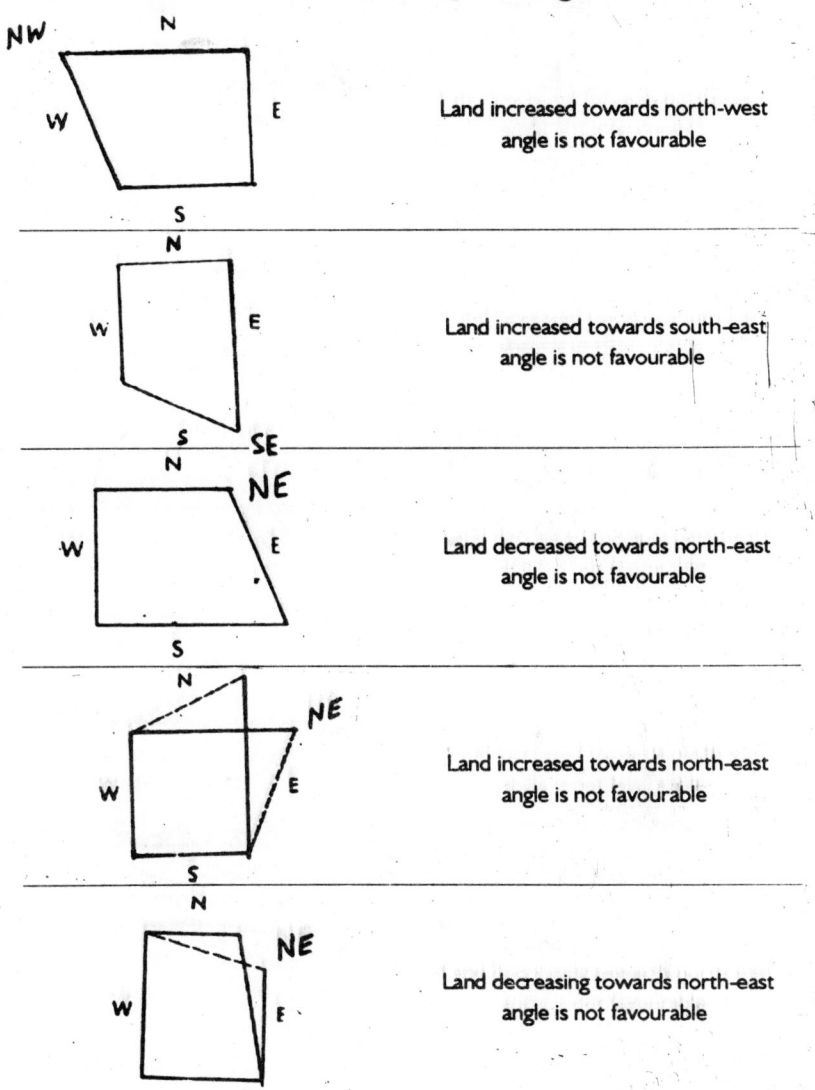

Land increased towards north-west angle is not favourable

Land increased towards south-east angle is not favourable

Land decreased towards north-east angle is not favourable

Land increased towards north-east angle is not favourable

Land decreasing towards north-east angle is not favourable

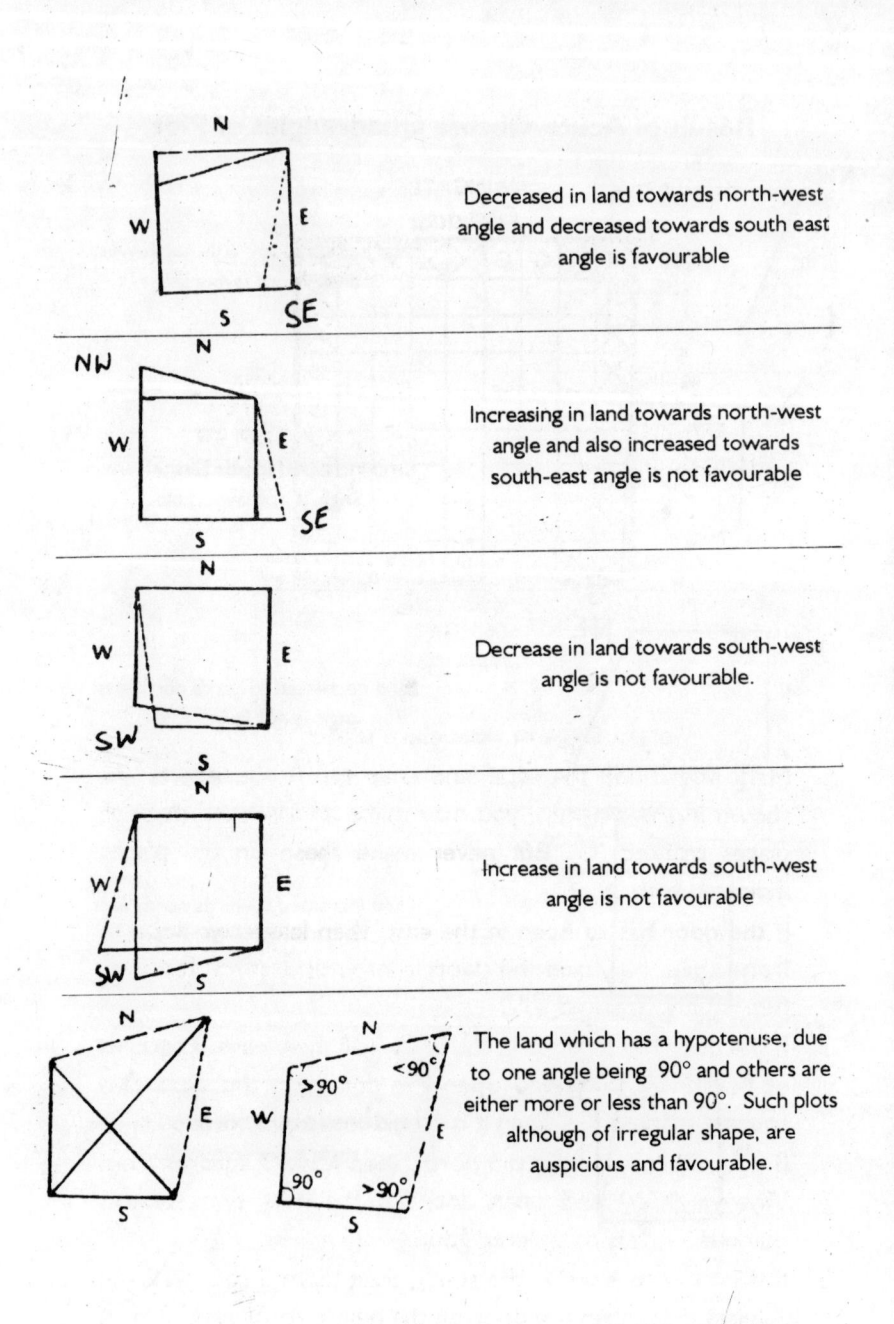

Decreased in land towards north-west angle and decreased towards south east angle is favourable

Increasing in land towards north-west angle and also increased towards south-east angle is not favourable

Decrease in land towards south-west angle is not favourable.

Increase in land towards south-west angle is not favourable

The land which has a hypotenuse, due to one angle being 90° and others are either more or less than 90°. Such plots although of irregular shape, are auspicious and favourable.

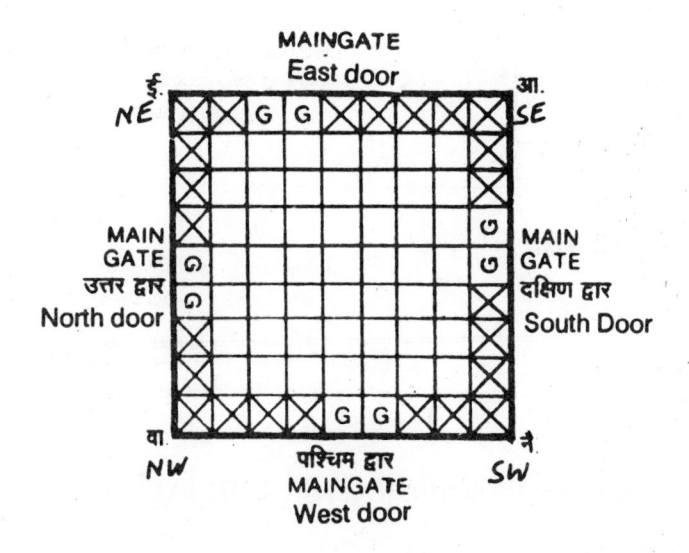

```
                MAINGATE
                East door
      ई                           आ.
    NE  ⊠⊠|G|G|⊠⊠⊠⊠⊠  SE
        ⊠                    ⊠
        ⊠                    ⊠
  MAIN  ⊠                    ⊠
  GATE  ⊠                    G  MAIN
  उत्तर द्वार  G                    G  GATE
        G                    ⊠  दक्षिण द्वार
  North door ⊠                ⊠  South Door
        ⊠                    ⊠
        ⊠                    ⊠
        ⊠⊠⊠⊠|G|G|⊠⊠⊠
      वा.                         नै.
    NW           पश्चिम द्वार      SW
                MAINGATE
                West door
```

Main Gate or Associate Door

1. Mark and divide the total land area into 9 equal parts. As shown in the diagram, you may make an associate door at places marked 'G'. But never make these on the places indicated with 'X'.

2. If the door has to open in the east, then leave two squares from Ishan (NE), and the doors can be opened on the next two squares marked 'G'.

3. If the door has to open in the west wall then leave 3 squares of Naishritya (SW) and open the doors on the next two squares marked 'G'. Then it is considered auspicious.

4. If door has to open in the north, then leave 3 squares from Vayavya (NW) and open door on the next two squares marked 'G'. It is considered good.

5. If door has to open in the south, then leave 3 squares from Agneya (SE), open the door on the next two squares. This is considered excellent.

Chapter 15

Selection of Plot (Site)

1. Situation of North-South Magnetic Poles in the Plot.

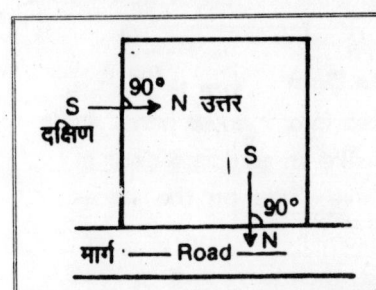

[diagram: plot with 90° angles at N उत्तर and S दक्षिण, मार्ग — Road]	The lay out of North-South magnetic poles should be parallel or perpendicular to the wall and road in front of the plot. One should follow precisely as shown in the diagram.

Result:— People living in such a plot will have proper sleep.

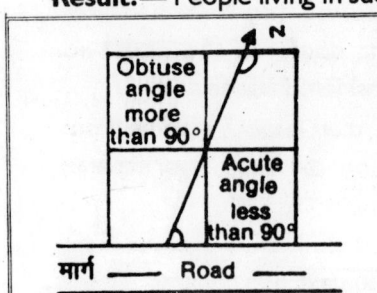

[diagram: Obtuse angle more than 90°, Acute angle less than 90°, मार्ग — Road]	The North-South magnetic pole of the plot should not be more than 90 degree and also it should not be less than 90°.

Result:— People sleeping in such a plot, will not get proper sleep and will feel tired on getting up in the morning.

2. Road towards the east of the Plot

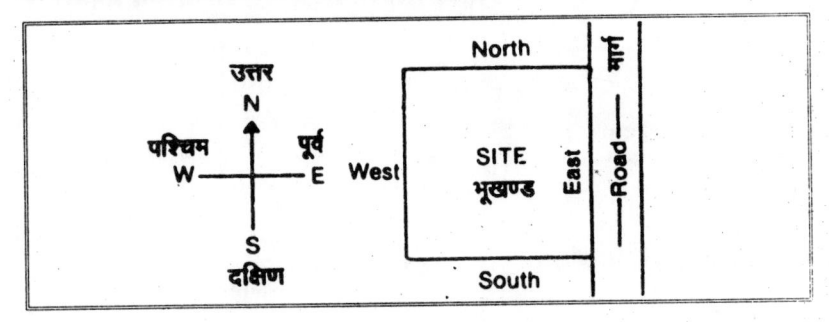

Result:— Such a plot provides an auspicious result to the plot owner.

Road towards the north of the Plot

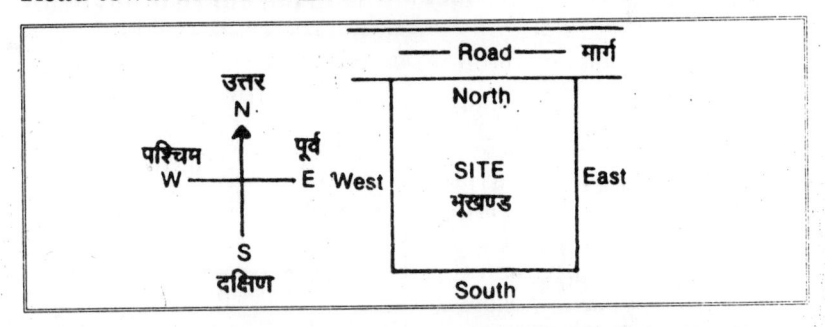

Result:— Such a plot provides an auspicious result to the owner.

Road towards the west of the plot

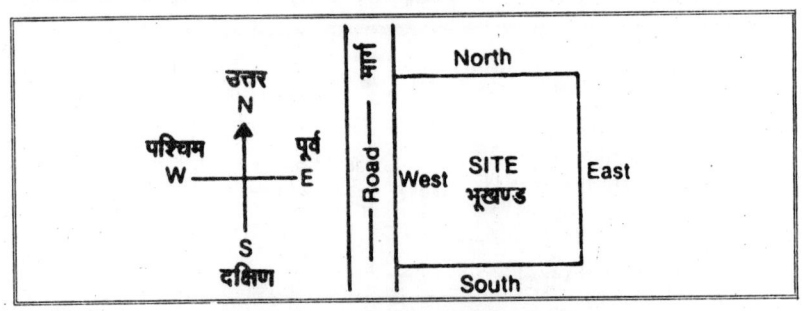

Result:— Such a plot is auspicious for the owner.

Road towards the south of the plot

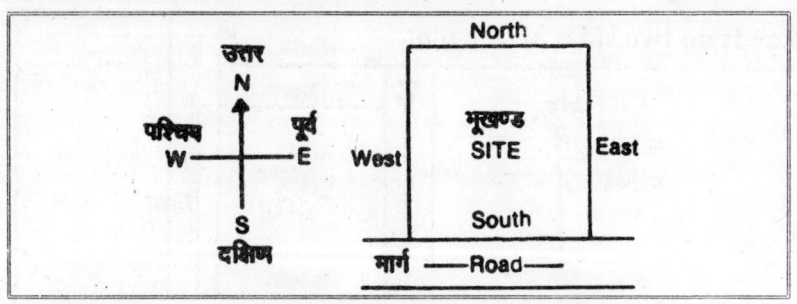

Result:—It gives mixed result to the owner, i.e., neither auspicious nor inauspicious. But the door, in south direction, is supposed to be inauspicious.

Road on both sides of the plot

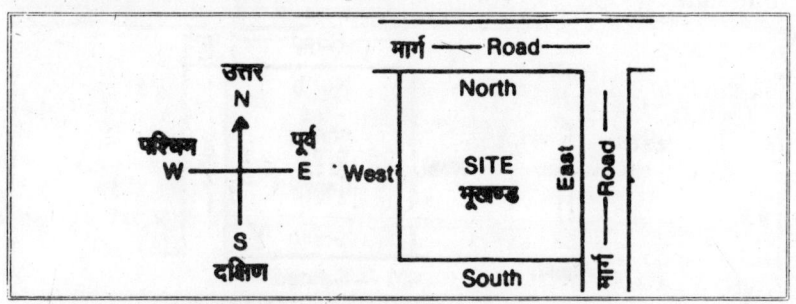

Result:— If the roads are towards the east and north of the plot, then it is very good and provides wealth.

Road on both side of the plot

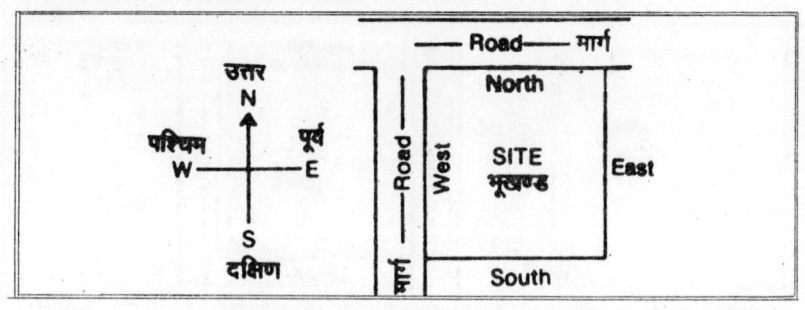

Result:— If the roads are towards North and west of the site, then such a site is normally fruitful to the owner.

Roads on two sides of the plot

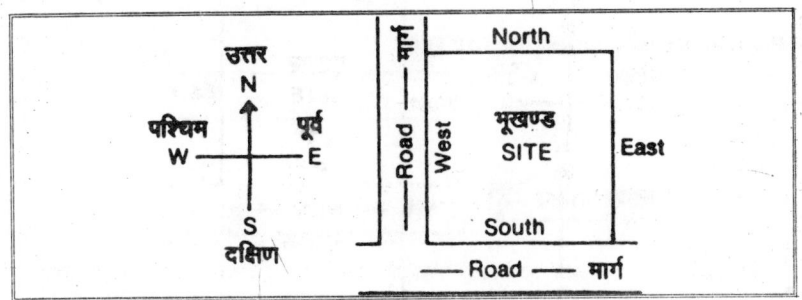

Result:— If the roads are in the west and south of the site, then it is normally fruitful.

Roads on two sides of the plot

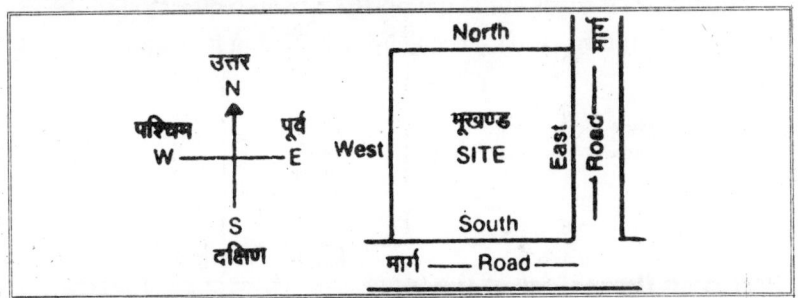

Result:— If the roads are in the south and east direction of the site then it gives bad consequences. The native becomes a pauper.

Roads on two sides of the plot

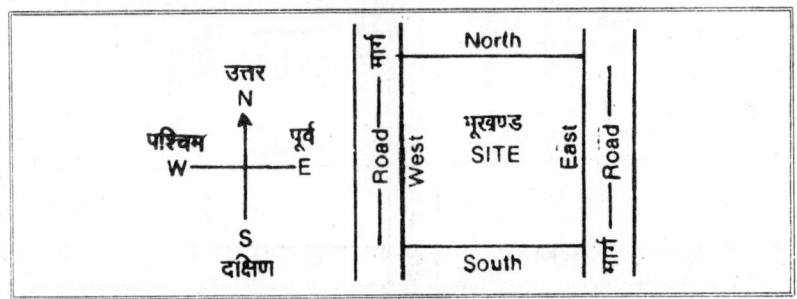

Result:— If roads are in east and west of the site, then the site provides mixed results to the owner.

Roads on two sides of the plot

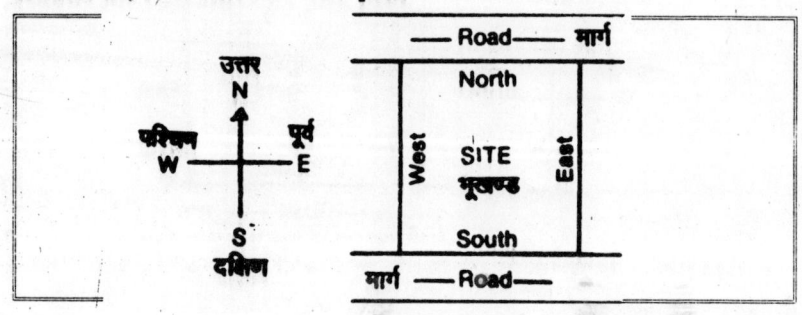

Result:— If roads are in the north and south direction of the site then it gives mixed result. People living in such a plot do not flourish much.

Roads on three sides of the plot

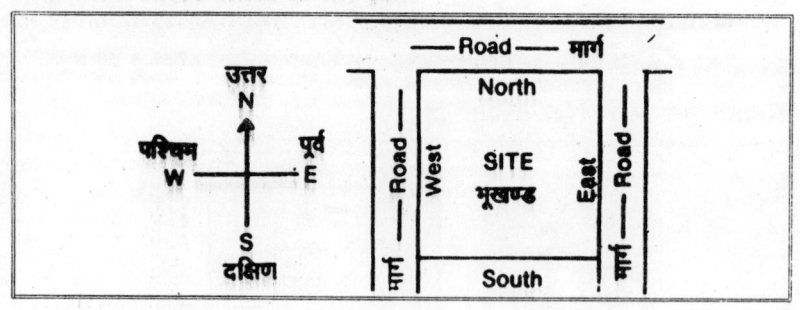

Result:— If roads are in east, west and north direction of the site, and southern side is closed then the site is not fruitful and it gives bad results.

Roads on three sides of the plot

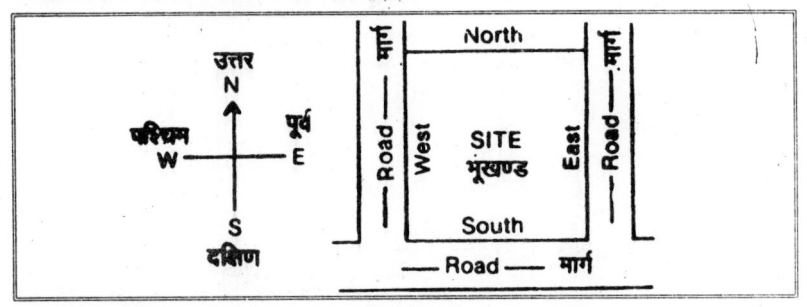

Result: — If roads are in east west and south and the northern direction is closed, then such a plot is not fruitful and gives bad results.

Roads on three sides of the plot

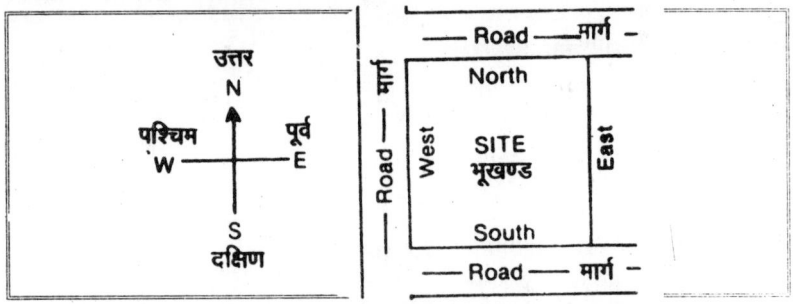

Result: — If roads are in north, south and west direction of the site and the east direction is closed, then it is not fruitful.

Roads on three sides of the plot

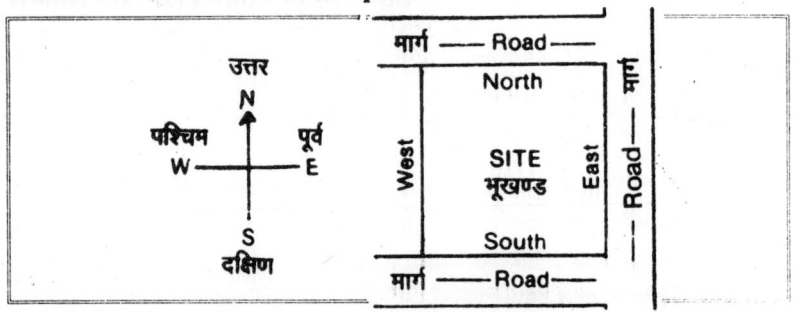

Result: — If roads are in east, north and south and the west direction is closed, then such sites are not fruitful.

Roads on all the sides of the plot

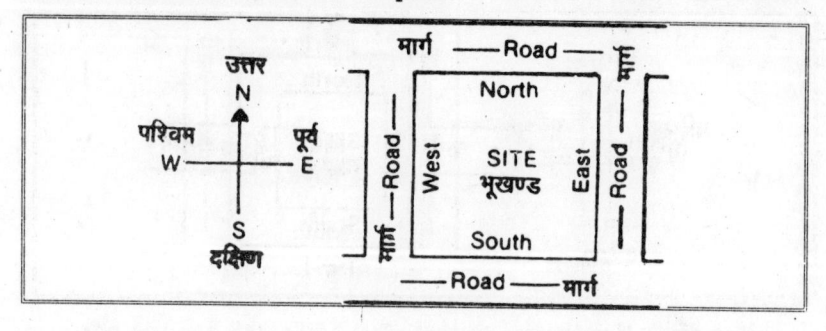

Result:— If, roads are all-round the site, as shown in the diagram and all directions are open, then such a site makes the owner rich and gives many auspicious results.

Roads on the four sides of the plot

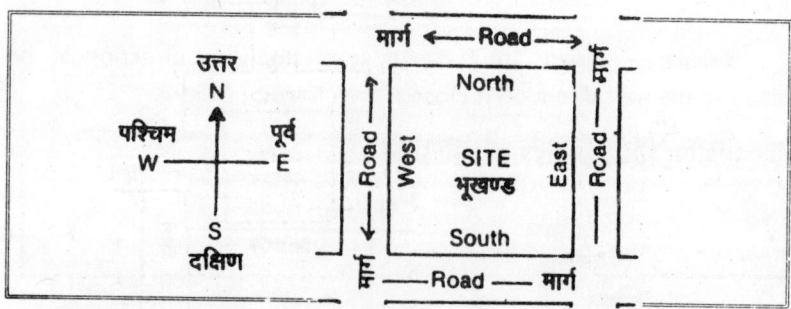

Result:— If roads are all-round the site, according to the diagram and all directions are open, in the form of crossing, then the site floods wealth in the owners house. House constructed, on such a site, gives maximum auspicious results.

Meeting place all-round the plot

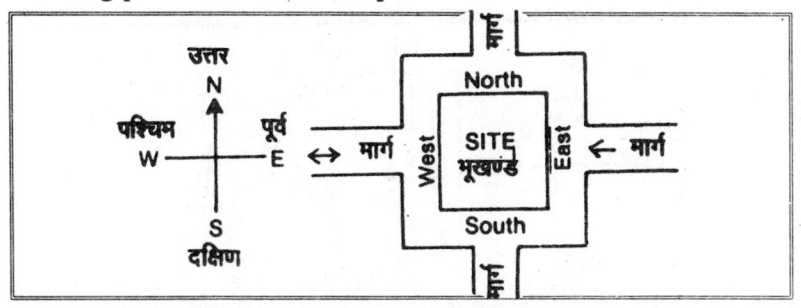

Result:— If meeting point or place be there, on all the sides of site, then such sites are extremely inauspicious and the house owner is not safe.

Meeting place on three sides of the plot

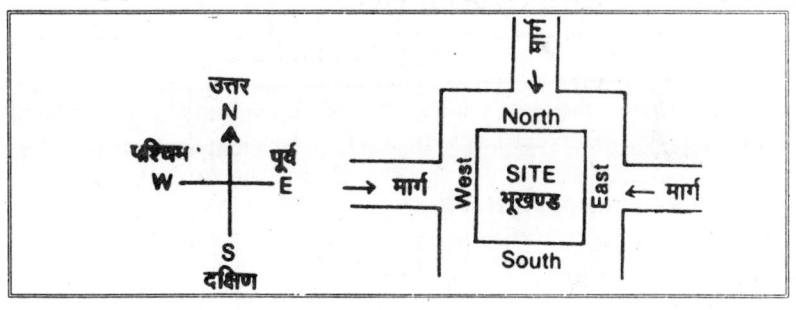

Result:— If any site is situated, as a triad, on the meeting places of three roads, and the south direction is closed, then it is extremely inauspicious and a matter of concern for the owner.

Meeting places on two sides of the plot

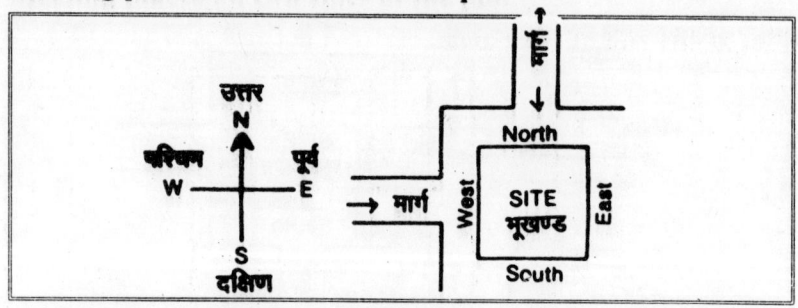

Result:— If the site is situated, on the meeting places of two roads and south and east directions are closed, then the site is inauspicious and causes bad consequences.

Meeting place on the two sides of plot

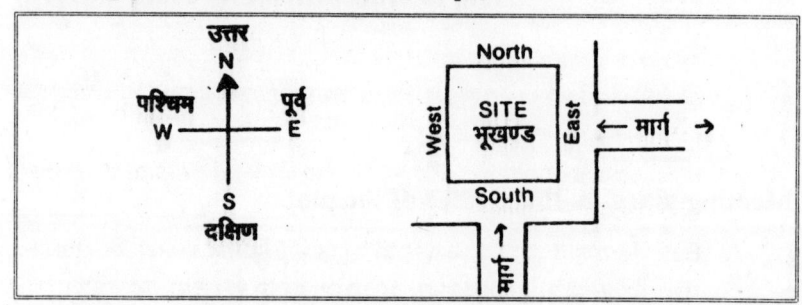

Result:— If site is on the meeting place, on two roads, and north and west directions are closed, then it provides extremely bad results.

Plot on a 'T' Shaped Road

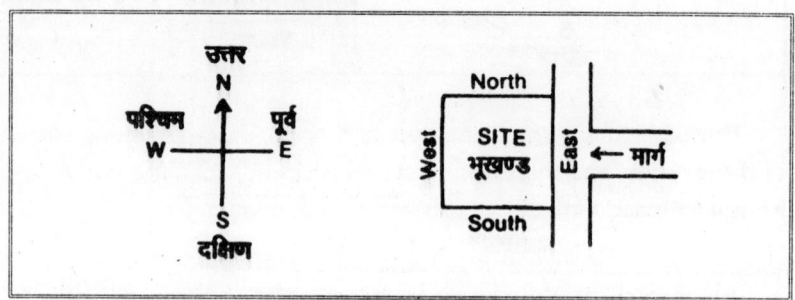

Result:— If the road is towards east of the site but is in the shape of 'T' as shown in figure then the result is inauspicious.

Plot at the end of the Road

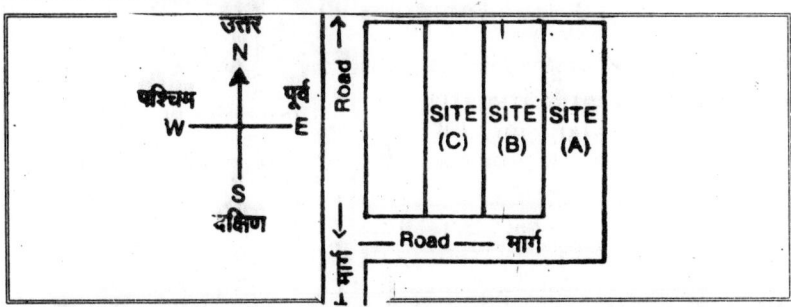

Result:— If the site as in the diagram, is having a door in the south i.e. road is in the south and all the other, directions are closed, then it is inauspicious. As in the diagram the front road of site 'A' is closed, the owner dies. Such a plot is extremely bad and inauspicious.

1. If roads are in the east and north on both the directions of the site, the main entrance should be in the east wall, even if the road is of short length.
2. If roads are open on both north and west of the site then main entrance should be in the shorter road.
3. Bear in mind that the depth of land should never be greater than its width. If roads are open on both west and south of the site then entrance should be from the west.
4. If roads are open on both the directions east and south then enter from east always.

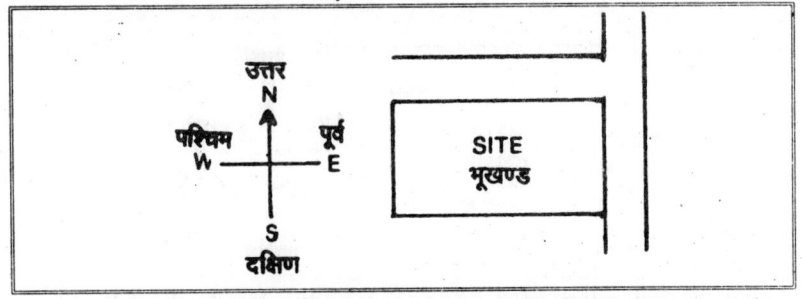

5. If roads of east and west are open, in both the directions then the entrance door should be always in the east.

6. If the roads of north and south in both the directions are open then keep entrance door towards the north direction.

About Temples

The shadow of any temple should not fall on the site or house between 9 A.M. to 3 P.M.

The temple of Sun, Brahma, Vishnu or Shiva should not be in front of main door of any house.

The shadow of any Jain temple should not fall on the rear portion of the house.

The temple of Goddess Durga and Chandi should not be near the house.

River Canal

River, gutter, canal should not exist parallel to west and south direction of site or house. But if these are, northwards and eastwards, then it is good. Specially the water flow should be from west to east or from south to north.

Cemetery or Mosque

Cemetery and Mosque should not be near house or site. Cemetery in the front or in the rear portion of house is prohibited.

Well, Tank or Handpump

Any well should not exist in the Agneya, Naishritya, Vayavya corner or in south direction. The place of well is supposed to be auspicious in the north, east, west and Ishanya angle.

Trees

Never plant Banyan tree in the east, Pipal in the west, Gular in the north and Pakad in the south, Inside or outside of house.

Slope of the Plot

1. The southern part of site should be on a higher elevation more than the northern part.

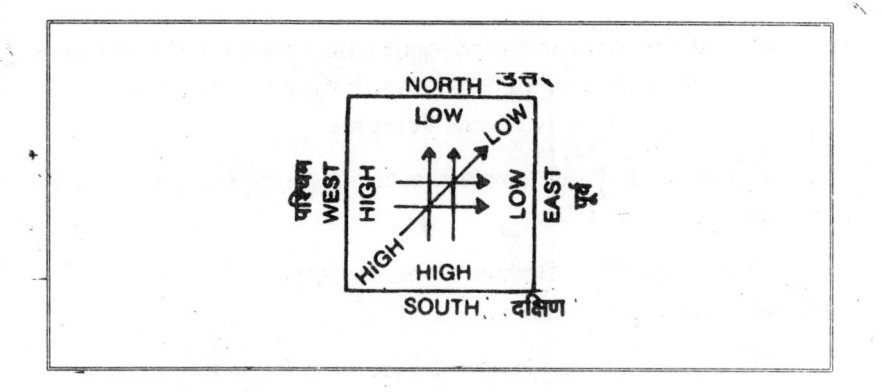

2. Western part of site should be on a higher elevation than the eastern part.
3. Naishritya part of site should be elevated more than the Ishanya.
4. The middle part of site should not be deep or lower.

Measurement of Site

1. The road in the middle of site (Length) should be longer than the breadth. As the following site is a bit larger than width.
2. If the site is in a square shape and the angles are of 90 degree then it is the best site and provides excellent result.
3. If the site be at right angles and the length is one and half times or double the width, then it is excellent, but length in excess of this is not very good.

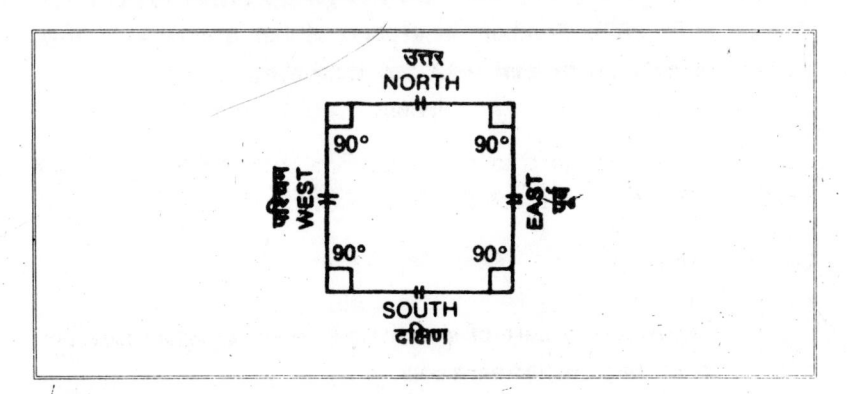

i.e. The best sized plots are 60' x 120', 45' x 90', 30' x 60', 20' x 40'. The plots of 30' x 90' or 20' x 60' sizes are of medium quality. The plots of 15' x 60', 20' x 90' measurements are inferior quality.

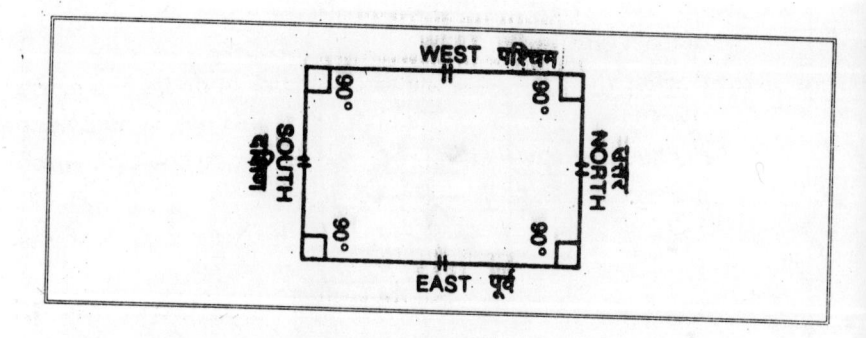

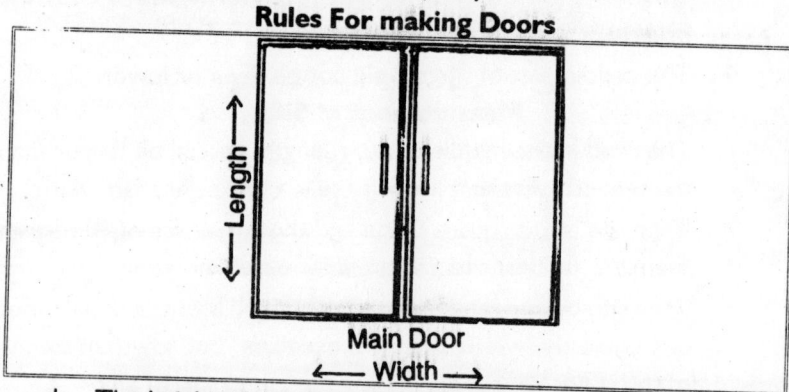

Rules For making Doors

1. The height of the door should be generally double the width. This height should not be of much length, or it should not be very short, much wide and much narrow.
2. Main gate should always be lengthy than other doors.
3. The main gate should always be with two flaps and should be very strong, firmly well fixed and more attractive than the other doors.

Dwar-Vedha

1. There should not be any obstruction or obstacles in the form of trees, wall corner, pole, pit, well, mud, shadow of temple, hand pump, any cemetery, upright 'gali' (narrow path) in front

of main gate.

2. Besides the main gate, the total number of doors in a house should be even. The doors of house should not be odd. Keep in mind that the total number should not be the digit which has zero at unit position e.g. 10, 20, 30.

3. The same rule is applicable for the windows, air-holes (Gawaksha), Ventilator and Almirahs in the house.

4. The doors and windows, in odd numbers, should never be in one line. Similarly, after entering the main gate, the number of doors should not finish in odd numbers.

5. The upper part of doors, windows and almirahs should be all at same level.

6. Door should not open outside but always inside. This should be kept in mind.

7. Door should not produce an unpleasant sound while opening or closing.

Place of Well or Water-tank in the house or outside the house

1. Well, handpump, water-tank in Ishanya (NE) corner inside house or outside the house, is always auspicious. Prosperity increases in the house and family is healthy.

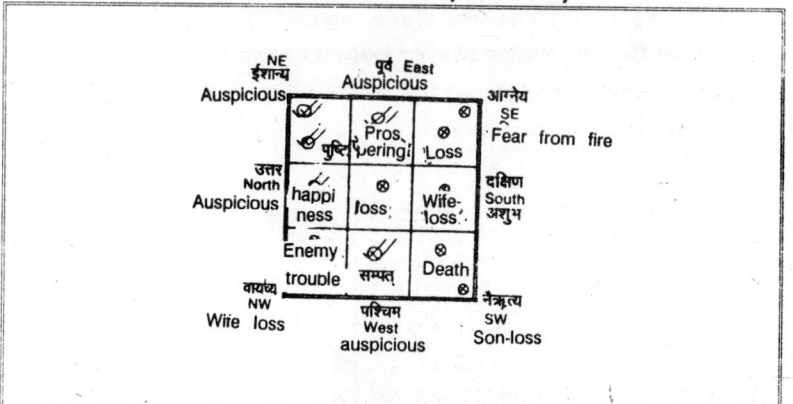

	NE ईशान्य Auspicious	पूर्व East Auspicious		आग्नेय SE Fear from fire
उत्तर North Auspicious	happiness	Pros. पुष्टि pering / loss	⊗ Loss	
			Wife-loss	दक्षिण South अशुभ
वायव्य NW Wife loss	Enemy trouble	सम्पत् पश्चिम West auspicious	⊗ Death ⊗	नैऋत्य SW Son-loss

2. Well, handpump, water tank or water reservoir, in the western part is good. Happiness and wealth increases in the

house.
3. If well, handpump, water tank or tank house are just in the east of house, it enhances prosperity.
4. If well, handpump, water tank or tank house are in just north of house, then it gives auspicious result, with increase in happiness.
5. If water resources, well, water tank be in Naishritya (SW), then the house owner meets with death of his close relatives and himself.
6. If these water resources are in Agneya (SE) corner then inhabitants of the house have fear from fire and if either of these are in Agneya direction, then the owner faces the death of his son.
7. If these water resources are in south direction of house then the wife of the owner dies; if either of these is in the middle of south then there is heavy loss of property.
8. If these are in the Vayavya (NW) direction, then the house owner is oppressed with enemy but, if any of water resources is just in corner of Vayavya (NW), then wife of house owner dies.

Place for the fire place, electric room, heavy motor or meter board in the house.

1. The Agneya (fire place) S-E of the house is the best place to put electric power or fire.

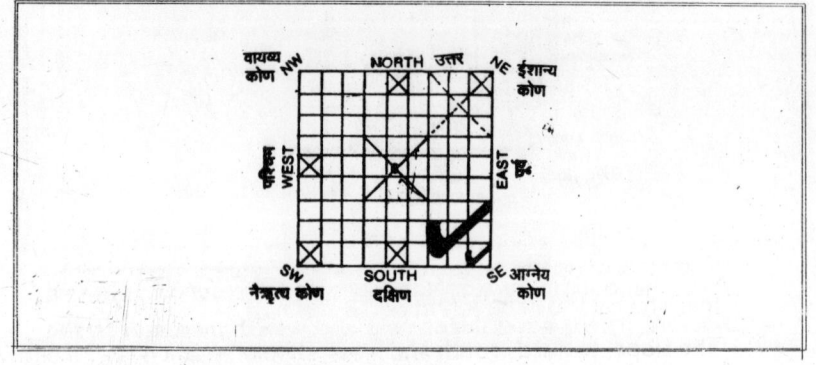

2. Don't establish and construct kitchen or fire place at the place marked 'X' in the diagram at any cost.

Construction work

1. The construction work on the site should be solid and according to measurement e.g. there should be equal space or distance in the east and west of a wall. Similarly the space between north and south wall should be balanced.
2. Similarly the boundary (safety wall) or 'Bagicha' (orchard), left in west and east outside house, should be equal.

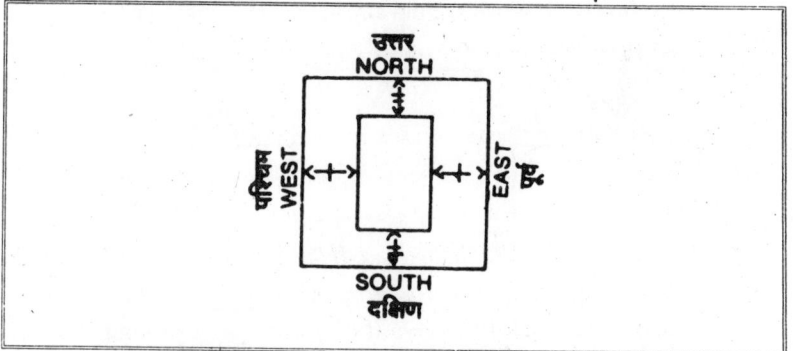

3. The slope of land, left in south and west direction, should be higher than the slope of land in north and east.

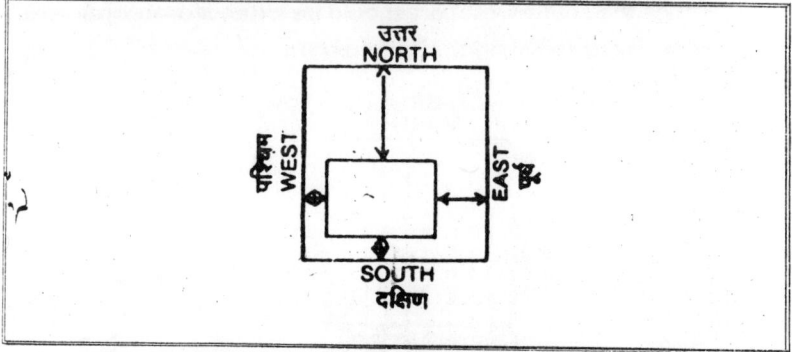

The ratio of open spaces, left in south and west, should be less than the ratio of land left in north and east.

The slope, towards south and west, should be at a higher level than slope in north and east.

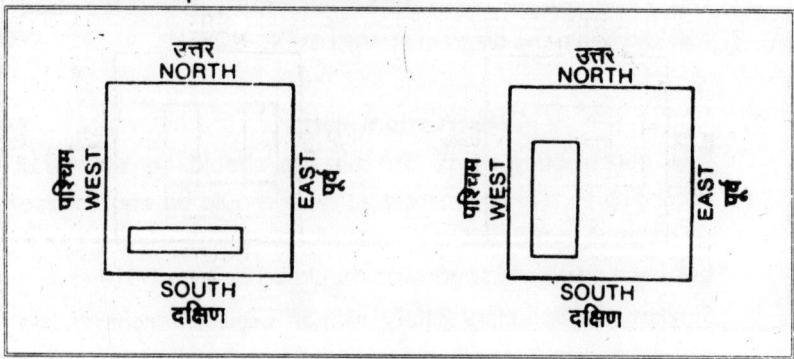

The foundation work should start from the first of all, in south and west directions.

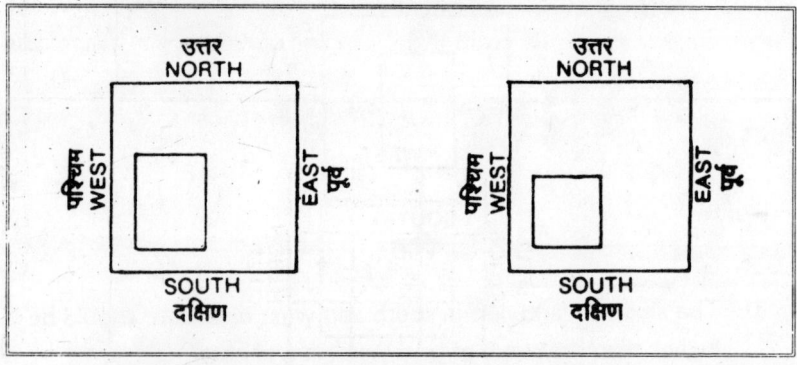

Hence the south-west part should be extended, according to necessity as shown in the first diagram.

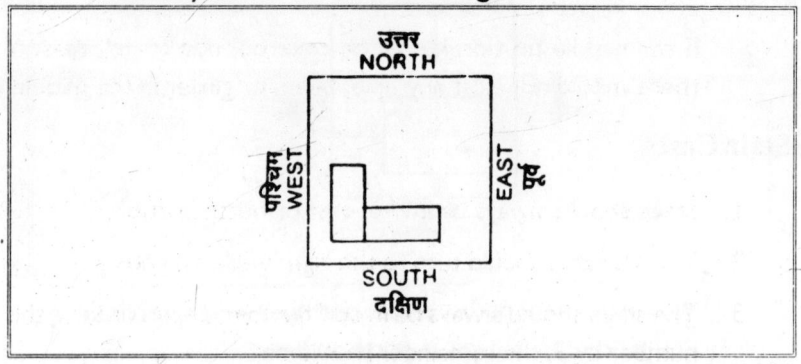

In the second stage of construction, it should proceed

towards south.

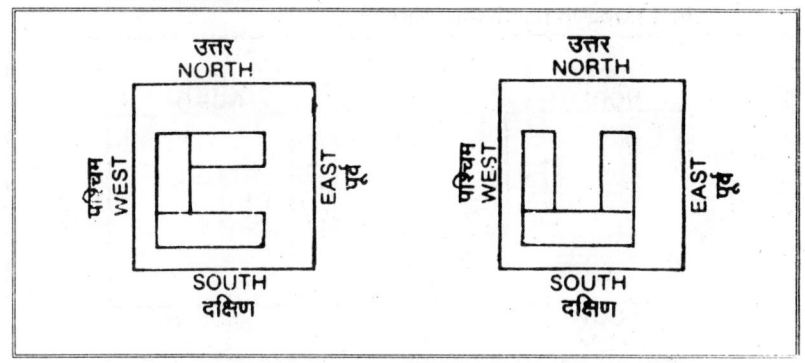

[Figure: Two diagrams showing construction stages with North, South, East, West orientations in English and Hindi (उत्तर, दक्षिण, पूर्व, पश्चिम)]

In the third stage of construction the work should proceed towards north or east. According to figure, construction work should proceed from 'A' to 'B'. Hence, work should proceed in the form of a quadrangle, keeping open space in the middle for air and light.

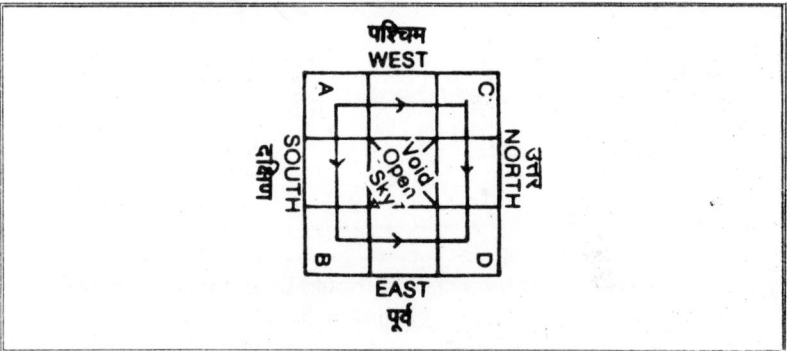

[Figure: Quadrangle diagram with Void/Open/Sky in middle, points A, B, C, D and directions marked in English and Hindi]

If the middle portion has to be covered, due to any reason, there should not exist any pole, beam or girder in the middle.

Stair Cases

1. Stairs should always be in the west or north portion.
2. The staircase should turn to the right while ascending.
3. The stairs should always be in odd number, i.e. on dividing this number by 3, the remainder should be 2.

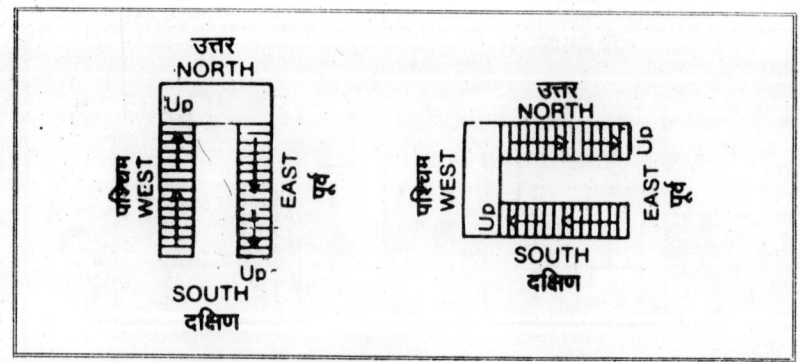

1. The map, angles, height, parts of the house should be constructed harmoniously.
2. The Naishritya (SW) part of house should be high in construction. Vayavya (NW) and Agneya (SE) corner should be medium but, if Ishanya (NE) is there, it should be lower in construction. Or the Naishritya (SW) should be elevated and other parts should be medium.

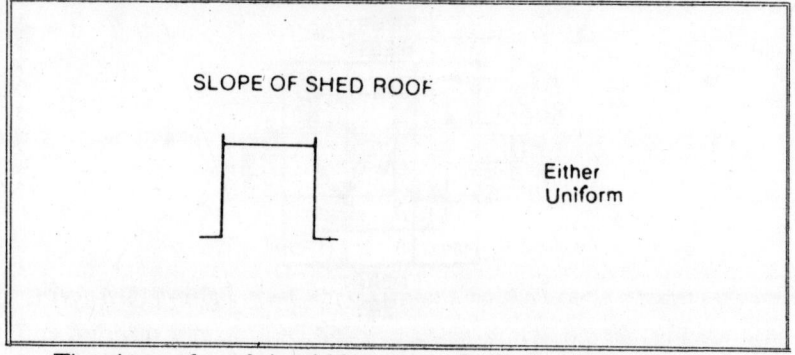

The slope of roof should be same. Both the sides of roof should be same and should not have difference even of a single thread.

[West or South] [East or North]

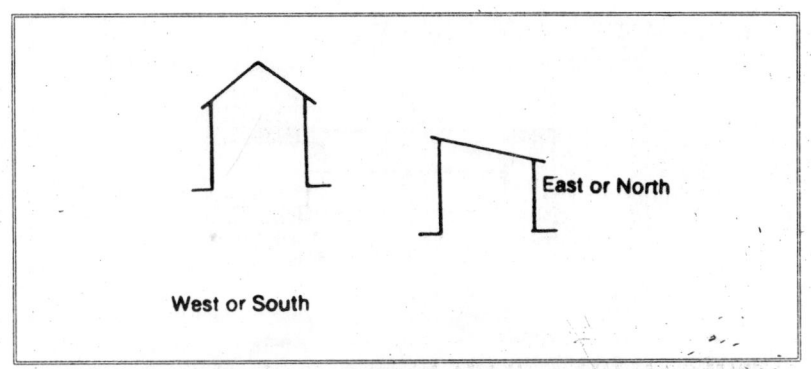

If slope or design has to be given then south and west should be higher or elevated and the wall of north and east should be shorter or lower.

Dining room and hearth fire place

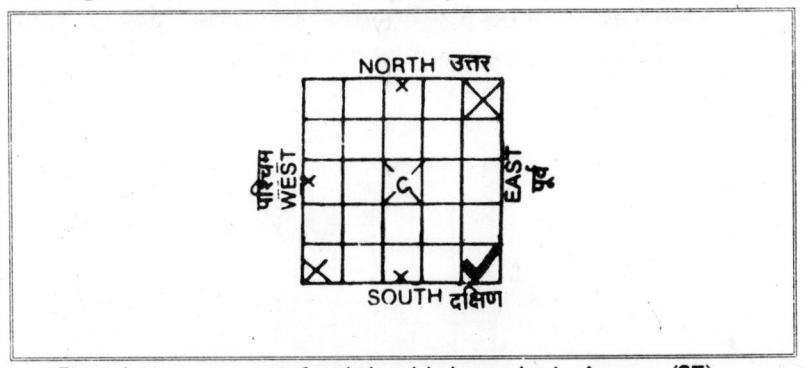

Fire place to prepare food should always be in Agneya (SE) corner and it should not be at the place marked 'X', in the diagram and especially in Ishanya (NE).

Toilet or W.C. (Water Closet) Work

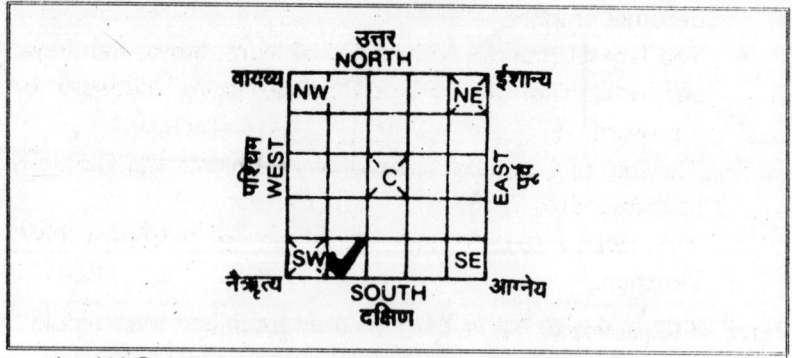

1. W.C., washing place, bath room should always be a little bit away from Naishritya (SW) corner, as shown in the also diagram.
2. Don't encourage W.C. work in the Ishan (NE) or in the middle of the house even by mistake.

Place of Worship

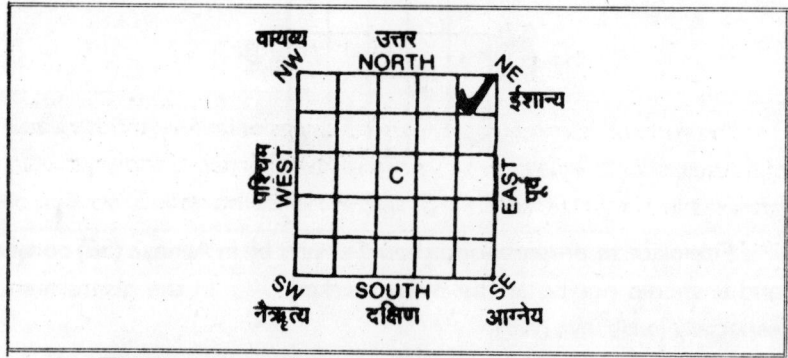

1. This is most important place in the house. The place for worship, 'bhajan', Kirtan (praise of god), study work should be done in Ishanya (NE) corner and the person should face eastward while praying.
2. The face of God or idol should be towards east, west or south.
3. As Kuber resides in the north direction hence put 'Galla' (Treasury box) cash box in north direction which increases

wealth. If 'Kuber-Yantra' is put in the locker, then it never becomes empty.
4. The face of Brahma, Vishnu, Shiva, Indra, Surya, Kartikeya, and other idol of Gods should be facing eastward or westward.
5. The face of Ganesha, Kubera, Durga, Bhairva and Shodasha Mrittika should be towards south direction.
6. The face of 'Hanumanji' should be in Naishritya (SW) direction.

Place of Godown or Place for keeping goods

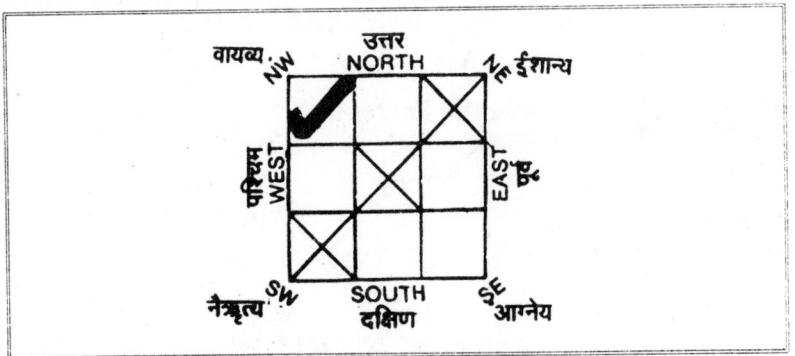

The godown, for keeping the useful things of factory, industry and of houses, should always be in Vayavya (NW) corner. Godown should not exist in Naishritya (SW), Ishanya (NE) or in the central portion of house.

Place to Keep Electrical Equipment

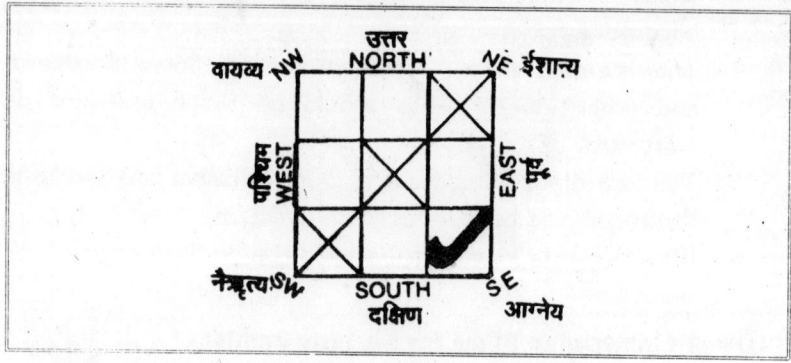

Boiler, heater, A.C. control, meter, oven, gas stove, drier etc., and things relating to fire, should be in Agneya (SE) corner.

Plant and Machines in the Factory

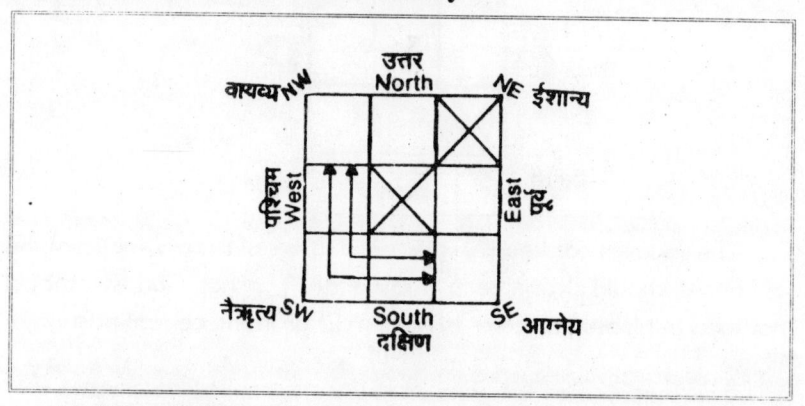

1. The machine of main plant of factory should be erected always either in Naishritya (SW), south and west according to need.
2. Useful and associate machines should be installed in east and north directions.
3. The on-off switch of machine should be in Vayavya (NW) corner.
4. Any heavy machine should not be in Ishanya (NE) or middle part.

The Raw Materials in Factory

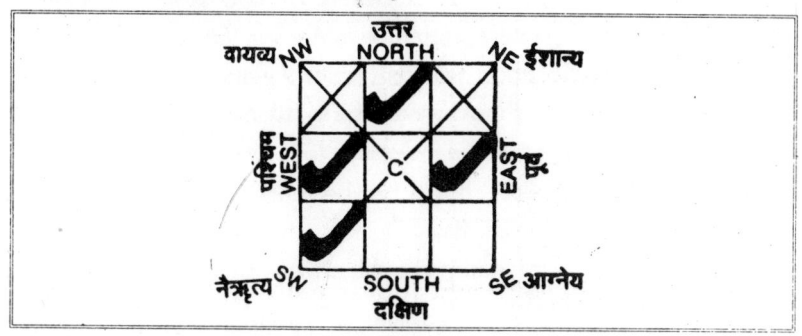

The raw material, to be used in the factory or industry should not be kept in Ishanya (NE), Vayavya (NW) and middle portion of the land. Use the places which are tick marked (✓)

Production-Place

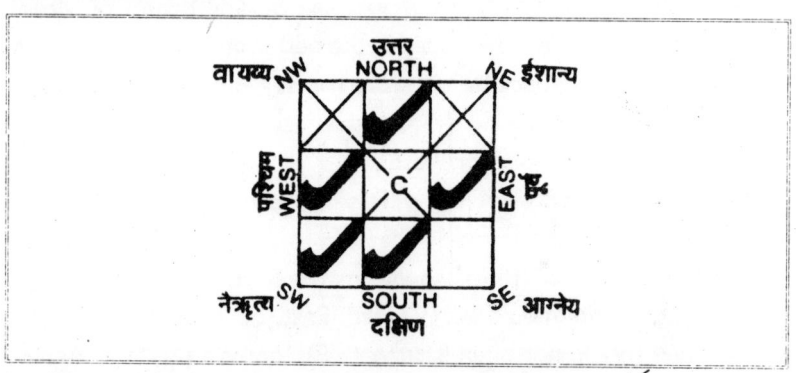

The production places should be at tick marked (✓) places.

The place of the information regarding Office and staff room:—

1. The room of senior manager, controller, director, should be in Naishritya (SW), west or south direction.
2. The room of middle level officer should be in the north or east.
3. The rooms earmarked for the worker and labourers working there, should be in Vayavya (NW) direction.

4. The staff room, for accounts, accountant, artist, map designer, engineers should be in Agneya (SE) corner.
5. Counter, reception hall, guest room, worship room, place for drinking water should always be in Ishanya (NE).
6. Store room should be in Agneya (SE) direction.
7. W.C., urinals etc. should not be in Ishanya (NE), Naishritya (SW), or middle portion.
8. The face of staff room should, always, be towards north and east directions.
9. Kitchen should be in Agneya (SE) corner.
10. Any bed or things relating to sleeping should not be in the depression of a corner.
11. Head should always be in east or south direction.
12. In the bedroom there should not be any beam, or girder, crossed border over head in the bed room.
13. There should not be any store room, near the bedroom.
14. When using latrine (W.C), the face of the person should always be in north or west.
15. The bed room for the elders, old people should be in the south or west.
16. The bed room of newly married couple, and younger generation should be in North-East, but, keep in mind that bed should not be in Ishanya (NE), Vayavya (NW) or Agneya (SE) corner.
17. The bed room for younger children should be in the east.

Conclusion

The house, which is a quandrangle with right angle, vacant in the middle, having doors all around, and having no 'vedha' (obstruction) on the door, is the best and excellent. People, living in such houses enjoy the riches and wealth like a king.

If Ishanya (NE), north and east possess water resources; Agneya (SE) corner be with fire place; shadow of any type of tree, temple does not fall on the house; pure air and natural light enters the house;

house is constructed on Vastu rules such that light, air, water is present, in abundance even if the electric light is put off; it is least dependant on artificial light and power, then such houses provide happiness, peace, prosperity, wealth, riches, from all directions and multiplies the property and wealth as well.

☐

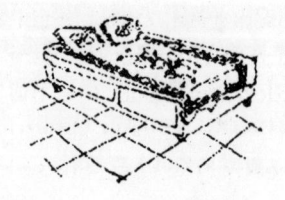

Chapter 16

Bed Room

There is a balanced discussion in 'Vastu Shastra' about the subject—How should a person sleep? It is said that "a person, desiring for good health and age, should always sleep with the head in the south and the leg in the north.

According to old treatise, Yam—the god of death, is lord of south direction. This is why the cemetery is always found in the south of villages and towns. The person, who sleeps putting his leg in the south, certainly seems to be tending towards death (Yamloka). The god of property 'Kubera' is also the lord of north. The person who sleeps, putting his leg towards north, seems to be moving towards north to get wealth and blessings of Kubera.

The King of gods, 'Indra', is said to be lord of east direction. With getting up in the morning, one who faces and sees the east is a blissful work, equivalent to getting the blessings for prosperity from Lord 'Devendra'. Hence, many people sleep with the head in the west and the legs in the east. God of water-Varun is said to be lord of west direction which effects our conscience, religious thought and emotion. Hence some learned one assumes the sleeping with head in the east and legs in the west as auspicious.

The person, who sleeps putting his head and legs in north and south directions respectively, will never get good sleep. Such people will be perturbed whole night and will get up in morning with tension and will feel pain in the body.

Scientifically, it is proved, that human body is affected by the magnetic waves and himself emanates very minute magnetic waves which creates attraction and repulsion in the 'Prabhamandal'(radiance world). As the earth has North pole, similarly the brain of the body is his north pole. The head of the body, due to the nature from the birth, is affected with the magnetic waves of the north pole. Hence, to get complete relaxation, the head part of the body should always be in south so that the magnetic wave could flow in right direction. On sleeping opposite to this direction, the magnetic flow will be disturbed, due to clash and due to unsuitable and opposite flow of rays. Hence the person will not get a proper sleep.

Our forerunner teachers—(Purvaacharyas) after their extensive research on this subject said—

सुप्ते प्रत्यक् शिरेमृत्युः वशाद आरुक् सुतार्तिदः।
अर्वाक् शिरेहयनिंद्रादा, दक्षिणे सुख संपदः॥
पश्चिमें प्रबला चिंता, हानिर्मृत्युत्तथोत्तरे॥
स्वगेहे प्राक्शिराः सुप्यात्, स्ववासे दक्षिणे शिरः।
प्रत्यक्‌मून॥ शिरः प्रवासेतु, नोदक्यां वै

Supte Pratyak Shiremrityuh Vashaad Aaruk Sutartidah.
Arwak Shirohaynindradaa, Dakshine Sukh Sampadah..
Paachichime Prabala Chinta, Hanihmrityuthatt Thottare.
Swagehe Praakshirah Supyat Swavaase Dakshine Shirah.
Pratyak Shirah Pravaasetu, Nodakyam Vai Kadacchan.

i.e., Sleeping with head in west, person is grabbed by different types of diseases, falling into the lap of death and his children get pain. By putting head in the north, person has false dream, sees useless and messy dreams and suffers from [insomnia] a disease. While sleeping with the head in the south, one gets happiness and wealth.

Intense tension in the west, and loss of wealth and pain equivalent to death, in the north are expected. Hence sleep in your house with head in east or south. Keeping west, as exception, some Teachers say that one can sleep with head in the west but one should never sleep with the head in the north. ☐

Chapter 17

Miracle of Feng-Shui

'Vastushastra' in China, Hongkong and south-east Asia is called 'Feng shui'. 90% of the people, living there construct their hotel, shop, commercial complexes, on the basis of Feng shui. This is the reason that Hongkong, Bankok, Singapore etc. are the biggest business centres of the world.

Five natural elements or things are the basics of 'Feng-shui' in which water, fire, land, gold and wood are the basics of constructing new house. If proportion of these things is exact and right, then the people living in the house are happy, otherwise invite lots of trouble and worries. The elements got prominence in India are following:—

(1) Earth, (2) water, (3) Fire, (4) Wind, (5) Sky.

According to western thought, the aforesaid five natural things, depend on the timing of birth of a person. For example, if a person takes birth at 8 a.m. then his element will be 'Bhumi' (soil). For the people having 'soil' element should start constructing in the direction of east and Agneya corner of the house and these directions should be cared much for cleanliness and decoration.

To understand this nicely, we should observe the following table on next page.

Five elements	Birth Time	Construction work
Wood	11 P.M.—1 A.M.	North(N)
	1 A.M—3 A.M.	North Ishanya (N-E)
Fire	3 A.M.—5 A.M.	East Ishanya (N-E)
	5 A.M.—7 A.M.	East (E)

Earth	7 A.M.—9 A.M.	East Agneya (S-E)
	9 A.M.—11 A.M.	South Agneya (S-E)
Gold	11 A.M.—1 P.M.	South (S)
	1 P.M.—3 P.M.	South Naishritya (S-W)
Water	3 P.M.—5 P.M.	West Naishritya (S-W)
	5 P.M.—7 P.M.	West (W)
	7 P.M.—9 P.M.	West Vayavya (N-W)
	9 P.M.—11 P.M.	North Vayavya (N-W)

Where should be the counter in Hotel or Commercial Complex:—

It has been thought and discussed much in 'Feng-shui' in connection with counter, reception centre and cashier's desk of the hotel. About this, the example of famous hotel 'Hayat' is observed. The entrance door, reception centre (counter) and the cashier counter, all the three of this hotel, were parallel to main road. According to 'Feng shui' the door, of any hotel or commercial complex, should not be in Vayavya corner because such doors help in making enter the evil spirit and the inauspicious elements. In any hotel the counter, main entrance door, and cashier's counter should not be parallel because this helps in flowing of wealth and money outside. Same case was here, for the incoming money used to be vanished and spent immediately.

At length the learned of Vastu treaties was called. He shifted the door in middle of hotel to a corner after making calculation and reconstructed it, which restricted the flow of money outside, unnecessarily. In the middle of the hotel and just in front of the main door was lying a very attractive artificial fountain which was the main cause for 'Dwar Vedha'. It was difficult to remove it hence parallel to it two more fountains beside, it were started. There was 'Vedha' (perforation or obstruction) of flag on the fourth storey. It was removed and worship with offering oblations was performed for purification. Now the monthly income of that hotel is in lakhs of dollars.

Similarly, 'Centaur' a five star hotel is situated on the main road near the Santacruz station aerodrome, in Bombay. A swimming pool is made, in the middle, to enhance its beauty. Existence of well, water reservoir or swimming pool is prohibited just in the middle of any hotel, commercial complex, or house. This hotel is also afflicted from this fault, hence less customers are coming here. Its situation is a matter of concern, in comparison to other hotels of Centaur group.

Where Telephone should be kept?

'Feng shui' has also glanced over telephone's position, as to where it should be kept, how it should be kept etc.

Power is communicated in Telephone. This is important medium, to talk through the ether rays which is conducted through electric waves. Hence its main place is Fire corner (Agneya). Second place is in Ishanya and east. The most important thing, notable here, is that there should not exist water reservoir or resources near telephone.

If glass with water, fruit juice, cup of tea or kettle is kept near telephone then one will have only wrong numbers. Wrong bell will start ringing. Blank-call or horrible call will start reaching. Your telephone will be uncontrolled and disordered. This is apparant effect of Vastushastra which is observed by me a lot of time. You can also test it. The scientific reason behind this is that fire and water are enemy of each other. Fire and water elements should always be kept separate, at distance. If fire element rests in Agneya and water elements rests in Ishanya or east then it is according to Vastu. There is a great effect of these tiny and little things which also affect our life.

Where the file of Court-case and the paper of litigation should be kept :—

It has been discussed in Feng Shui as to where the case-file and papers of litigation should be kept, just like the currency notes. The papers of court-case and litigation are the important documents in the life of human being, for which a person always remains worried.

Be careful and never keep the court case-file in Agneya. With this the litigation will go on prolonging. Don't keep it in the south, otherwise you will loose the case and enemy will kill you. Litigated paper should not be kept in treasure box, with F.D.R. or in cash box. This will drain out your wealth and money will be spent on expenditure in court-case mostly. Keep the court case file always in east, Ishanya direction. As far as possible, it should be kept below the gods place, then you will win the case by the grace of God. These small things of daily routine will affect all the three—present, past and future.

Don't administer powerful slap on main gate or door:—

Both the miracles mentioned above was of fire element. Now I tell you about the miracle of wind element which you will feel immediately. You may experiment it in your home or of others, if you desire.

When all the persons are sleeping in the early morning you get up and after slapping with force the main door, you sleep again. Due to hammering of the wind the atmosphere of the house will be polluted and any one member of the house must quarrel upto noon. Peace will be disturbed in the house and hot discussion and quarrel will take place. This is a felt example. You may examine it. It has also been found that the main door of the house, if produces noise during opening or shutting, that house meets skirmishes and quarrel daily. This is the visible example of unpleasant wind disturbance. Vastushastra, in fact, teaches us about the excellent use of proportionally balanced mixture of wind, fire, water, sky and earth. Various types of disturbances breed, due to breaking of these proportional rythms. Vastushastra teaches us to pacify these distrubances also.

Don't spoil the Daily routine

It is also mentioned in 'Feng shui' that don't disturb and make your daily routine irregular; don't spoil it. This also disturbs the house atmosphere. If one work or act gets late, automatically all the programmes of the day become haphazard and the whole day becomes inauspicious.

I have an example which is experienced. You may also examine it.

Suppose that the youngest member of a family any day gets up early with no reason and gets free of latrine, bath etc. Then be definite, that there will be an unexpected occurrence in that house. Hence, according to rule, the eldest member of the family should get ready, first of all daily.

Such type of timing and behaviour should be natural. Preplanned Programme has no place in it. For example, crossing the road by cat, snake are inauspicious, but if any enemy or jealous person deliberately puts cat or snake to cross the path during your movement, this has no value, for its having artificiality. This is unnatural and is lacking super powers indication.

There are so many examples relating 'Omens'; for which read our book 'Study of Omens'. The remedy, to save against bad-omens, is given in it, based on classical treatise.

☐

Chapter 18

About the Author

A son was born, with 'Cancer Ascendant', in the house of 'Kula Bhushan, Shrimali Brahman Kulaguru Vedia Pandit Jai Narayan Dwivedi in Samvat 2006, on Dewjhulni Ekadashi of Shukla Pakhsh of Bhadra month, corresponding to 5.9. 1949, at the exact 'Brahmmuhurta' time 04:04 a.m. when Kaliyugi incarnation of God Baba Ramadeva was born. A very surprising incident occurred before his birth, his mother, Srimati Rama Pyari Devi's soul left her physical body, while sleeping. His mother reached heaven straight away where she met her great grandfather and grandfather. Her grandfather said, after offering her a divine mango, she blessed by a brilliant son who would be the pride of your Vedia family. Her grandfather took her to God Chitragupta and repeated the sentences. Chitragupta checked his accounts and ledger and begged pardon for the mistake committed to her grandfather and directed the messenger of Lord Vishnu to send her to earth again. His mother, reawakened after ten hours at the burial ground. Instaneously a lady, having the same name, Rampyari died in Dundara village.

After this incident his mother got divine power and 'Siddhi'. She could immediately tell the thoughts of strangers or people coming to her, to the enact word. Telling about lost things or thing robbed was very common for her. She was always surrounded by multitude of people both male and female. Old people of Jodhpur town, tell queer stories of his mother with great fervour now-a-days. After one year of her return from heaven Shri Dwivedi was born on 5.9.1949 in the morning. Shri Dwivedi was very logical and showed reasoning from his early childhood. His mother was alive, till Sri Dwivedi was married. He was married to Janaki Devi of a village named Samdari in Barmer district. He was blessed with two obedient daughters and one gem-like son.

Shri Dwivedi passed B.A.(Hon) with Sanskrit in first class. In M.A. (Sanskrit) and philosophy, he got first class with the highest marks. and thus enabled him to get a scholarship, from the university. Thereafter he conducted research on astrological subject by Varahmihir, in Sanskrit department of Jodhpur University.

In 1977 A.D. under the inspiration of Dharma Samrat 'Karpatriji' and from Puripithadhishwar Jagat Guru Shankaracharya, Shri Niranjandevatirth's hands he started the quarterly astrological magazine named Agyatdarshan. The magazine now appears fortnightly. It is the only fortnightly, Jyotish Patrika, which is recognised and affiliated with Rajasthan Government and Indian Government and it is being published from the last 18 years under the editorship of Dr. Bhojraj Dwivedi.

In Samvat 2034 there was confusion and discussion about the Shrawan-Asaad Adhikmas. There were two groups of learned people at country level, and Shastrarth (discussion) was held finally in Sri Ganganagar, at Nohar, with the association of Jagat Guru Shankaracharya. Late Pt.Ramdatt Agnihotri was neutral. Dr. Bhojraj Dwivedi defeated all the learned ones in the Shashtrarth (discussion) and emerged triumphant. On account of this, Jagatguru Shankaracharya crowned him with the title 'Shashrarth Kesari' and gave him Rs.501 and a shawl as a gift. His initial achievements are as follows:—

On December 24, 1979 he was given shawl and certificate, for his selfless work, for the cause of people by Rajmata of Gwalior, in the All India Indian Astrology Conference, organised by 'Indian Astrological Council' in Bhopal.

He was awarded the highest honour in astrology as 'Jyotish

Shiromani' by Brihat Gujarat Astrological society on January 11, 1981.

Prachya Vidya Maha Mahapaadhyaya' was conferred on him in Lucknow (U.P) for his research work in April, 1982. On 4th October, 1982 Chief Justice of Rajasthan High Court, Shri K.D. Sharma, gave him a 'gold medal' in All India Jyotisha Conference, held in townhall of Jodhpur.

He was given a cash award of Rs.5000/ by 'Samanvay Seva Trust, London' and gold medal by Mahamandaleshwar Swami Sri Satyamitranand Giri in 1983. He was honoured with title of 'Jyotish Bhaskar', a shawl and admiration paper by 'Jyotisvidyapith' of Pune in 1983.

Bestowed with a certificate on Oct. 21, 1983 by 'All India Astrological Conference, Cuttuck (Orissa)' He was awarded with Jyotirmartand and given 'gold medal' and a shawl by Maharani of Jaipur, Srimati Gayatridevi, in the precincts of Dadu Sanskrit University in June 1984.

Thereafter, he started regular correspondence courses on old Indian and classical subjects, through Jyotish University after the registration of 'All India Astrological Journalist Association' on 15.11.1984. Now-a-days his many disciples are spreading and canvassing the scientific base of astrology, Mantra-Tantra and other subjects.

'Sri Chandmartand Panchang' started publishing regularly from october 1986 under his editorship and this Panchang covered the whole of India and is highly in demand in Arabic countries.

On August 7, 1988 in Lajpat Bhawan Motijhil, in Kanpur he was honoured with title 'Jyotish Bhushan' and was given a bag with rupees and shawl at a public reception.

In a public address in Bhavnagar (Saurashtra) on May 11, 1989, under the chairmanship of All India Indian Shrimali Brahman Conference in Mahua (Kathiawar) and Jamnagar, he was honoured with respect and praise. On 17th January 1990 an astrological computer office was established, under the chairmanship of Jodhpur

Maharaja Sri Gajraj Singh, Maharani Srimati Hemlata Rajye, and Rajmata Sahiba.

On April 22, 1990 he was awarded with the title 'Daivagya Maharshi' in the Ravindra hall, in Bhopal, on the occasion of All India Astrological Conference. On 14th July, 1990 he travelled to Dubai, Sharjah, Abu dhabi, Aline, Muscat and other Arab countries for the canvassing of astrology through Pravachan (Preachings), Journalist's interview, T.V. interview etc.

On December 9, 1990 he was given the highest title of 'Jyotish Samrat' by him a shawl, putting on him a crown of embossed gold, and making him sit on elephant, by former president Sri Gyani Jail Singh at India International Centre, Delhi.

He was honoured, with garland, certificates in Tirupati for his correct prediction in the context of Srividya on January 1, 1991.

In All India Astrological Conference held on Feb. 8, 1991 in Faridabad (Haryana) he was crowned with 'Gold embossed Sri Yantra', shawl and title of 'Doctor of Astrology' title, by the then Union Health Minister Shri Makhan Lal Fotedar.

On March 8, 1991 in All India Astrological Conference, Mavalankar Hall, Delhi, he was crowned with title 'Tantra-Martanda' On Aug 4, 1991, he was crowned with the title 'Jyotish Maharshi* by the All India Brahm Jyotirvid Mandal (Regd.) Conference held in Ahmedabad.

He performed 108 Kundiya Sri Yagya on 1.1.92 and an All India Learned men's Conference was held and managed by him, He was honoured by the then Home Minister of Rajasthan, Sri Lalit Kishore Chaturvedi and many other ministers.

At a public reception in Jaipur on 30.3.92, the Chief Justice of Rajasthan High Court, Shri K.P. Agrawal paid his respect by putting a red shawl on his shoulder.

On April 8, 1992 on the occasion of All India Medical Astrological Conference held in Modinagar, he was given title of 'Jyotisha Ayurvigyan Vibhushan' and was given a shawl and a big trophy for being the best orator.

On 18.6.92, he travelled to Bangkok, Hongkong, Pattaya, Singapore, Macua and China for the canvassing of astrology and delivered many speeches over a period of one month.

Lion's Club International

In July 1992 he became the secretary of Lions Club Marwar, which was earlier associated with Lions International', working for public cause. He took active part in International Conference held in Bangkok. He was awarded as 'Best Secretary' and performed successful experiment in publishing 'Jyotish Diary' every year in Lions Club. In 1993 he was selected as 'Director of Board' for two years and worked as President of the club during the period 1996-97. And again elected as charter president of Lion's Club Jodhpur Central for 1997-98.

On 22.9.93, he was honoured by the public, at Birla Play Centre in Bombay and he released the book named 'Kaala Sarpa Yoga'.

On 13.12.93 started publishing fortnightly magazine named 'Shrimali Pradip' from Shiv-vadi, Jodhpur.

On 16.12.94, he released the book. 'Shrimal Puraan' in Bombay and performed 'All India Shrimali Brahman Conference'. He translated five thousand Sanskrit Shlokas into Hindi and got fame as old-treatise compositor for which the association of 24 villages' Shrimali Brahman Lunikantha Mahasabha' praised and respected him by offering him 'Safa', 'Shrifal', 'Yagyopavit' and garland. On 24.2.95, in Gwalior, he chaired the All India Astrological Conference on the occasion of 108 Kundiya Sri Rama Mahayagya' which was praised by the public.

On 4.6.95, he was honoured with 'Vishwakarma Award' the highest title of Vastushastra, and was offered a shawl, garland in Bangalore Assembly during All India Vastu Conference held in association with the then Karnataka's Chief Minister H.D. Deve Gowda (Present Prime Minister of India), Sri T.N. Sheshan, and Sri Ramkrishna Hegde. Awarded Highest award of 'Vaastu Samrat at Inter-state Symposium on Vaastu by Jagadguru Shankaracharya on

15.12.1996 in presence of State Ministers.

The words and paper will be short in giving details, about the achievements and life style of Dr. Bhojraj Dwivedi. He has done a lot for the society, Srimali Brahman Society, to which he belongs and has held many important posts. He has worked, not only for caste and society only, but also for the progress of human beings which can't be effaced. The respected Gurudev was born in such an auspicious Nakshtra and Muhurta that he got splendid success in every work he under took in his hand. The fate was changed, as soon as the object he touched. He wrote many columns in various papers and magazines like Dainik-Jagran, Tarun Rajasthan, Dainik Pratinidhi, Dainik, Jalte Deep, Rajasthan Patrika, Kadambani, Sanmarg, Blitz, Sunday Mail, Chitralekha, Gujarat Samachar, Shrimale Sandesh, Jyotishbodh etc. and has published many stories and episodes. He chaired many national and international conferences. His name is continuously published in 'Who is Who in India', 'Asia's whose who' and 'International Directory'.

Lot of books have been written in the field of astrology and 'Mantra-Tantra' of which about a seventy books have already been published and many costly books and 'granthas' are under publication. The word uttered by him effortlessly became immortal as if spoken by divine guidance. More than two thousand predictions of national and international events have been published which proved correct. More than fifty discussions, on radio have been relayed and about one and half thousand research-articles have already been published to relating astrology. Due to his sharp intellect and good writing, so much of literature about astrology has been produced that the age of a person is short to read and understand the whole literature. No sect relating science and knowledge is untouched by him. Hundreds and thousands of families in India and abroad are impressed with his peculiar life-style and mode of work. The present book is a collection of words and speeches from Sri Gurudeva's mouth. Hence we are feeling much happiness and are thrilled by offering our regards in his blissful respected feet. **—Publisher**

PERSONALITY DEVELOPMENT

Management Guru Bhagwan Shri Ram
Author: Dr. Sunil Jogi

Management Guru Hanuman
Author: Dr. Sunil Jogi

Management Guru Chankya
Author: Himanshu Shekhar

Gandhi and Management
Author: Dr. Pravind Shukl

Management Guru Ganesha
Author: B.K. Chandrashekhar

Unlock the Doort to Success
Author: Ashok Jain

Secrets Of Success Through Bhagwadgeeta
Author: Kapil Kakkar

Time Management
Author: Dr. Rakha Vyas

Be An Achiever
Author: K G Varshney

Power of Positive Thinking
Author: G.D. Budhiraja

Think And Grow Rich
Author: Napoleon Hill

Golden Sutras Of Success
Author: P. Gopal Sharma

Dare to Dream Dare to Excel
Author: Dr. H. Devsare

Yes You Can
Dr. Harikrishan Devsare

Tips of Success
Author: Sunil Jogi

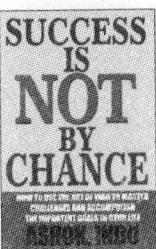

Success Is Not By Chance
Author: Ashok Indu

DIAMOND BOOKS
X-30, Okhla Industrial Area, Phase-II, New Delhi-110020,
Phones: 41611861-65, 40712100, Fax: 011-41611866
E-mail: Sales@dpb.in, Website: www.dpb.in

BEST BOOKS ON PERSONALITY DEVLOPMENT

Book By: Joginder Singh (Former CBI Director)

SUCCESS MANTRA
This book is a masterpiece by Sh. Joginder Singh, IPS (Retd) who is a former Director of the CBI. Hailing from a poor farmer's family, he scaled the pinnacles of success through sheer motivation and hard work. The saga of success he has enunciated through his win-win story is worth emulating for any young aspirant for achievements and glory in life: to be on top!

HOW TO EXCEL WHEN CHIPS ARE DOWN
Excellent suggestions with suitable examples have been cited in the book which will guide youngesters about the importance of objective thinking and to erase unwanted thoughts from their memory.

FOR A BETTER TOMORROW
This magnum opus by Sh. Joginder Singh is a treatise on self improvement. This win-win sory is based on the secrets of success as to how to become an achiever. And the success mantra that he espouses for you. Make the best of all opportunities; dream big and work hard-dreams will turn sheer realities. Price : 150.00

WINNING WAYS
The mantra he unveils for success, through this book, is potent enough to lift the young and ambitious to the highest peaks. These winning tips will inspire your morale to achieve greater glories - you simply need to tune up your mindset and hone your skills.

• • • • • • • • • • • • • •

Books By: Dr. Ujjwal Patni

GREAT WORDS, WIN HEARTS
Great Words, Win Hearts will tell you the powerful ways to get noticed, to get heard, to impress the listeners, to remove public and stage fear. The author, Dr. Ujjwal Patni assures that after reading this book every common man can speak effectively and strongly, everywhere and everywhere without any fear, hesitation or inferiority complex.

WINNERS & LOSERS
This book can shake you, hurt you, make you feel ashamed, arouse you, encourage you or bring forward bitter facts. **Price : 150.00**

• • • • • • • • • • • • • •

Books by: Surya Sinha

A GUIDE TO NETWORK MARKETING
This book will prove to be a milestone to all those who are already associated or desire to Join this Business. It has been written in a simple language and manner by the well known thinker, inspirer & human trainer Surya Sinha. **Price : 100.00**

WHY NETWORK MARKETING
In this book you will know how network marketing works. How to earn extra income, economic freedom, self employment, time freedom, personality Development, helping others, making new contacts learning Inheritance..

LEARN TO SAY I LOVE YOU
The book is meant to make you more practical, professional and well-connected. The book - Learn to say I Love You- bridges distance, eliminates isolation and inculcates in us a new feelings and a new thinking, for our all round happiness and success.

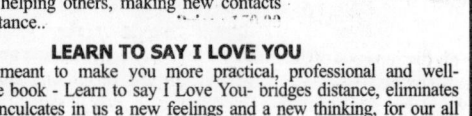

DIAMOND BOOKS X-30, Okhla Industrial Area, Phase-II, New Delhi-110020,
Phones : 41611861- 65, 40712100, Fax: 011- 41611866
E-mail : Sales@dpb.in, Website: www.dpb.in

COMPUTER BOOKS

DYNAMIC MEMORY COMPUTER COURSE
Biswaroop Roy Chowdhury

In today's cyber world, not knowing about computer is nothing less than illiteracy. Knowing about computer and its uses is no more a luxury but a necessity. This book has been brought out keeping this necessity in mind. In this book the fantastic story of the computer from its inception to its vital state on covered. Every nuance from hardware to software, interest to networking & from MS-Office to Window XP/Vista, a reader will get all he wants to know about computers. Computer will be as clear as your drinking water.

Dynamic Memory Windows Vista & Office 2007
Devender Singh Minhas

The technology of Windows and internet to computer system has created an open run way for new introductions. In this field as well, every new version overrides old version and comes forward with yet more power & features. Window Vista is one such latest version & this book updates its readers, with the novality. Devender Minhas has once again done his wonderful job.

Dynamic Memory Windows 98/XP & Internet
Devender Singh Minhas

In the hi-tech world, not knowing about the computer is nothing less than illiteracy. Computer has become an intergral part of our life. Computer touches our every aspect of life making it easier and comfortable. So, knowing about computer and its uses are no more a knowledge but a necessity. This book has been brought forth keeping this necessity in mind.

Dynamic Memory Internet & E-mail
Davinder Singh Minhas

In today's educated world, not knowing about Internet is nothing less than illiteracy. This book will be a handy tool to become an expert on Internet. Every step from the equipments you need to have an Internet to the method of approaching an Internet Service provider. From E-mail to Internet safety and from Web browser to e-commerce, a reader will get all in this book. **Rs. 110.00**

Dynamic Memory Internet Dictionary
Tarun Chakarborty

This Internet Dictionary contains almost all the necessary Internet Terminology. Surely, it will benefit all those who are NET savvy and willing to know more about the endless world of WorldWide Web (WWW).

Dynamic Memory Computer Dictionary
Tarun Chakarborty

This dictionary is an essential guide to modern computer terminology and jargon and contains hundreds of straightforward definitions, example sentences and usage tips. The terms are illustrated wherever possible for the convenience of the readers.

Books can be requisitioned by V.P.P. Postage charges will be Rs. 20/- per book.
For orders of three books the postage will be free.

FUSION BOOKS
X-30, Okhla Industrial Area, Phase-II, New Delhi-110020,
Phone : 41611861 Fax : 41611866
E-mail : sales@dpb.in Website : www.dpb.in

BIOGRAPHIES BOOKS

Maharana Pratap
Author: Dr. B. S. Rana

Chhatrapati Shivaji
Author: Dr. B. S. Rana

Chandra Shekhar Azad
Author: Dr. B. S. Rana

The First Woman President of India - Pratibha Patil
Author: Ayushma Sharma

Bhagat Singh
Author: Dr. Bhawan Singh Rana

Rani of Jhansi
Author: Dr. Bhawan Singh Rana

Veer Vinayak Damodar Savarkar
Author: Dr. Bhawan Singh Rana

Dr. Bhimrao Ambedkar
Author: Mahesh Ambedkar

Indira Gandhi
Author: Meena Agrawal

Rajiv Gandhi
Author: Meena Agrawal

Ramakrishna Paramhansa
Author: Dr. B. R. Kishore

Dr. A.P.J. Abdul Kalam
Author: Mahesh Sharma,

Sonia Gandhi (A Biography)
Author: Arun Bhanot, S. P Verma, Mahesh Sharma

The Making of Mahatma (A Biography)
Author: Anuradha Ray

Munshi Premchand
Author: Rekha Sigi

Gandhi and Gandhigiri
Author: Praveen Shukla

DIAMOND BOOKS
X-30, Okhla Industrial Area, Phase-II, New Delhi-110020,
Phones: 41611861- 65, 40712100, Fax: 011- 41611866
E-mail: Sales@dpb.in, Website: www.dpb.in

BOOKS ON PERSONALITY DEVELOPMENT

AMBANI & AMBANI
Tarun Engineer

The presented volume deals with the dazzling rise of Dhirubhai Ambani and his sons, Mukesh and Anil. Only a few minds have been able to create unprecedented waves of success in the world of business. Dhirubhai Ambani tops that distinguished list. He dared to dream; and he realized it through imagination, a unique business style and dare.

STEEL KING LAKSHMI MITTAL
Prateeksha M. Tiwari

Lakshmi Niwas Mittal, usuallly known as steel king is a London-based Indian billionaire industrialist. He has actually revolutionized the world economy through his tremendous business skill. So he is a force to be reckoned with.

NANDAN NILEKANI
Rajiv Tiwari

In this book, readers would learn a lot about Nilekani's life, his colleagues and other projects he and his family had been associated with. The much talked about Unique Identity Card project has also been discussed.

RATAN TATA
Prateeksha M. Tiwari

Ratan Tata is one of the renowned personalities of India. He is the Brand Ambassador of India on international state. For him, quality is not a mantra, but the road to the customer's doorstep. The book gives a detailed description not only of Ratan Tata but also of the evolution of Tata industries on the world map.

YOUTH ICONS OF INDIA
Kumar Pankaj

The results of the 15th parliamentary elections indicate that the coming Lok Sabha will be having abundant fresh faces which will decide the leadership of the country. This book, narrating the saga of youth leadership will undoubtedly prove to be inspirational for the people relating to or having interest in political and social sectors.

BE AN ACHIEVER
K.G. Varshney

The book 'Be an Achiever' authorised by Mr.K.G.Varshney offers 26 achievement mantras to convert the readers into achievers by promoting nobility of humble behaviour and cultivating a culture for accomplishment of the task. The unique style of presentation in the form of twin letter alliterations of the English alphabet is going to compel you to read the book and to make you an achiever.

| World famous Women... | Famous Indian Women... |  Great Indian Personalities... | Great Personalities of the world.. | Novel Prize Winners of the world.. | World Famous Scientists... |

DIAMOND BOOKS
X-30, Okhla Industrial Area, Phase-II, New Delhi-110020,
Phones : 41611861- 65, 40712100, Fax: 011- 41611866
E-mail : Sales@dpb.in, Website: www.dpb.in

Now you can
Improve your Memory

Without problem
choose book of your favourite author
Biswaroop Roy Chowdhury

The 4th Idiot
'The 4th Idiot' is written by Biswaroop Roy Chowdhury, the only person to hold mind and body world records on the earth. Actually, it is the collection of RARE S^3 (Scientific Super Shortcuts) which can guide you towards your goal faster. It is inspired by the Indian cinema 3 Idiots which give a clear message i.e. if you achieve excellence, then success will follow.

One Minute Mind Memory
In the present spell of highly competitive time, where knowledge, qualifications and skills are so richly available is people, the next parameter which can decide the overall merit is memory. It is an art of quick retrival of what you have in the stock of your mind. Means what you have is alright, but what you can pull out instantly from your mind system, on the hour of need, is paid most. This book is designed to make your mind capable to earn that premium.

Memory Unlimited
This book is a collection of examples from various areas of science, commerce and arts showing how Advanced Mnemonics can be helpful in improving the learning speed.

Memory, Mind & Body
Memory, Mind & Body is the masterpiece by a master mind. It is another magnum opus by the renowed memory master. Biswaroop Roy Chowdhury, whose amazing work Dynamic Memory Methods was a record-breaking bestseller of the millennium, running into several reprints in a short span.

Dynamic Memory Methods
Dynamic Memory Methods is a bestseller on memory developing techniques. This book deals with the use of scientific memory techniques. This book deals with the use of scientific memory techniques for memorising faster and retaining it longer.

Impossible.. Possible...
This book is about change. Poeple by nature are status quoists. This book will tell you how you can change the way you think, act and behave. The chronic patients can recover, the habitual failures can turn around.

Vocabulary@100 Words/hr
Whether you are a businessman, or a student, if you want to remember everything this book is a must for you. It deals with how to improve concentration Memorising difficult biological diagrams.

Memorising Dictionary Made Easy
Memorising Dictionary Made Easy will be immensely useful to all. The book identifies every new word with a Key and Memory Link, which connect the new word with a more identifiable word and in the process get firmly lodged in the reader's mind.

Books can be requisitioned by V.P.P. Postage charges will be Rs. 20/- per book.
For orders of three books the postage will be free.

⊚ FUSION BOOKS
X-30, Okhla Industrial Area, Phase-II, New Delhi-110020,
Phone : 41611861, 40712100, Fax : 41611866
E-mail : sales@dpb.in Website : www.dpb.in